800-762-2974

CHEAT SHEET

Installing the Disk

To use the files on the disk that comes with this book, you first have to *install* them on your computer. Follow these steps to do so:

1. Insert the *Dummies 101* disk in your computer's 3½-inch floppy disk drive (the only drive in which the disk will fit).
2. Double-click on the My Computer icon.
3. Double-click on the Control Panel icon.
4. Double-click on the Add/Remove Programs icon.
5. Click on the Install button.
6. Click on the Next button
7. Follow the directions on-screen.

Unless you *really* know what you're doing, accept the settings that the installation program suggests. If you decide to forge into the unknown and change the folder in which you install the files that you'll use with this book, write the pathname of that folder here.

Folder in which this book's files reside: _____

(Problems with the installation process? Call the IDG Books Worldwide Customer Support number: 800-762-2974.)

Start Menu Tips

The Start menu contains the following items in these menu groups. When you install additional programs, they usually create their own, new menu groups.

Menu Window	Items	Description
Programs	Accessories	Windows 95 programs like games, Media Player, Sound Recorder, Calculator, HyperTerminal, Notepad, Paint, Phone Dialer, and WordPad.
	Applications	Larger Windows 95 programs that you've paid for, as well as old programs that Windows 95 found on your computer when it installed itself.
	Startup	Any icon living in here automatically starts up its program when Windows 95 loads itself.
Documents	Filenames	Lists the last ten files you opened. Click on a filename to load the file.
Settings	Control Panel, Printers, Taskbar	Use for changing your computer's settings, adjusting printer settings, and changing the settings of your taskbar.
Find	Files or folders	Can search your entire computer for a particular filename or for filenames containing certain words.
Help	Help program	Click here for general help with Windows 95.
Run	Program	Runs a program when you type the launcher program's filename and location in the box.

☑ Progress Check

D1529969

CHEAT SHEET

Popular Keystrokes in Windows

To Do This	Press These Keys
Bring up Windows	Type **exit** at the DOS prompt (that C:\ thing)
Call up the Help menu	F1
See a list of open programs	Alt+Tab
Undo the mistake you just made	Ctrl+Z or Alt+Backspace
Close a window	Alt+F4
View the Start menu	Ctrl+Esc

To press a key combination such as Ctrl+Esc, press and hold down the first key (Ctrl), press the second key (Esc), and then release both keys.

Handling Files within a Program

To Do This	Press These Keys
Start a new file	Alt, F, N
Open an existing file	Alt, F, O
Save a file	Alt, F, S
Save a file under a new name	Alt, F, A
Print a file	Alt, F, P

To press a key combination such as Alt, F, N, press and release the Alt key, press and release the F key, and then press and release the N key. (You don't have to worry about typing uppercase letters.)

Working in My Computer or Explorer

To Do This	Do This
Copy a file to another location	Hold down Ctrl and drag the file there on the *same* disk drive
Copy a file to a *different* disk drive	Drag the file there or move a file to another location on the *same* disk drive
Move a file to a *different* disk drive	Hold down Alt and drag the file there
Select several files	Hold down Ctrl and click on the files' names
Make newly opened windows replace the current window	Hold down Ctrl while clicking on folders and drives
Load a program as an icon	Hold down Ctrl while double-clicking on the program name

IDG BOOKS WORLDWIDE

®

COMPUTER BOOK SERIES FROM IDG

References for the Rest of Us! ®

Are you intimidated and confused by computers? Do you find that traditional manuals are overloaded with technical details you'll never use? Do your friends and family always call you to fix simple problems on their PCs? Then the *...For Dummies*® computer book series from IDG Books Worldwide is for you.

...For Dummies books are written for those frustrated computer users who know they aren't really dumb but find that PC hardware, software, and indeed the unique vocabulary of computing make them feel helpless. *...For Dummies* books use a lighthearted approach, a down-to-earth style, and even cartoons and humorous icons to diffuse computer novices' fears and build their confidence. Lighthearted but not lightweight, these books are a perfect survival guide for anyone forced to use a computer.

Already, hundreds of thousands of satisfied readers agree. They have made *...For Dummies* books the #1 introductory level computer book series and have written asking for more. So, if you're looking for the most fun and easy way to learn about computers, look to *...For Dummies* books to give you a helping hand.

TM

IDG BOOKS WORLDWIDE

7/96r

DUMMIES 101:™
WINDOWS® 95
2ND EDITION

by Andy Rathbone

IDG Books Worldwide, Inc.
An International Data Group Company

Foster City, CA ✦ Chicago, IL ✦ Indianapolis, IN ✦ Southlake, TX

Dummies 101™: Windows® 95, 2nd Edition

Published by
IDG Books Worldwide, Inc.
An International Data Group Company
919 E. Hillsdale Blvd.
Suite 400
Foster City, CA 94404
http://www.idgbooks.com (IDG Books Worldwide Web Site)
http://www.dummies.com (Dummies Press Web Site)

Library of Congress Catalog Card No.: 96-80284

ISBN: 0-7645-0181-X

Printed in the United States of America

10 9 8 7 6 5 4 3 2 1

2B/SX/QS/ZX/IN

Distributed in the United States by IDG Books Worldwide, Inc.

Distributed by Macmillan Canada for Canada; by Contemporanea de Ediciones for Venezuela; by Distribuidora Cuspide for Argentina; by CITEC for Brazil; by Ediciones ZETA S.C.R. Ltda. for Peru; by Editorial Limusa SA for Mexico; by Transworld Publishers Limited in the United Kingdom and Europe; by Academic Bookshop for Egypt; by Levant Distributors S.A.R.L. for Lebanon; by Al Jassim for Saudi Arabia; by Simron Pty. Ltd. for South Africa; by Pustak Mahal for India; by The Computer Bookshop for India; by Toppan Company Ltd. for Japan; by Addison Wesley Publishing Company for Korea; by Longman Singapore Publishers Ltd. for Singapore, Malaysia, Thailand, and Indonesia; by Unalis Corporation for Taiwan; by WS Computer Publishing Company, Inc. for the Philippines; by WoodsLane Pty. Ltd. for Australia; by WoodsLane Enterprises Ltd. for New Zealand. Authorized Sales Agent: Anthony Rudkin Associates for the Middle East and North Africa.

For general information on IDG Books Worldwide's books in the U.S., please call our Consumer Customer Service department at 800-762-2974. For reseller information, including discounts and premium sales, please call our Reseller Customer Service department at 800-434-3422.

For information on where to purchase IDG Books Worldwide's books outside the U.S., please contact our International Sales department at 415-655-3172 or fax 415-655-3295.

For information on foreign language translations, please contact our Foreign & Subsidiary Rights department at 415-655-3021 or fax 415-655-3281.

For sales inquiries and special prices for bulk quantities, please contact our Sales department at 415-655-3200 or write to the address above.

For information on using IDG Books Worldwide's books in the classroom or for ordering examination copies, please contact our Educational Sales department at 800-434-2086 or fax 817-251-8174.

For press review copies, author interviews, or other publicity information, please contact our Public Relations department at 415-655-3000 or fax 415-655-3299.

For authorization to photocopy items for corporate, personal, or educational use, please contact Copyright Clearance Center, 222 Rosewood Drive, Danvers, MA 01923, or fax 508-750-4470.

is a trademark under exclusive license to IDG Books Worldwide, Inc., from International Data Group, Inc.

About the Author

Andy Rathbone started geeking around with computers in 1985 when he bought a boxy CP/ M Kaypro 2X with lime-green letters. Like other budding nerds, he soon began playing with null-modem adaptors, dialing up computer bulletin boards, and working part-time at Radio Shack.

In between playing computer games, he served as editor of the *Daily Aztec* newspaper at San Diego State University. After graduating with a comparative literature degree, he went to work for a bizarre underground coffee-table magazine that sort of disappeared.

Andy began combining his two interests, words and computers, by selling articles to a local computer magazine. During the next few years, Andy started ghostwriting computer books for more famous computer authors, as well as writing several hundred articles about computers for technoid publications like *Supercomputing Review, CompuServe Magazine, ID Systems, DataPro,* and *Shareware.*

In 1992, Andy and *DOS For Dummies* author/legend Dan Gookin teamed up to write *PCs For Dummies,* which was runner-up in the Computer Press Association's 1993 awards. Andy subsequently wrote the first edition of *Windows For Dummies* plus *OS/2 For Dummies, Upgrading & Fixing PCs For Dummies, Multimedia & CD-ROMs For Dummies, MORE Windows For Dummies,* and *Windows 95 For Dummies.* He also cowrote *VCRs and Camcorders For Dummies* with Gordon McComb and *Windows NT 4 for Dummies* with Sharon Crawford.

Andy lives with his most-excellent wife, Tina, and their cat in San Diego, California. When not writing, he fiddles with his MIDI synthesizer and tries to keep the cat off both keyboards.

ABOUT IDG BOOKS WORLDWIDE

Welcome to the world of IDG Books Worldwide.

IDG Books Worldwide, Inc., is a subsidiary of International Data Group, the world's largest publisher of computer-related information and the leading global provider of information services on information technology. IDG was founded more than 25 years ago and now employs more than 8,500 people worldwide. IDG publishes more than 275 computer publications in over 75 countries (see listing below). More than 60 million people read one or more IDG publications each month.

Launched in 1990, IDG Books Worldwide is today the #1 publisher of best-selling computer books in the United States. We are proud to have received eight awards from the Computer Press Association in recognition of editorial excellence and three from *Computer Currents'* First Annual Readers' Choice Awards. Our best-selling *...For Dummies®* series has more than 30 million copies in print with translations in 30 languages. IDG Books Worldwide, through a joint venture with IDG's Hi-Tech Beijing, became the first U.S. publisher to publish a computer book in the People's Republic of China. In record time, IDG Books Worldwide has become the first choice for millions of readers around the world who want to learn how to better manage their businesses.

Our mission is simple: Every one of our books is designed to bring extra value and skill-building instructions to the reader. Our books are written by experts who understand and care about our readers. The knowledge base of our editorial staff comes from years of experience in publishing, education, and journalism — experience we use to produce books for the '90s. In short, we care about books, so we attract the best people. We devote special attention to details such as audience, interior design, use of icons, and illustrations. And because we use an efficient process of authoring, editing, and desktop publishing our books electronically, we can spend more time ensuring superior content and spend less time on the technicalities of making books.

You can count on our commitment to deliver high-quality books at competitive prices on topics you want to read about. At IDG Books Worldwide, we continue in the IDG tradition of delivering quality for more than 25 years. You'll find no better book on a subject than one from IDG Books Worldwide.

John J. Kilcullen

John Kilcullen
CEO
IDG Books Worldwide, Inc.

Eighth Annual
Computer Press
Awards ≥1992

Ninth Annual
Computer Press
Awards ≥1993

Tenth Annual
Computer Press
Awards ≥1994

Eleventh Annual
Computer Press
Awards ≥1995

IDG Books Worldwide, Inc., is a subsidiary of International Data Group, the world's largest publisher of computer-related information and the leading global provider of information services on information technology. International Data Group publishes over 275 computer publications in over 75 countries. Sixty million people read one or more International Data Group publications each month. International Data Group's publications include: **ARGENTINA:** Buyer's Guide, Computerworld Argentina, PC World Argentina; **AUSTRALIA:** Australian Macworld, Australian PC World, Australian Reseller News, Computerworld, IT Casebook, Network World, Publish, Webmaster; **AUSTRIA:** Computerwelt Osterreich, Networks Austria, PC Tip Austria; **BANGLADESH:** PC World Bangladesh; **BELARUS:** PC World Belarus; **BELGIUM:** Data News; **BRAZIL:** Annuário de Informática, Computerworld, Connections, Macworld, PC Player, PC World, Publish, Reseller News, Supergamepower; **BULGARIA:** Computerworld Bulgaria, Network World Bulgaria, PC & MacWorld Bulgaria; **CANADA:** CIO Canada, Client/Server World, ComputerWorld Canada, InfoWorld Canada, NetworkWorld Canada, WebWorld; **CHILE:** Computerworld Chile, PC World Chile; **COLOMBIA:** Computerworld Colombia, PC World Colombia; **COSTA RICA:** PC World Centro America; **THE CZECH AND SLOVAK REPUBLICS:** Computerworld Czechoslovakia, Macworld Czech Republic, PC World Czechoslovakia; **DENMARK:** Communications World Danmark, Computerworld Danmark, Macworld Danmark, PC World Danmark, Techworld Denmark; **DOMINICAN REPUBLIC:** PC World Republica Dominicana; **ECUADOR:** PC World Ecuador; **EGYPT:** Computerworld Middle East, PC World Middle East; **EL SALVADOR:** PC World Centro America; **FINLAND:** MikroPC, Tietoverkko, Tietoviikko; **FRANCE:** Distributique, Hebdo, Info PC, Le Monde Informatique, Macworld, Reseaux & Telecoms, WebMaster France; **GERMANY:** Computer Partner, Computerwoche, Computerwoche Extra, Computerwoche FOCUS, Global Online, Macwelt, PC Welt; **GREECE:** Amiga Computing, GamePro Greece, Multimedia World; **GUATEMALA:** PC World Centro America; **HONDURAS:** PC World Centro America; **HONG KONG:** Computerworld Hong Kong, PC World Hong Kong, Publish in Asia; **HUNGARY:** ABCD CD-ROM, Computerworld Szamitastechnika, Internetto online Magazine, PC World Hungary, PC-X Magazin Hungary; **ICELAND:** Tolvuheimur PC World Island; **INDIA:** Information Communications World, Information Systems Computerworld, PC World India, Publish in Asia; **INDONESIA:** InfoKomputer PC World, Komputek Computerworld, Publish in Asia; **IRELAND:** ComputerScope, PC Live!; **ISRAEL:** Macworld Israel, People & Computers/Computerworld; **ITALY:** Computerworld Italia, Macworld Italia, Networking Italia, PC World Italia; **JAPAN:** DTP World, Macworld Japan, Nikkei Personal Computing, OS/2 World Japan, SunWorld Japan, Windows NT World, Windows World Japan; **KENYA:** PC World East African; **KOREA:** Hi-Tech Information, Macworld Korea, PC World Korea; **MACEDONIA:** PC World Macedonia; **MALAYSIA:** Computerworld Malaysia, PC World Malaysia, Publish in Asia; **MALTA:** PC World Malta; **MEXICO:** Computerworld Mexico, PC World Mexico; **MYANMAR:** PC World Myanmar; **NETHERLANDS:** Computer! Totaal, LAN Internetworking Magazine, LAN Networks Buyers Guide, Macworld Netherlands, Net, WebWereld; **NEW ZEALAND:** Absolute Beginners Guide and Plain & Simple Series, Computer Buyer, Computer Industry Directory, Computerworld New Zealand, MTB, Network World, PC World New Zealand; **NICARAGUA:** PC World Centro America; **NORWAY:** Computerworld Norge, CW Rapport, Datamagasinet, Financial Rapport, Kursguide Norge, Macworld Norge, Multimediaworld Norge, PC World Ekspress Norge, PC World Nettverk, PC World Norge, PC World ProduktGuide Norge; **PAKISTAN:** Computerworld Pakistan; **PANAMA:** PC World Panama; **PEOPLE'S REPUBLIC OF CHINA:** China Computer Users, China Computerworld, China InfoWorld, China Telecom World Weekly, Computer & Communication, Electronic Design China, Electronics Today, Electronics Weekly, Game Software, PC World China, Popular Computer Week, Software Weekly, Software World; **PERU:** Computerworld Peru, PC World Profesional Peru, PC World SoHo Peru; **PHILIPPINES:** Click!, Computerworld Philippines, PC World Philippines, Publish in Asia; **POLAND:** Computerworld Poland, Computerworld Special Report Poland, Cyber, Macworld Poland, Networld Poland, PC World Komputer; **PORTUGAL:** Cerebro/PC World, Computerworld/Correio Informático, Dealer World Portugal, Mac*In/PC*In Portugal, Multimedia World; **PUERTO RICO:** PC World Puerto Rico; **ROMANIA:** Computerworld Romania, PC World Romania, Telecom Romania; **RUSSIA:** Computerworld Russia, Mir PK, Publish, Seti; **SINGAPORE:** Computerworld Singapore, PC World Singapore, Publish in Asia; **SLOVENIA:** Monitor; **SOUTH AFRICA:** Computing SA, Network World SA, Software World SA; **SPAIN:** Communicaciones World España, Computerworld España, Dealer World España, Macworld España, PC World España; **SRI LANKA:** Infolink PC World; **SWEDEN:** CAP&Design, Computer Sweden, Corporate Computing Sweden, Internetworld Sweden, it.branschen, Macworld Sweden, MaxiData Sweden, MikroDatorn, Nätverk & Kommunikation, PC World Sweden, PCaktiv, Windows World Sweden; **SWITZERLAND:** Computerworld Schweiz, Macworld Schweiz, PCtip; **TAIWAN:** Computerworld Taiwan, NEW ViSiON/Publish, PC World Taiwan, Windows World Taiwan; **THAILAND:** Publish in Asia, Thai Computerworld; **TURKEY:** Computerworld Turkiye, Macworld Turkiye, Network World Turkiye, PC World Turkiye; **UKRAINE:** Computerworld Kiev, Multimedia World Ukraine, PC World Ukraine; **UNITED KINGDOM:** Acorn User UK, Amiga Action UK, Amiga Computing UK, Apple Talk UK, Computing, Macworld, Parents and Computers UK, PC Advisor, PC Home, PSX Pro, The WEB; **UNITED STATES:** Cable in the Classroom, CIO Magazine, Computerworld, DOS World, Federal Computer Week, GamePro Magazine, InfoWorld, I-Way, Macworld, Network World, PC Games, PC World, Publish, Video Event, THE WEB Magazine, and WebMaster; online webzines: JavaWorld, NetscapeWorld, and SunWorld Online; **URUGUAY:** InfoWorld Uruguay; **VENEZUELA:** Computerworld Venezuela, PC World Venezuela; and **VIETNAM:** PC World Vietnam.

1/24/97

Dedication

To my wife, parents, sister, and cat.

Author's Acknowledgments

Thanks to Dan Gookin and his wife Sandy, Matt Wagner, Jim Trageser, Mike Kelly, Colleen Rainsberger, Pam Mourouzis, Tammy Castleman, Joe Jansen, Jim McCarter, Chris Collins, Michael Sullivan, Constance Carlisle, Steve Hayes, Rob Rubright, Valery Bourke, and all the Production folks at IDG Books Worldwide, Inc. Thanks also to Access Technology for designing the *Dummies 101* series disks.

Publisher's Acknowledgments

We're proud of this book; please send us your comments about it by using the Reader Response Card at the back of the book or by e-mailing us at feedback/dummies@idgbooks.com. Some of the people who helped bring this book to market include the following:

Acquisitions, Development, and Editorial

Senior Project Editors: Colleen Rainsberger, Pamela Mourouzis

Acquisitions Editor: Mike Kelly, Quality Control Manager

Media Development Manager: Joyce Pepple

Copy Editors: Tamara S. Castleman, Joe Jansen

Technical Editors: Jim McCarter, Rob Rubright

Editorial Manager: Seta K. Frantz

Editorial Assistants: Constance Carlisle, Chris H. Collins, Steven H. Hayes, Michael D. Sullivan

Production

Project Coordinator: Valery Bourke

Layout and Graphics: Cameron Booker, Maridee Ennis, Drew Moore, Mark Owens, Brent Savage, Kate Snell

Proofreaders: Laura L. Bowman, Nancy Reinhart, Rachel Garvey, Dwight Ramsey, Karen York

Indexer: Richard Shrout

Special Help

Kevin Spencer, Associate Technical Editor; Access Technology; Stephanie Koutek, Proof Editor

---

General and Administrative

IDG Books Worldwide, Inc.: John Kilcullen, CEO; Steven Berkowitz, President and Publisher

IDG Books Technology Publishing: Brenda McLaughlin, Senior Vice President and Group Publisher

Dummies Technology Press and Dummies Editorial: Diane Graves Steele, Vice President and Associate Publisher; Judith A. Taylor, Brand Manager; Kristin A. Cocks, Editorial Director

Dummies Trade Press: Kathleen A. Welton, Vice President and Publisher; Stacy S. Collins, Brand Manager

IDG Books Production for Dummies Press: Beth Jenkins, Production Director; Cindy L. Phipps, Supervisor of Project Coordination, Production Proofreading and Indexing; Kathie S. Schutte, Supervisor of Page Layout; Shelley Lea, Supervisor of Graphics and Design; Debbie J. Gates, Production Systems Specialist; Tony Augsburger, Supervisor of Reprints and Bluelines; Leslie Popplewell, Media Archive Coordinator

Dummies Packaging and Book Design: Patti Sandez, Packaging Specialist; Lance Kayser, Packaging Assistant; Kavish+Kavish, Cover Design

◆

The publisher would like to give special thanks to Patrick J. McGovern, without whom this book would not have been possible.

◆

Files at
a Glance

ABC 123

Contents at a Glance

Table of Contents

Introduction

Welcome to *Dummies 101: Windows 95,* the textbook for people who want to learn Windows 95 as quickly as possible so that they can move on to the truly important things in their lives.

Of course, you're no dummy; it's just that the awkwardness of Windows sometimes makes you *feel* like a dummy. And no, you're not alone, either: Almost everyone feels like a dummy when he or she first sits in front of a computer. (Some people are a little better at hiding their grimaces, that's all.)

Don't think of this book as another boring school course, where you learn something snoozable like computer theory. Instead, it's more of a hands-on wood shop — a place where you can come to build your own Windows knowledge at your own pace.

Learning How to Use Windows 95

Learning how to control a computer with Windows 95 is a little like moving into a new house. A house is just a big, empty room. Sure, the house probably has basics like paint or wallpaper and a stove and refrigerator. But it doesn't have anything that you've added or rearranged.

The same holds true with Windows 95. Your computer probably came with a couple of Windows programs already on it. But until you begin arranging Windows so that it meets your personal needs, working with it is like living in an empty house — and that's not very fun or relaxing.

In fact, computers often seem so frustrating for that very reason: They seem sterile, rigid, and uncontrollable. But when you know how to push *them* around a little bit, things change for the better. And that's where this book comes in.

This book teaches you how to push the right buttons so that the right things happen, which makes Windows 95 much less intimidating and much easier to use.

Why You're Reading This Book

You could be peering through these pages for any of the following reasons:

- ♦ The manual that came in the Windows 95 box is too hard to read.

Notes:

- Someone is making you learn Windows 95 at work. (If so, consider yourself lucky — at least you're getting paid to learn it.)

- You already know how to use Windows 3.1 or Windows 3.11, but this new version — Windows 95 — leaves you feeling a little sketchy.

- You're tired of looking through *Windows 95 For Dummies* (IDG Books Worldwide, Inc.) whenever you need instructions for installing a program. Or worse yet, your office copy disappeared — Fred from Receiving never returned it after he promised to borrow it "just over the weekend."

- You want to become a little more serious about computing because you know that the beasts aren't going away. In fact, they're so trendy that *Vogue* magazine listed Iomega's Zip drives as #2 on its "Ten most wanted objects of desire" list (right between the Charles David boot and S-Papa tote bag).

- You don't have time for one of those evening-college computing courses, and you sure aren't giving up a weekend for one, either.

- You don't want to be a know-it-all computer guru, but you want to gain some basic knowledge of Windows 95 so that you can hold your own when the guru's nowhere to be found.

That's where this book comes in handy. It won't make you a Windows 95 expert, but it will teach you how to use Windows 95 in a day-to-day setting. And when your friends find out that you know how to make party flyers by using the Paint program, you'll start to be pretty popular around the office, too. But when people ask you Windows 95-related questions, toss the book at them. Let them do their own homework.

How to Use This Book

This book's a textbook, plain and simple. Very plain and simple, hopefully. It starts by teaching you how to turn on your computer and bring Windows 95 to the screen. From there, it shows you how to maneuver a mouse and move windows around on-screen. Step by step, this book teaches you how to load programs. And eventually, as you progress through the units, you'll learn how to write letters, create drawings, dial other computers with a modem, and copy files to and from your computer's assortment of disks.

You're free to move at your own pace, starting on page 1 and finishing the course with the last unit. Or if you want to learn only the exact steps required to write and print a letter, for example, head straight to the unit on WordPad, the word processor that comes with Windows 95.

If you're determined to learn — and *remember* — the information, feel free to take the quiz at the end of each unit. That shows you which areas you've mastered and which (if any) you may need to brush up on. (You can find the correct answers to the quizzes in the Appendix.) Then practice what you learned by completing the Unit Exercise.

To make things easier for you, this book follows certain conventions. For example, if you have to type something into the computer, you'll see easy-to-follow text that looks like this:

In the dialog box, type **these letters**.

That's your cue to type the words *these letters* in the box on-screen and then press the Enter key.

Whenever I describe a message or information that you'll see on-screen, I present it as follows:

`This is a message on-screen.`

(And don't worry, you'll see plenty of pictures along the tops of the pages, too.)

Don't know whether you can handle a unit? The first page of the unit contains a Prerequisites section that lists the skills you need to complete that unit's lessons.

Right below the Prerequisites, you'll find a list of files that you'll need for the unit; the files are found on the disk that comes in the back of this book.

Have a question? Q/A Sessions pop up throughout the text to answer particularly nagging questions.

Finally, people who prefer traditional course work will enjoy the review and test at the end of each part, as well as a Lab Assignment, which lets you bring together the skills that you learned in that part's units.

How about the Technical Stuff?

You don't need to know the mechanics of internal combustion to drive a car. And you don't need to know technical programming information to use Windows 95. So this book filters out the technical stuff that just gets in the way anyway.

Of course, I'll have to slip a few of the "why's" in there so that you know why the heck Windows 95 is making you go through so many convoluted steps to do such a simple task. (Otherwise, you'd never believe me.)

Also, all the really nasty computer words are set in italic type and humanely defined in the text.

How This Book Is Organized

The information in this book is arranged like a long line of bread crumbs, along which you can move at your own pace. If you're ravenous for information about Windows 95, start at the beginning and scoop 'em up as fast as you can. Or if you just have time for a snack, pick up the book, start where you left off, and spend a few minutes with some exercises. Either way, you'll eventually reach the end of the trail and have all that Windows knowledge under your belt.

The parts

The book's divided into 5 parts and 19 units, but that's really not as much work as it sounds. Here's the breakdown.

Part I: Bare Bones Basics

First-time Windows users should definitely start here, learning how to start your computer and load Windows. You'll learn how to use that mouse by "clicking" in certain places on-screen in order to get some work done. Finally, you'll learn the best part: exiting Windows and getting away from the computer.

Part II: Rearranging Your Desktop

Windows 95 turns your computer screen into a computerized desktop, complete with folders, stick-on notes, and random office tools. This part of the book shows you how Windows 95 handles *programs* — computerized tools for getting your work done. You'll learn how to put little "push-buttons" on your desk that automatically find your favorite programs and put them to work.

Programs make you store your work in *files* — computerized collections of information such as your letters, spreadsheets, and other important things you don't want to lose. Unit 5 in this book teaches you what to do with your files: copy them, delete them, move them to and from floppy disks, store them in folders, and perform other often-complicated tasks.

Oh, yeah — you'll learn how to find the files you thought you'd lost, too.

Part III: Getting into Windows

The bulk of the mechanics of Windows 95 is in here. You'll learn how to load a program like a word processor or spreadsheet. Then you'll learn how to load information — a *file* — into that program. Changed the information? Then you'd better save it — a process that's explained fully, of course. Finally, you'll learn how to send a copy of your work to the printer so that you can do something with it.

You'll also learn about that "cut and paste" stuff for moving information to and from different programs. (That's how most of those computer owners get maps into their spiffy party flyers.)

Part IV: The Free Programs

You've probably seen some of those little on-screen push-buttons — *icons* — with names like WordPad, Paint, and other oddities. This part teaches you how to do something with those programs, from start to finish: write a letter, make a party flyer, connect to other computers through the phone lines, and perform other Windows tasks.

You'll also learn how to get your toes wet on the Internet; yep, you learn how to use Internet Explorer to surf the World Wide Web.

Part V: Fixing Problems

Windows 95 stuck by the roadside? No help in sight? You'll find information about the Windows equivalent of changing a flat tire here. You'll learn how to install a new program, tell Windows about a new computer part, and fine-tune its various settings. Plus, if Windows 95 is still giving you trouble, you'll learn how to wring the most help out of its built-in Help program.

The icons

Because Windows uses *icons* — little symbols — to stand for things, this book does the same. The icons in the book's margins mean the following:

If you spot this icon, look for filenames sitting next to it; you'll need those files for any exercises coming up in the unit.

Better remember this snippet of information so that you can spit it back out for the quiz at the unit's end or the test at the end of the part.

Like what you learned? Then delve a little deeper by reading the extra credit section. This section is entirely optional, however.

Watch out — this icon points to tasks or steps that may trip you up. Some of these tasks may be a little tricky or not work as you expect them to.

Nothing sneaky here. The word *Notes:* just means that you can write your own notes in the margins. (Highly paid psychologists say that simple action often transforms hard-to-remember stuff into easy-to-find stuff.)

Think you're ready to move on to the next lesson? Then take the simple "quiz" that follows this Progress Check icon. If you can do all the things listed there, check them off to show that you've mastered that lesson. You may even be able to skip a lesson and move ahead, you lucky dog.

The tests (Well, you wanted a tutorial, didn't you?)

To make sure that you've absorbed the information in each unit, you'll find a quiz at the end of each unit. Hold on, though — that can be good news as well as bad. If you can pass the quiz without reading the unit, you've passed. You don't have to read the unit!

If some of the questions catch you off guard, you'd better budget some time for a little review.

Finally, if you want to really jump ahead of the game, you'll find a full-fledged exam at the end of each of the book's five parts. By looking at these exams, you can start reading the book and taking its lessons at your own level of knowledge.

(And if you *do* need to read the book from the beginning, don't worry — the tests aren't too hard. A distinctive "on the test" icon appears in the margin next to nearly every snippet of information that you'll need to know.)

You'll find the answers to all the unit quizzes and part tests in the Appendix. If you miss a question, this appendix will tell you which lesson or unit to go back and review.

About the Disk

You can use the files on the disk that comes with this book to work through the practice exercises. But first you need to install those files on your computer. The disk includes a handy installation program that makes the installation process a cinch for you to complete; you just stick the disk in the computer, click on a few things, and then follow the instructions on-screen. If you're brand-new at this Windows stuff, though, you may want to complete Part I of this book before you try installing the disk — but make sure to put the disk in a *very* safe place so that you'll have it when you're ready for it.

With Windows 95 running, follow these steps:

1 Insert the *Dummies 101* disk into your computer's 3½-inch floppy disk drive (the only drive that it will fit in — if you have two 3½-inch drives, use the one on top or on the left), which is probably called the A drive (or it may be the B drive).

2 **Double-click on the My Computer icon along the left edge of the screen.**

A window opens up.

3 **Double-click on the Control Panel icon.**

Another window opens up.

4 **Double-click on the Add/Remove Programs icon.**

A dialog box pops open.

5 **Click on the _Install button.**

Another dialog box pops open.

6 **Click on the _Next button.**

7 **Follow the directions on-screen.**

The installation program asks you some questions, such as where you want to install the files and whether you want to install all the files or just some of them. Unless you know what you're doing (and you folks know who you are), go ahead and accept the defaults that the program suggests by clicking on the Next button when those windows appear. That way, the files will be placed in the folder used throughout this book, and you'll be able to access all the files on the disk. If at any time during the process you need more information, click on the Help button.

After you complete the installation process, all the files you'll need for this book will be ready and waiting for you in the C:\Dummies 101\Windows 95 folder. Store the disk where it will be free from harm so that you can reinstall a file in case the one that's installed on your computer gets messed up.

If you have problems with the installation process, you can call the IDG Books Worldwide Customer Support number: 800-762-2974.

Where to Go from Here

Never used Windows 95 before? Then flip ahead to Unit 1 and start reading. If you've already used Windows a little bit, skim Part I to make sure that you've caught all the basics, and then jump ahead to Part II for a little more advanced information.

Although this book is a full-fledged tutorial course, you don't *have* to learn how Windows works. Because the book contains step-by-step instructions for most of the tasks that you'll do in Windows, you can simply turn back to those pages when you want. Later, if you tire of looking stuff up and want to memorize the steps, master the quiz at the end of the unit.

Either way, this book teaches you how to make Windows 95 work the way you want it to with as little pain as possible. Good luck!

Notes:

Bare Bones Basics

Part 1

In this part . . .

Windows 95 works like those expensive picture-in-picture TV sets, where viewers can watch the Raiders yet still keep an eye on the Chargers game playing in the corner window.

Windows, too, lets you put more than one program on the computer screen, each visible in its own little window. Or if your multimedia computer has a TV card, you can put the Chargers game in a corner window while typing business reports in the foreground.

To introduce you to this world of Windows, this book starts at the most elementary level: how to turn your computer (and Windows) on and off. The procedure is only a little more complicated than turning on your TV set and less complicated than anything involving recording on your VCR.

When windows start filling your screen, you'll have to learn ways to manipulate them. A unit in this part of the book shows you how to shuffle programs around, pushing their windows aside when you don't need them and bringing them to the forefront when desired. You'll learn how to make the important windows bigger and shrink or delete the unnecessary ones.

Finally, you'll learn to make a Windows program do your bidding, which is usually as simple as ordering food from a restaurant's menu.

Note: When Windows 95 is capitalized, it refers to the software that's sold on little floppy disks or CD-ROMs in computer stores. When windows is lowercase, the word refers to the little square box on-screen containing a program. Also, don't confuse Windows 95 with earlier versions of Windows, like Windows 3.1 or Windows 3.11. Windows 95 will run most programs written for earlier versions of Windows, but most earlier versions of Windows won't run programs written for Windows 95.

Starting and Exiting Windows 95

Prerequisites
- A computer
- Windows 95 installed on the computer

Objectives for This Unit

- ✓ Turning on your computer
- ✓ Loading and exiting Windows
- ✓ Turning off the computer and monitor

Right after firing up the coffee machine, turning on your computer and starting Windows are probably your first steps of the day. So this unit starts with the absolute basics: finding the computer's On switch, flipping it in the right direction, and watching Windows jump to life.

Or if Windows doesn't jump onto your screen automatically, you'll learn the easiest ways to drag it up there yourself.

Finally, this unit explains how to shut down Windows and your computer at the day's end. Plus, it explores the topic that's been plaguing computer users for years: Should computers *really* be turned off at night?

Lesson 1-1

Turning On Your Computer

Notes:

If your computer isn't making any noise, it's either turned off, unplugged, or broken. The good news is that turning the computer on usually brings it to life.

The bad news is that computer designers didn't hang out at the same bar when designing the On/Off switch. Sometimes a big red lever on the side controls the power; other times the switch is a little nub along the front. However, it's almost always the biggest switch on the computer.

Found the switch? Then here's how to turn on the computer:

1 **Turn on the monitor.**

Most monitors make a "click" sound when you turn them on, just like a TV set. They usually don't display anything until you turn on the computer, though.

2 **Flip the computer's On/Off switch in the opposite direction**.

Some On/Off switches have little symbols on them; the side with the little line means On, and the side with the little circle means Off. Your computer should gently whir itself to life and make high-tech clicking noises.

Doesn't work? Try this: If the computer still doesn't start making noise, turn the On/Off switch back to off. Then check to make sure that the computer's power cord is plugged securely into its rear. Check to see where the cord plugs into the wall or power strip, too. Are the connections tight? Try flipping the switch again.

Still doesn't work? Check the *power strip* — a collection of outlets that powers some computers. Power strips have their own On/Off switch that controls *everything* plugged into them.

If you're lucky, Windows 95 appears on your screen, as shown in Figure 1-1. If you're not so lucky, you get something called a *DOS prompt,* which looks like this: `C:\>`.

Got Windows on-screen? Skip ahead to the "Exiting Windows" section near the end of Lesson 1-2.

Stuck with a funny looking `C:\>` prompt instead of Windows? The beginning of Lesson 1-2 shows you how to bring Windows 95 to the forefront.

Either way, congratulations! You've taken the first step toward computer literacy.

Note: See the little welcome note that Windows 95 tosses your way as a greeting? To get the note off the screen, click on the button marked Close. Or if you're getting sick of seeing those notes whenever you turn on your computer, first click in the little box where it says `Show this Welcome Screen next time you start Windows`. (The mouse arrow is pointing at that box in Figure 1-1.) Windows 95 will then stop trying to be so helpful. Don't know how to click your mouse? Jump ahead a few pages to Lesson 2-1 for a quick tutorial.

☑ Progress Check

If you can do the following, you've mastered this lesson:

❑ Turn on your monitor.

❑ Turn on your computer.

❑ Know the difference between Windows and the DOS prompt.

Loading and Exiting Windows

When you turn on the computer, it almost always loads Windows 95 automatically. If it doesn't, this lesson teaches you how to load Windows yourself. Plus, you'll learn how to exit Windows when you're through working. Whew!

Loading Windows

If Windows doesn't automatically appear when you turn on your monitor, perhaps your computer has been left at the DOS prompt. To bring Windows 95 back to life, follow these instructions:

1 **Type** exit **at the DOS prompt, as shown in the following line:**

```
C:\>EXIT
```

2 **Press Enter. Your computer should immediately start loading Windows.**

Exiting Windows

heads up

Never simply turn off your computer while Windows is on-screen. First, that doesn't give Windows a chance to save your work. Second, Windows often stores information in the background, and it subsequently fumbles it if it doesn't have a chance to pack up. Always exit Windows by using the following steps:

never turn off computer when Windows is running

1 **Find the Start button and click on it.**

If you can spot the Start button, shown in the bottom-left corner of Figure 1-1, head for Step 2. If you don't see it, holding down the Ctrl key and the Esc key at the same time brings the Start button to the forefront.

The Start button contains the buttons that let you start other programs and get some work done.

on the test

2 **Click on the words Sh**u**t Down from the Start menu.**

Sh**u**t Down is the official Off switch, and clicking on it tells Windows 95 to shut itself down. First, however, Windows sends out the warning shown in Figure 1-2.

Although the Start button is labeled Start, you also use it for stopping Windows 95 when you're ready to stop working.

on the test

3 **Click on the** **Y**es button.

After being convinced that you really want to exit, Windows shuts itself down, making sure that you've saved all your work in your Windows programs. (Just in case, make a habit of saving your work whenever you think of it; you'll find more information about saving files in Unit 8.)

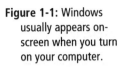

Figure 1-1: Windows usually appears on-screen when you turn on your computer.

Figure 1-2: When you choose Sh<u>u</u>t Down from the Start menu, Windows 95 sends a warning to make sure that you want to shut it down.

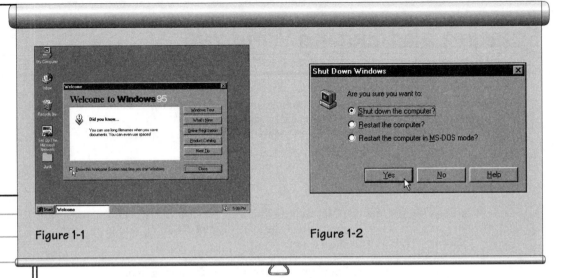

Figure 1-1   Figure 1-2

☑ Progress Check

If you can do the following, you've mastered this lesson:

❑ Load Windows.

❑ Find the Start button.

❑ Exit Windows by choosing the Start menu's Sh<u>u</u>t Down command.

Running any DOS programs? Then you'd better shut them down before trying to shut down Windows. Windows refuses to close DOS programs, leaving that chore up to you.

extra credit

Hey, what's a double-click?

See that mouse attached to the computer by its tail? See the little buttons on the mouse? Rest your right hand on the mouse and look at the button that your index finger touches. When you click the button once, you've *clicked* the mouse. Click the button twice in rapid succession, and you've *double-clicked.*

See how the arrow on-screen moves when you move the mouse with your hand? That's how you control things in Windows: by pointing the mouse's arrow at buttons on-screen and pushing the mouse's buttons with strategic clicks. (Mice — and their subsequent double-clicks — get their own section in Unit 2.)

Lesson 1-3   Turning Off Your Computer

Both sides of the "Should I turn off my computer at night?" debate are covered at the end of this lesson; I'm not going to tackle that issue here. In the meantime, *everybody* agrees that you should follow these basic steps before leaving your computer at the day's end (Step 5 is optional):

1 Save your work and exit your Windows and DOS programs.

Make sure that you save all your work before turning off your computer — that's the most important step of all. (Not sure how to save a file? Here are the basic steps, but Unit 8 has the full details: Click on the word Eile along the program's top edge; when a menu drops down, click on the word Save. If you haven't saved the file before, type a short, descriptive name and press Enter.)

DOS programs aren't always shut down in the same way, unfortunately, but you need to shut them down, too.

2 Back up your computer's information.

If you have a backup program — a tape system, Zip drive, or some other device that the guy at the store talked you into buying — now's the time to use it. (You really should have bought one, you know.) Store the backups in a safe place, preferably away from the computer.

3 Exit Windows.

You already learned this trick — you choose Shut down the computer from the Start menu's Shut Down command — in Lesson 1-2.

4 Turn off the monitor.

Flip that same switch that you flipped in Lesson 1-1. *Everybody* turns off their monitors at night except the security guy in the lobby.

5 Turn off the computer (optional).

Again, flip that same On switch that you flipped in Lesson 1-1. Or if you prefer to leave your computer on, just make sure that nobody puts a cover over it so that it won't heat up at night.

extra credit

What are those other Shut Down options?

Windows 95 gives you a few other options under the Shut Down command, as shown in Figure 1-2. Although computers differ, you'll probably encounter these options:

▶ **Shut down the computer?**

If you want to turn off your computer, choose this option in order to close down Windows 95 first.

▶ **Restart the computer?**

Many newly-installed programs want you to restart your computer by choosing this option.

▶ **Restart the computer in MS-DOS mode?**

Some temperamental DOS programs don't like to run from within Windows 95. So choose this option to temporarily run your computer in MS-DOS mode, which often treats MS-DOS programs in a more friendly way.

▶ **Close all programs and log on as a different user?**

Some Windows users set up Windows 95 so that different people can work on the same computer but still keep their work separate. If your computer is set up this way, this option appears in the Shut Down box, ready for different users to play with Windows at different times.

Notes:

☑ **Progress Check**

If you can do the following, you've mastered this lesson:

❏ Safely exit Windows.

❏ Turn of your monitor.

❏ Turn off your computer.

Notes:

extra credit

Debating the merits of leaving the computer on

Some people don't turn their computers off. Ever. See, when you turn off the computer, its sensitive internal components cool down. When you turn it back on, they heat up again. Because most of the components sit on a big fiberglass plate called a *motherboard*, all that flexing can cause them to loosen. Keeping the temperature constant keeps the fluctuation down, which keeps everything more comfortable inside.

Other people turn their computers off at night, saying that 24-hour wear and tear can't be good for the fans and hard drives. Plus, the computer will catch any power surge that comes down the wire.

Which method works best? You'll have to decide that one yourself. (Some of my computers are on constantly, and the others are on for only a few hours a day.)

Unit 1 Quiz

For each question, circle the letter of the correct answer or answers. Some questions may have more than one right answer.

1. **When trying to fix a broken computer, you should try this:**

    A. Make sure that its power switch is turned on.

    B. Make sure that it's plugged in.

    C. If it's plugged into a power strip, make sure that the power strip is turned on.

    D. Raise your hand and slowly wave it back and forth.

2. **To shut down Windows 95, you do this:**

    A. Choose Sh<u>ut</u> Down from the Start menu.

    B. Click on the Close button.

    C. Just flip the computer's Off switch.

    D. Just turn off the monitor.

3. **Should you leave your computer turned on at night?**

    A. Yes.

    B. No.

    C. Maybe.

    D. There are more important things to worry about.

4. **What does "backing up" your data mean?**

    A. Putting the computer into reverse and hitting the gas.

    B. Copying important files onto floppy disks, tape drives, or other storage devices.

    C. Storing your programs and boxes in a safe place.

    D. Making sure that you have two copies of your most important files.

Unit 1 Exercise

1. Turn on the monitor and computer.

2. If Windows 95 doesn't load itself automatically, load it yourself.

3. Find the Start button.

4. Close down Windows by choosing Shut Down from the Start menu and clicking on the Yes button.

5. Turn off your monitor and your computer, if you choose to.

Using a Mouse and Keyboard

Prerequisites
▶ Turning on your computer (Lesson 1-1)
▶ Loading Windows 95 (Lesson 1-2)

Objectives for This Unit

✓ Clicking the mouse

✓ Double-clicking the mouse

✓ Dragging and dropping

✓ Using the function keys

✓ Using the Alt and Ctrl keys

✓ Using the Esc key

✓ Using the arrow keys

Just as you control a car by moving the steering wheel, you control Windows by moving the mouse and pressing keys on the keyboard. (Talking at computers — or even yelling at them — doesn't control them nearly as well, as most people have discovered.)

This unit shows you how to use the mouse to press buttons and make choices from on-screen menus. You'll learn how to *drag and drop* bits of important information from one program window to another. Plus, you'll learn about some of those extra keys that computers have on their keyboards: Alt, Ctrl, Esc, the function keys, and the four little arrows.

This unit also shows you how to get into Solitaire, that card game that you see on everybody's screens.

Lesson 2-1

Using the Mouse

Notes:

In the days of olde, people merely typed text into computers. To control the programs, they pushed little arrows on their keyboards.

Today's computer users don't get as much exercise because they rely on a *mouse*. Shown in Figure 2-1, the mouse is a palm-sized contraption with a wire that connects to the back of the computer.

Moving the mouse with your hand moves an arrow across the computer screen. By pointing at buttons on-screen — and pushing a button on the mouse — you can boss programs around.

You can manipulate your mouse in three basic ways, which are described in the following sections.

Making a click

Whenever you press and release a button on the mouse, the mouse makes a *click*. Computer programmers used that scientific phrase to describe pushing one of the mouse's buttons with your finger. To give a click a try, follow these steps:

1 Load Windows 95.

Don't have Windows 95 on your screen? Unit 1 is waiting for you.

2 Move your mouse and watch the arrow or cursor move across the screen.

Moving the mouse means sliding it across the desktop with the clickable buttons facing upward. (The mouse doesn't slide against the face of the monitor, and yes, people have certainly tried.)

3 Aim the mouse's arrow at the Start button, shown in Figure 2-2, and click the left mouse button.

See how the mouse's arrow is pointing to the Start button in the lower-left corner of your screen? When you click the left mouse button, a menu shoots up, just as it does in Figure 2-2.

Click the mouse by quickly pressing and releasing its left mouse button with your right index finger.

The menu reveals a bunch more options to choose from, but you don't have to play with any of those now; menus are covered in Unit 3. But you've mastered clicking, and that's a *big* part of using Windows. (To get the menu back down, click on the Start button again. Or you can press the Esc key, but that trick is covered in Lesson 2-2.)

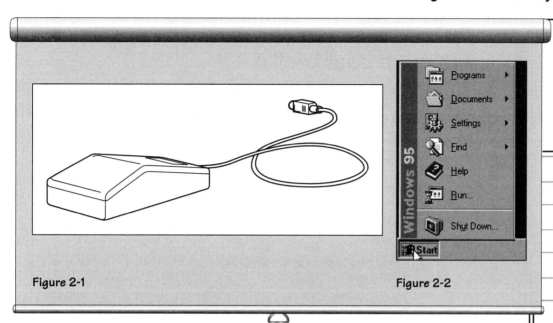

Figure 2-1

Figure 2-2

Figure 2-1: The mouse.

Figure 2-2: Press and release the mouse button with the mouse arrow over the Start button to "click" the mouse on that spot.

on the test

Windows 95 — and all earlier versions of Windows — normally prefers that you use the *left* mouse button (unless, of course, someone switched the functions of your left and right mouse buttons, in which case Windows prefers the *right* mouse button). Windows 95, however, also makes use of the right button. In fact, whenever you're curious about what an icon or window can do, click on it with your right mouse button. A menu appears, listing the things that you can do with that icon or window.

extra credit

Getting helpful hints from the mouse

Windows 95 dumps a lot of information onto the screen at one time. How can you tell which button, box, or window does what? Luckily, your mouse can help you out.

First, if a button or icon in a Windows 95 program has you confused, simply point at it and wait a few seconds. Sometimes that's enough to make the program send a little window to the screen, explaining that button or icon's reason for existence.

Or if an icon, window, or menu item has you confused, click on it with your *right* mouse button. Windows 95 usually brings up a menu listing the things that you can do with that icon or window.

on the test

For the most part, Windows 95 doesn't care where the mouse pointer happens to be resting on-screen — *until you click the mouse.* So when you move the mouse pointer to where you want the action to happen, click the mouse button to make Windows notice your presence.

Notes:

Making a *double-click*

Got the mouse click down pat? Then get ready for the *double-click*. The double-click is just like it sounds: pointing the mouse's arrow at someplace on-screen and clicking the mouse's left button with your index finger twice in rapid succession. In other words, you make two clicks, one right after the other. Follow these steps for some practice:

1 Load Windows 95.

By now, you probably have Windows on-screen most of the time, so I'll soon start leaving it off as the first step. (Feel free to keep loading Windows, though.)

2 Move your mouse and watch the arrow or the cursor move across the screen.

Most new computer owners get mouse pads for Christmas; a good mouse pad lets the mouse roll more smoothly.

3 Aim the mouse's arrow at the My Computer button in the screen's top-left corner (shown in Figure 2-3), and double-click the left mouse button.

Instead of just clicking the mouse button like you did in the last set of steps, *double-click* the mouse by quickly pressing and releasing the left mouse button twice with your right index finger.

The My Computer program, shown in Figure 2-4, opens to reveal even more buttons — called *icons.* By double-clicking on the icons in this My Computer contraption, you can view the files and programs stored inside your computer. (You'll find a lot more My Computer information in Part II.)

4 Click on the little X in the My Computer window's upper-right corner to close the window.

To close down any window in Windows 95, just click on the X in its upper-right corner. (Figure 2-4 shows the arrow pointing at the proper place.)

Although a double-click sounds easy — just two rapid clicks — getting the hang of it can be hard at first. However, double-clicking is the key to making just about anything happen in Windows.

Is all this clicking stuff too easy for you? Then jump ahead to the quiz at this unit's end. You may be able to flip ahead a few pages and save yourself some time.

extra credit

Q/A Session

Question: My double-clicks don't work!

Answer: You're probably not keeping the mouse pointer steady enough while you press the mouse button. See, your mouse's arrow needs to hover over the object while you press *and* release the button twice. If you push too hard — or too quickly — you may slide the mouse arrow off of its destination before the last click release has a chance to register. Also, your mouse click speed may be set too fast for your fingers; Unit 17 shows you how to fine-tune the speed of a recognizable double-click.

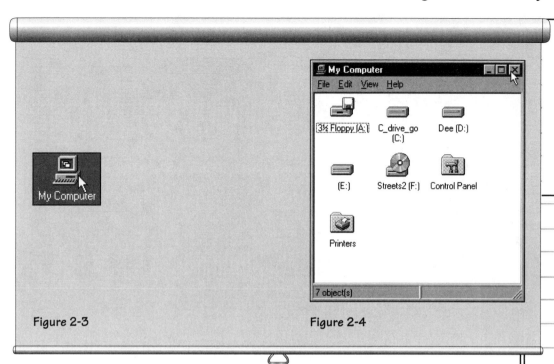

Figure 2-3

Figure 2-4

Figure 2-3: Double-click on the My Computer icon to see the folders and disk drives stored inside.

Figure 2-4: Click on the little X in any window's upper-right corner to close it down and get it off the screen.

Dragging and dropping

A *drag and drop* is really a slow, slow click, when you think about it. Basically, it's a slick trick for moving something across the screen, and it works like this:

Point the mouse's arrow at the object you want to move — a window or box on-screen, for example — and then *hold down* the mouse button. Now, while holding down the mouse button, move the mouse across your desktop. When the arrow hovers over the place you'd like to drop the object, let go of the mouse button, and you *drop* the object there.

extra credit

Q/A Session

Question: Hey, I'm left-handed. Can I switch my mouse buttons?

Answer: Sure. The Windows Control Panel lets you switch the mouse button to work on either the left or right side, whichever feels best. (Changing Windows settings is covered in Unit 17.)

I'll use the Solitaire game to teach dragging and dropping, for two reasons. First, Solitaire is a game, so working with it is fun. Second, loading Solitaire teaches you how to load any program by using the Start button's menus, which is another task you need to know in Windows 95. Follow these steps:

Figure 2-5: Click on the Start button, and a menu pops up.

Figure 2-6: Click on the word Programs, and another menu pops up.

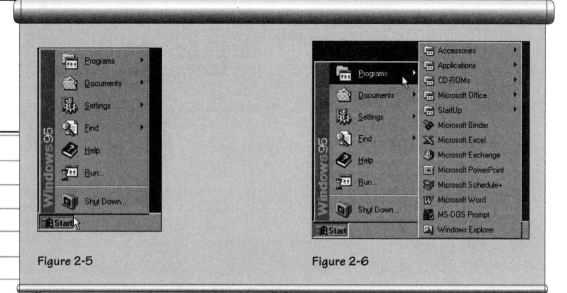

Figure 2-5   Figure 2-6

1 Click on the Start button.

By now, you probably know that the Start button lives in the bottom-left corner of your screen. A menu pops up, as shown in Figure 2-5.

2 Click on the word Programs.

Yet another menu pops out, as shown in Figure 2-6.

3 Click on the word Accessories.

Yep — it's yet another menu, as shown in Figure 2-7.

4 Click on the word Games.

Yawn. *Another* menu pops out, as shown in Figure 2-8.

extra credit

Q/A Session

Question: What's that funny-looking wheel on top of my mouse?

Answer: Microsoft recently released an *IntelliMouse* that features a strange wheel along its top. Spinning the wheel back and forth with your finger affects your program in different ways. You can make portions of the screen larger or smaller, for example, or you can change font sizes in Microsoft Word. The Microsoft AutoMap

Streets Plus program lets you spin the wheel to "zoom in or out" of the map, quickly changing the view from an entire county to individual streets. The catch? The IntelliMouse only works if a program specifically supports it, and so far, very few programs have rolled onto the IntelliMouse bandwagon. If it's not working with your favorite program, that program probably doesn't support the IntelliMouse.

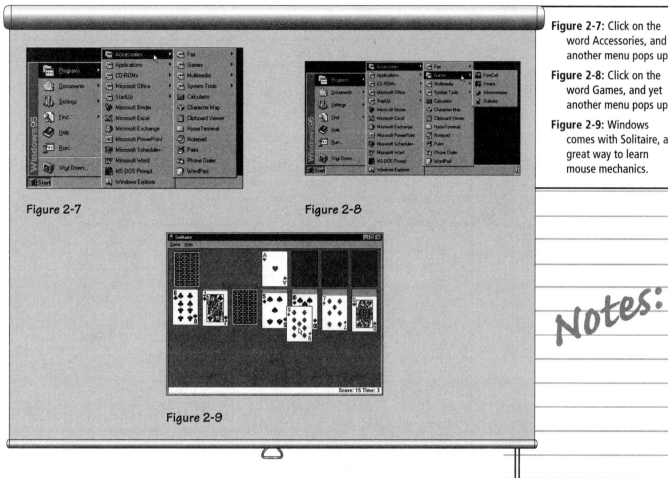

Figure 2-7

Figure 2-8

Figure 2-9

Figure 2-7: Click on the
word Accessories, and
another menu pops up.

Figure 2-8: Click on the
word Games, and yet
another menu pops up.

Figure 2-9: Windows
comes with Solitaire, a
great way to learn
mouse mechanics.

Notes:

heads up

What? No listing for Games on your menu? That means that the person who
installed Windows 95 on your computer didn't install any games. Luckily,
Unit 19 shows how to use the Control Panel's Add/Remove Programs icon to
install them. Look for the "My version of Windows 95 doesn't have the right
programs!" section in Unit 19.

5 Click on the word Solitaire.

Shown in Figure 2-9, Solitaire is an officially endorsed method of learning how
to use Windows. In fact, many people around the office never stop using this
valuable tool.

6 Practice dragging and dropping cards with a game of Solitaire.

If you don't know how to play Solitaire, just point at a card, hold down the
mouse button, and move the mouse across the desk. See how the card moves
across the screen? Let go of the mouse button, and you drop the card. If you
drop it in a spot approved by Hoyle, the card stays put; otherwise, Solitaire
whisks the card back to its stack and you have to try dragging another.

extra credit

A first-time Solitaire user

Most people have a copy of Hoyle's around, so I'll stick with the mouse mechanics. Basically, you drag the face-up cards around from stack to stack, trying to sort them into the right order on-screen. For example, in Figure 2-9, the mouse pointer is dragging the nine of diamonds off of one stack and dropping it onto the ten of spades.

If you drag a card off of a stack, click on the face-down card that's left in its place on-screen; doing so flips the card over. If you drag the last remaining card off of a stack, then you can drag a king over and drop it on the blank stack.

One more basic rule exists: After you drop an ace onto any of the four card areas in the upper-right corner, you can start dropping other, similarly suited cards on top. (In numerical order, of course. And you can drop big chunks of cards, too.)

To start the game, look at the cards that Solitaire's stub-stogied dealer dumps on-screen. Can you immediately drag any aces to the piles along the top? Can you drop any cards from the seven bottom stacks onto those freshly dropped aces? Can you drag and drop any of the cards

around on the seven stacks? The more cards you're able to expose, the better you'll be able to plan your strategy.

Tip: If you have a card that can be dragged and dropped to the piles along the top, just double-click on the card. Windows moves the card to the pile automatically.

If you can't make any moves with what's currently showing, click on the deck of cards sitting in the upper-left corner to begin turning them over. Can you play that first exposed card anywhere? If so, go for it. If not, keep clicking on that stack of cards, turning them over until you find one that you can play.

When the deck's completely turned over, double-click the spot where the deck used to rest and it flips over. And over. And over.

Finally, if Solitaire still seems too complicated, give its Help system a whirl: Click on the word <u>H</u>elp along its top edge. When the menu drops down, click on <u>H</u>elp Topics. When the Help Topics window appears, click on the words How to play Solitaire. (A little icon with a question mark sits next to those words.) You'll find more information about the Windows Help system in Unit 18.

Although Unit 3 is packed with this stuff, Table 2-1 provides a preview of the kinds of things that Windows lets you drag and drop.

☑ Progress Check

If you can do the following, you've mastered this lesson:

❏ Aim the mouse pointer.

❏ Click the mouse pointer on a button.

❏ Double-click the mouse pointer.

❏ Drag and drop an item on your desktop.

❏ Load a game of Solitaire and begin to play (you don't have to win).

Table 2-1	Things That Windows Conveniently Lets You Drag and Drop
Accomplish This	*By Doing This*
Change a window's on-screen size	Dragging its corners or borders around on-screen
Move an entire window across the screen	Dragging the window's top-most edge, which usually contains the program's name
Change settings	Sliding levers back and forth

Accomplish This	By Doing This
Create organized batches of push buttons	Dragging and dropping *shortcut* icons to ease program launching on your desktop
"Scroll" your on-screen view of something contained in a window	Dragging the little "elevator" up or down the shaft on the window's right side and dropping it onto a new location
Customize your desktop	Dragging icons into new or different groups
Copy files from place to place	Dragging the file's names and dropping them in different locations in the My Computer folder or Explorer program
Move just about any item that's not nailed down	Pointing at the item, dragging it to a new place, and letting go of the mouse button

Using the Keyboard   Lesson 2-2

The keyboard's a little more familiar than a mouse to most new Windows users, but it's often just as awkward — especially because computers come with some sneaky extra keys that everyone's supposed to learn. And of course, those strange new keys are harder to reach than Q and Z. Plus, the keys are never in the same place on a friend's keyboard, either.

This lesson covers the four main types of sneaky keys that you'll find yourself using with Windows 95: function keys, arrow keys, the Alt key, and the Ctrl key.

Using a function key

Perched like spectators along a keyboard's top edge, function keys let you boss Windows around quickly and easily. Shown in Figure 2-10, for example, the function keys often appear listed next to the particular menu items they stand for. Pressing the function key works just like clicking the mouse on the menu item, and it's often a quick shortcut.

One function key almost always summons the Windows built-in Help program no matter what you happen to be doing. Here's how it works:

1 Load Windows 95, and click anywhere on its background.

Don't click on any programs, just aim for the background. (In fact, you may have to move some of the programs out of the way in order to see the background.) Although you won't see anything happen on the surface, that background click turns Windows' attention to its *desktop*, the platter that everything rests on.

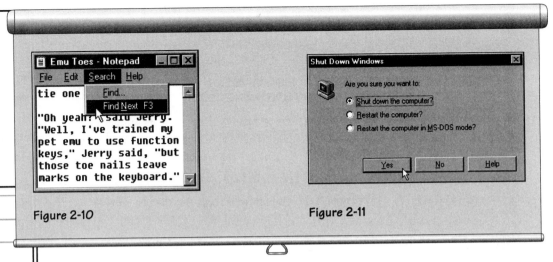

Figure 2-10: Some menus list their function key shortcuts; pressing F3 tells Notepad to perform the Find Next command.

Figure 2-11: Click on the No button if you don't want to exit Windows.

Figure 2-10   Figure 2-11

press the F1 key near the top-left corner of the keyboard, and Windows 95 usually offers information that's helpful to the current situation

pressing Alt+F4 shuts down a window, just like double-clicking in the window's upper-left corner

2 Press F1.

The Help program pops up, ready to dish out information about the currently running window. In this case, the Help system explains basic Windows 95 information, complete with tips and tricks, troubleshooting, and a short instructional tour.

The Windows Help system is covered completely in Unit 18; the desktop gets its due in Unit 4.

Whenever you see something in Windows, or in this book, like Ctrl+F1 or Alt+Backspace, that means that you press those two keys simultaneously. You don't have to be lightning fast; just press the first key listed, press the second key, and then let go of both of them.

Using the Alt and Ctrl keys

The Alt and Ctrl keys don't do anything by themselves. No, they almost always need another key as a buddy to make things happen on-screen. For example, here's how to close Windows — or any window, for that matter — without double-clicking on anything. (It's a handy trick to know if your mouse ever dies on you, heaven forbid.)

1 Click on your Windows 95 desktop.

Don't click on any programs, just click on the desktop that all your programs run on.

2 Press F4 while holding down the Alt key.

Known as Alt+F4, this simultaneous combination of keys tells the currently running program to close itself down. Because shutting down the desktop also shuts down Windows 95, ever-cautious Windows sends you the message shown in Figure 2-11.

3 Click on the No button.

Doing so brings you back to Windows 95, but now you've got some function key know-how under your belt.

extra credit

> ## Undeleting accidental deletions
>
> Just erased a key paragraph with your word processor? Then hold down Alt and press the Backspace key. If you press Alt+Backspace before typing anything else, Windows may be able to spit your accidental deletion back onto the screen.

press
Alt+Backspace to
undo deletion

Using the Esc (Escape) key

Although it sounds like a lifesaver from a bad computing situation, the Esc key is a pretty weak hero. But pressing Esc is worth a shot if nothing else is going right and things look weird.

For example, if you click on something and a menu shoots out, how do you make the menu pop back down without fuss? By pressing the Esc key, as shown in the following steps:

1 Click on the Start button.

A menu pops up, listing bunches of choices that you'll hear about in Unit 4.

2 Press the Esc key, usually found in the upper-left corner of most keyboards.

The menu goes away.

on the test

The Esc key doesn't do much by itself, but it's often a good first bet for clearing the screen of a popped-up menu.

Using the keyboard's arrow keys

No big surprises here. Pushing the keyboard's arrow keys simultaneously pushes your computer's cursor across the screen. In fact, the keyboard's arrow keys are often called *cursor keys.* The big thing to remember is that your *cursor* differs from your mouse *pointer,* and here's how.

When you move your *mouse,* you're moving your pointer. Doing so helps you choose among different options on-screen or move items to different on-screen locations. The mouse's little arrow can point just about anywhere on the monitor, and when you click on different spots, you're telling Windows where you want to work.

When you push your keyboard's *arrow keys,* you're only moving your cursor on-screen. The cursor stays stuck in the single window or program that you're currently working with; no big travels here. The following example shows a little of the difference between the two:

☑ **Progress Check**

If you can do the following, you've mastered this lesson:

❑ Use function keys as shortcuts.

❑ Uses the Alt, Ctrl, and Esc keys.

❑ Use a keyboard's arrow keys.

use mouse pointer
for switching
between programs
or moving cursor to
new location inside
programs

use arrow keys for
more subtle cursor
movements within
programs

1 **Click on the Start button.**

As always, a menu shoots up.

2 **Press the keyboard's up arrow key.**

See how the word Sh<u>u</u>t Down is now highlighted? Pushing the arrow lets you control the Start button's menu with the arrow keys instead of the mouse.

3 **Press the up arrow again.**

The word <u>R</u>un is highlighted now.

4 **Press the up arrow until it highlights the word <u>P</u>rograms.**

5 **Press the right arrow key.**

A menu pops out listing the available programs. Notice how pressing the arrow keys lets you explore — but not leave — the Start menu.

6 **Click on the desktop's My Computer icon in the upper-left corner of your desktop, and watch the Start menu disappear.**

See how the mouse's arrow lets you leave the confines of the Start menu and head to the desktop area instead? Although the keyboard cursor and mouse arrow both perform similar functions, the mouse arrow has much more get-up-and-go.

The mouse pointer and the arrow-key cursor are two separate things on-screen, but they often look and act alike. Here's a big clue, though: If it blinks, it's probably an arrow-key cursor, because a mouse pointer never blinks.

Unit 2 Quiz

For each question, circle the letter of the correct answer or answers. Remember, each question may have more than one right answer, so don't be afraid to chew that pencil stub a little.

1. **Windows 95 programs use only the left mouse button.**

    A. True.

    B. False.

2. **Double-clicking a mouse is an easy task.**

    A. True, because it's simply like knocking twice on a door.

    B. False, because everything's so darn small.

    C. False, because you're sunk if you accidentally jostle the mouse pointer off the target while clicking.

    D. Performance depends on mood.

Notes:

3. **Windows lets you adjust your mouse's double-click speed to match your finger speed.**

    A. Impossible.

    B. It's pretty easy, actually, and it's covered in Unit 17.

4. **To make Windows shift its attention to another place on-screen, do the following:**

    A. Move the mouse until the little on-screen arrow points at that spot.

    B. Move the mouse until the little on-screen arrow points at that spot, and then click the left mouse button.

    C. Move the mouse until the little on-screen arrow points at that spot, and then click the right mouse button.

    D. Push the keyboard's little arrow keys.

5. **You use the Esc key for the following tasks:**

    A. Fixing any computer mistakes you've made.

    B. Avoiding bad situations.

    C. Leaving work early.

    D. Making pop-up menus go back down.

6. **The expression "Press Ctrl+Esc" means the following:**

    A. Everybody should escape other people's control.

    B. You should press the Ctrl key, release it, and then press the Esc key.

    C. You should press the Esc key, followed by the Ctrl key.

    D. You should press the Esc key *while holding down* the Ctrl key.

Unit 2 Exercise

1. Click on the Start button.

2. Choose Programs from the Start menu.

3. Choose Accessories from the Programs menu.

4. Click on Notepad from the Accessories menu.

5. While pointing at the words Untitled - Notepad in the Notepad window's top edge, drag and drop the window a quarter of an inch in any direction.

6. Click on the word File located near Notepad's upper-left corner.

7. Press the Esc key to make the File menu disappear.

8. Press Alt+F4 to close down Notepad.

Understanding Windows and Menus

Prerequisites
- Turning on your computer and loading Windows (Lessons 1-1 and 1-2)
- Pointing and clicking the mouse (Lesson 2-1)
- Double-clicking the mouse (Lesson 2-1)
- Dragging and dropping with the mouse (Lesson 2-1)
- Using the keyboard (Lesson 2-2)

Objectives for This Unit

- ✓ Understanding window basics
- ✓ Finding and moving windows around on-screen
- ✓ Changing a window's size
- ✓ Minimizing and closing windows
- ✓ Choosing options from menus and buttons
- ✓ Filling out forms in Windows 95

In the old days, people worked on a plain-old desktop, grabbing and sliding around pieces of paper until it was time to go home. The newfangled software known as Windows 95 creates a new type of desktop on your computer monitor. Instead of making you work with pieces of paper, however, Windows makes you work with *windows* — boxes of information that light up your computerized desktop.

Embedded along the edges of these windows are little buttons and menus for controlling the work inside. (Yeah, all this stuff sounds weird at first, but you'll get used to it.)

In fact, you *have* to get used to it; this window/button/menu concept appears in every Windows program.

You have to get used to a few other oddities as well. For starters, your computerized desktop is probably just a little over one square foot in size, meaning that the windows constantly overlap each other. Adding to the clumsiness, the windows don't let you reach over and grab them. Instead, you manipulate them with the computer's mouse and keyboard, which can be as awkward as grabbing logs with fireplace tongs.

This unit teaches you how to open and close the windows and programs on your new, computerized desktop. You'll learn how to move the unwanted windows out of the way and bring the desired ones to the forefront. You'll learn the locations of a window's most sensitive spots so that you'll know where to point and click. Finally, Unit 3 teaches you some shortcuts for scurrying past one of the most frequent and least entertaining Windows 95 activities: filling out on-screen forms. Yaaaaawwwwnnnn.

Lesson 3-1 — Maximizing and Minimizing Windows

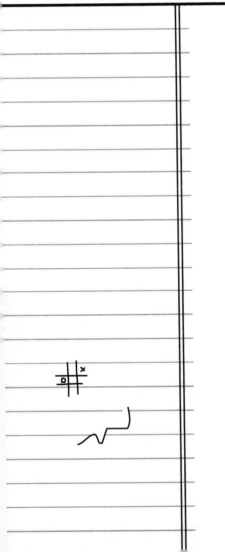

When installed in a house, windows come with two basic options: open or shut. Anything else requires a contractor, a fancy decorator, or a big rock.

Microsoft Windows jazzes things up in a few other ways. Its programs can run inside little windows on-screen, as you saw in Unit 1, or a program can fill the entire screen for easier access. If other windows get in the way, you have yet another option: You can shrink currently unused windows into tiny icons that rest along the bottom of the screen.

By combining these skills, you can simultaneously juggle several programs on the desktop without dropping them all.

Opening and closing a window

Whenever you want Windows to do something, you load a *program:* a bunch of computerized instructions that tell the computer to get off its duff and do something. Some programs balance checkbooks, for example; others process words or create party flyers.

To make a program appear on-screen, double-click the program's *icon,* located on the Start menu. Windows 95 finds the program's instructions and loads them into your computer's memory, and the program appears on-screen, ready for action. (Don't worry if this sounds confusing at first; the Start menu gets complete coverage in Unit 4.)

Opening a window works like this:

1 Click on the Start button.

Unit 1 teaches this step; the Start button appears along the bottom-left corner of your screen whenever you turn on your computer and start Windows. Start button not visible? Press Ctrl+Esc to bring the Start menu to life.

2 **Click on Programs from the Start menu.**

A list of programs shoots out from the side of the word Programs.

3 **Click on Windows Explorer at the bottom of the Programs menu.**

When you click on an item on the Start menu, that item comes to life, either revealing another menu or loading itself and appearing as a program on your screen. In this case, the Windows Explorer program pops onto the screen in its own window. (Explorer, a complicated-looking little beast, lets you move files around on your computer, but you don't have to worry about using it until Unit 5.)

4 **Close Windows Explorer.**

As you learned in Lesson 2-1, close any program by clicking on the little X in the window's upper-right corner. Doing so always makes Windows shut down the program, whether the program is taking up the whole screen or living inside a window.

Or if a program happens to be a little icon at the bottom of the screen, click on the icon once with the right mouse button and choose Close from the menu that pops out of its head.

Some programs take up the entire screen when they're loaded; others automatically jump into a window, and still others load themselves as little icons along the bottom of the screen. The rest of this lesson teaches you how to toggle a program among all three varieties.

A window's borders enable programs to overlap on-screen without their contents getting mixed up. The borders also let you change the window's size and shape, a simple task described in the next lesson.

After you load some programs, you can move their windows around on-screen until they're easy to see and work with. The lessons later in this unit teach you all the ways to move windows, but be sure to check out the unit's last lesson; it teaches you some quick window-positioning tricks that everybody else spent three months learning through trial and error.

You can load Windows programs a few other ways, but the Start button (covered in Unit 4) is by far the easiest and most common way.

Making a window fill the screen (Maximizing)

Running programs in little on-screen windows often makes your work easier. You can glance back and forth between windows, grabbing information from one program and "pasting" it into another.

But sometimes you want a window to fill the entire screen. When writing a letter, for example, you don't want the sentences running off the edges.

Notes:

Figure 3-1: Double-click the bar along the Windows Explorer window's top edge to maximize the window and make it completely fill the screen.

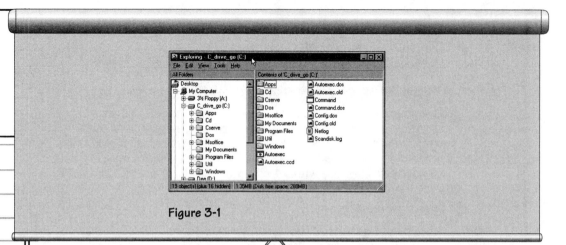

Figure 3-1

To satisfy people who want their programs running at maximum size, Windows lets you *maximize* its windows. For example, here's how to maximize the Windows Explorer window:

1   Click on the Start button and load Windows Explorer.

You learned how to do so in the preceding lesson.

2   Double-click on the bar along Explorer's top.

In Figure 3-1, see that bar along the top that starts with the word *Exploring*? A double-click on that bar toggles the window's size between two positions, making it either fill the entire screen or fit inside a window.

Also in Figure 3-1, see the three little icons in the window's top-right corner? Clicking on the middle icon — the one with the square inside it — maximizes a window as well.

If double-clicking on your window's *title bar* — that little bar along the window's top edge — shrinks the window into a *smaller* window, then the window was maximized to begin with. (Why? Because double-clicking on the title bar *toggles* the program between full-screen and window-sized.)

on the test

The little bar along a window's top that lists a program's name is called the *title bar*.

on the test

You can tell when a window has been maximized because much of its window paraphernalia disappears; the borders drop off and the corners vanish.

Changing a full-screen program back into a window

If a program has been maximized — the window is borderless and filling the screen — you can push it back into a window with a single click, as described in the steps that follow.

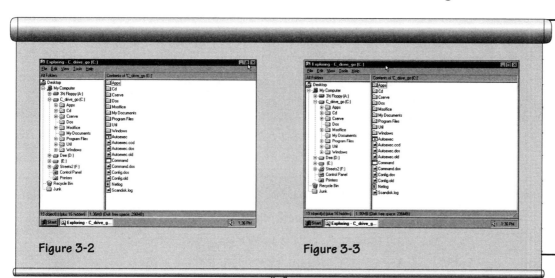

Figure 3-2: A click on the restore button in the upper-right corner shrinks a full-sized program back into a window.

Figure 3-3: Although Windows Explorer fills the screen here, the ultra-thin borders around its outside edge mean that it's still running inside a window, unlike the way Windows Explorer is running in Figure 3-2.

Figure 3-2   Figure 3-3

1 Maximize a window.

Follow the instructions in the preceding section; they give you a maximized window to practice on.

2 Click on the middle icon containing the two little squares, located near the window's upper-right corner.

Shown in Figure 3-2, the middle icon with the two little squares lets you toggle the window between filling the screen and living inside a window. The little button with the two arrows is called a *restore button*, by the way.

on the test

Tip: You can also turn a full-screen program back into a window by double-clicking on the title bar along the top of the window. Because the title bar is bigger and easier to reach than the restore button, it's often the quickest way to toggle programs from big screen-fillers into more manageable window sizes.

Sometimes a window can be big — so big, in fact, that it fills the screen, just like the full-screen program did. That confuses things, because double-clicking on the title bar doesn't appear to do anything: Simply too little of a difference exists between that huge window and a full-screen program! Look carefully, however, at the screen-filling Windows Explorer window in Figure 3-3; you'll still be able to see the window's borders around its edge, as well as two little overlapping squares in one of the icons on its upper-right side. So to change the program's size, you can drag and drop the borders, a trick that Lesson 3-2 teaches.

Turning a window into an icon (Minimizing)

Even if you can afford enough memory to have bunches of programs running simultaneously on your computer, you still have a problem: Your computerized desktop is simply too small for spreading everything out. Sooner or later, you're going to have to move some of those windows out of the way.

double-click title bar to toggle between window-size and full screen

Notes:

Luckily, Windows offers a way to keep programs loaded in your computer's memory — and ready for quick action — yet still away from view.

Windows simply hides the program in its memory and then puts a little push button called an *icon* on a strip that runs across the bottom of your screen. Click on that little icon, and the hidden program comes back to the screen almost instantly.

If your screen's getting crowded, here's how to turn a currently running program into an icon along that strip at the bottom of your screen:

1 Load Windows Explorer from the Start button's Programs menu.

You learned how to do so earlier in this lesson.

2 Click on the little box containing the line in the window's upper-right corner.

That third icon over from the top right — the one containing the tiny line — is known as the *minimize* button. Click on it, and the window immediately shrinks into a little icon and awaits further duty along the screen's bottom.

You'll find yourself toggling programs between icons and windows throughout the day. Sometimes you'll want a program in a big window for easy access; other times you'll want the same program minimized as an icon for later reference.

Minimized programs can still run in the background. For instance, telecommunications gurus can be *downloading* a file from the Internet while the telecommunications program sits as an icon at the bottom of the screen.

If you minimize one of your programs — turning it into an icon along the screen's bottom — and then load that program from the Start menu, that program comes to the screen. But it is a *second copy* of the program! The first version of your program is still waiting for you along the bottom of the screen.

heads up

Watch out for accidentally running second copies of Windows programs simultaneously. The second copy usually just causes confusion and takes up memory.

Tip: Don't know whether or not your program is currently running? Press Alt+Tab to make Windows 95 display a list of all your currently running programs. Keep pressing Tab until your program's icon is highlighted and its name appears; then let go of the Alt key. The program rises to the surface.

If you have one of those big, expensive computer monitors, you have more surface area to work with. To spread things out, you can tell Windows to change its video *resolution,* a chore covered in Unit 17.

on the test

An icon living along the bottom of the screen stands for a program that's already loaded; clicking on the icon merely brings the program back to a visible location on your desktop. The icons on the Start menu are push-buttons that launch a program — even a second copy of a program that's already running. If your program's icon rests along the screen's bottom, then that program is already loaded and ready for action. Don't load it again by clicking on its icon on the Start menu.

press Alt+Tab to display currently running programs

Turning an icon back into a window

Programs that squat inside the bar along the bottom of your screen have been *minimized* — they're still loaded in your computer's memory for quick reference, yet they're stashed away from that cramped, computerized desktop.

When it's time to bring a program back to life — to bring Windows Explorer back to the forefront for moving files around, for example — follow these instructions:

1 Find the Explorer icon on your desktop.

Although the icon is probably lined up inside the *taskbar* — that strip of icons that runs along the screen's bottom — it might be hard to spot, especially if the taskbar is hidden from view. If you can't spot the icon, try pointing the mouse at the bottom of the screen (or its outside edges); sometimes that action brings the taskbar into view. If other windows still cover the taskbar, try pressing Ctrl+Esc. (On the rare occasion that you still can't find the taskbar or icon, you may need to jump ahead to the taskbar section in Unit 4.)

2 Click on the Explorer program's icon.

The icon immediately turns back into a program, and Windows Explorer jumps back onto the screen.

If you can't find the program even after you double-click its icon, head for Lesson 3-3 for tricks on tracking down wanton Windows programs.

☑ **Progress Check**

If you can do the following, you've mastered this lesson:

❑ Open and close a window.

❑ Make a window fill the screen (maximize it).

❑ Turn a full-screen program into a window.

❑ Turn a running program into an icon (minimize it).

❑ Turn an icon back into a running program.

Carefully Adjusting a Window's Size   Lesson 3-2

The preceding lesson showed you how to shovel windows around on-screen with a heavy hand, making them appear and disappear, for example. You learned how to make them fill the screen or turn them into tiny push-button-sized icons at the bottom of the screen.

But how can you handle windows with a more delicate touch, moving them around the desktop until they're just the right size? This lesson teaches you how to move windows without breaking them.

Dragging a window's edges

If your window is not the right size, then change it. Luckily, you can do so with the "drag and drop" trick that you learned in Lesson 2-1: Just point at the window's edge, hold down your mouse button, slide the mouse until the window is the desired size, and then let go of the mouse button. Here's how to change a window's size, step by step:

1 Double-click on the My Computer icon.

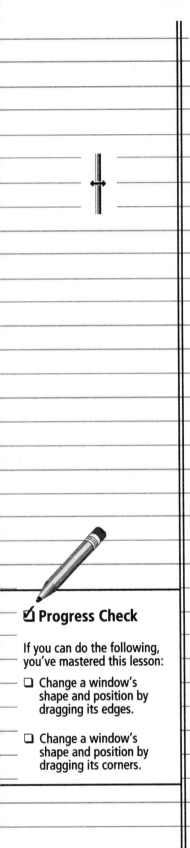

The My Computer program, found in the upper-left corner of your screen, leaps into view, listing all your computer's disk drives. (My Computer is covered in Unit 5, by the way.) Make sure that My Computer appears in a window and doesn't fill the entire screen.

Can't tell whether it's in a window or not? As you learned in Lesson 3-1, windows have visible borders that disappear when the window runs at full-screen size. (Lesson 3-1 also shows you how to toggle between window and full-screen size.)

2 Point the mouse pointer at the window's border.

Hit Lesson 2-1 for mouse maneuvering instructions. When you point at the window's edge, the mouse pointer grows two arrows, pointing in the direction in which you can drag the window's border.

3 Hold down the left mouse button.

4 Slide the mouse to maneuver the border.

As you slide the mouse inward, the border moves inward as well. Slide the mouse back and forth until the border is sitting where you want it.

5 Let go of the mouse button when the border is positioned correctly.

When you release the mouse button, the window's border snaps to its new position and stays put.

By dragging and dropping your window's borders, you can change their sizes until they're all easy to see and work with on-screen. Borders slide in two directions: inward and outward.

Started to move a border and then changed your mind? Press Esc before letting go of the mouse button, and Windows immediately puts the border back where it was, ignoring your faux pas.

Dragging and dropping a window's corners

There's nothing much new to learn here (unless you skipped the section immediately before this one).

You drag a window's *corners* in the exact same way you drag a window's borders; just point at the window's corner instead of its edge. Many people prefer to drag and drop corners because of the method's built-in speed; it lets you drag two borders simultaneously.

1 Double-click on the My Computer icon.

Or if you left the My Computer program running from the preceding example, move ahead to Step 2.

2 Point at the window's corner.

If you look really closely, you see that the mouse pointer grows two heads, each one pointing diagonally, as shown in Figure 3-4.

3 Hold down the mouse button.

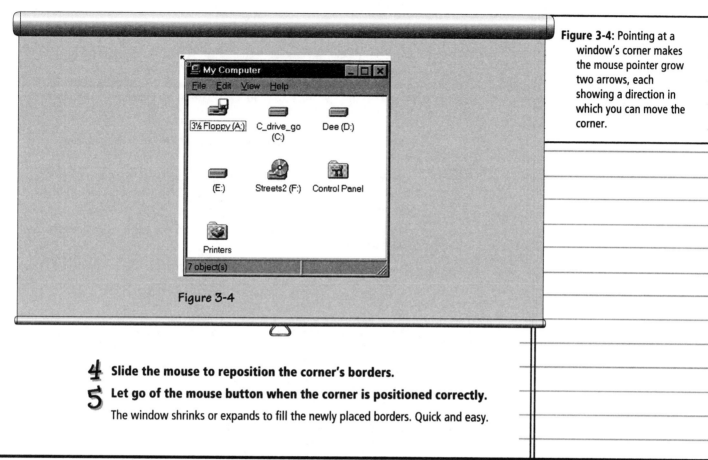

Figure 3-4

Figure 3-4: Pointing at a window's corner makes the mouse pointer grow two arrows, each showing a direction in which you can move the corner.

4 **Slide the mouse to reposition the corner's borders.**

5 **Let go of the mouse button when the corner is positioned correctly.**

The window shrinks or expands to fill the newly placed borders. Quick and easy.

Finding and Changing a Window's Location On-Screen

Lesson 3-3

When you start running more than one Windows program on your desktop, you face a big problem: trying to keep track of all those programs on a desktop that's the size of your computer monitor.

The preceding lessons showed you how to change the window's shape; this lesson shows you how to find lost windows and move them around on-screen until they're easy to work with.

Finding a program that's hiding somewhere on-screen

As soon as you start loading more than one program, windows start covering each other up. Following are ways to find a lost window, ranging in order from least to most effort. (True to form, Windows provides about as many ways to *find* windows as to lose them.)

Notes:

Notes:

For this lesson, repeat the following steps until you locate every program currently running on your desktop. (Doing so won't take nearly as long as it sounds — maybe a minute or two.) If you don't have any programs running, load a few from the Start menu's Games or Accessories area, as described in Lesson 2-1, so that you have something to work with.

1 If you spot any part of a window on your desktop, click on any portion of it.

Windows turns its attention to that window, immediately bringing it to the forefront even if it was buried beneath a pile of other windows. From there, you can change the newly emerged window's size, as Lesson 3-2 describes.

2 If you spot the window's icon listed along the bottom of the screen, click on the icon.

I'm talking about a minimized icon that's living in the taskbar along the bottom of your screen, not an icon that's sitting in the Start menu or living on your desktop. Clicking on that minimized icon kicks the program back onto the screen.

3 Press Alt+Tab to bring up a list of all your currently running programs.

The Alt+Tab window, shown in Figure 3-5, lists all the programs that Windows currently has loaded in its memory, ready to serve you. Do you spot your program on the list? Then move to Step 4 and retrieve it. (If your program isn't listed, it's not currently running. You'll have to load the program from its place on the Start button, described earlier in this unit. Using the Start button is discussed more fully in Unit 4.)

4 Find and click on your program's icon in the Alt+Tab window.

Spot the name or icon of your missing program? Keep pressing Tab until you spot its name, and then let go of the Alt key — the program jumps to the top of the pile of windows on your desktop. From there, you can rearrange the windows by using the tricks that you learned earlier in this unit.

Moving a window around on the desktop

Most people like to have more than one item on their "real-life" desktop: a paper-clip holder as well as a fast-food sandwich, for example. When something's in the wrong place, you simply pick it up and move it out of the way.

Moving windows around on the Windows "virtual" desktop is almost as simple when you learn the following steps:

1 Find the window's title bar.

As explained in the preceding lesson, that's the top edge of the border where the program's name lives.

2 Point at the title bar and move the mouse while holding down the mouse button.

Yep, you're simply *dragging and dropping* the window's border. Let go of the border, and you move the window to its new location. Watch closely as you move the mouse, and you see a faint outline of the window's border.

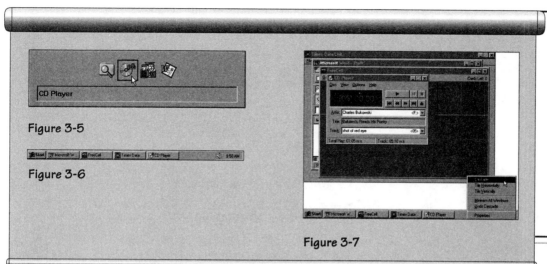

Figure 3-5

Figure 3-6

Figure 3-7

Figure 3-5: Pressing Alt+Tab lists all your currently running Windows programs.

Figure 3-6: The taskbar lists your currently running programs.

Figure 3-7: Click the taskbar's Cascade button, and Windows deals all your open windows across the screen like playing cards.

on the test

By watching a window's outline move as you drag and drop its title bar, you can tell where you're repositioning the window.

Tiling and cascading windows on the desktop

Windows offers two quick ways to organize windows on your desktop. Both of them involve the taskbar, and these steps teach you how they work:

1 Bring up the taskbar.

The taskbar normally rests along the bottom of your screen, where it displays icons for your currently open programs. If it's not there, you can summon the taskbar by pressing Ctrl+Esc. Still not there? Try pointing at the bottom edge or sides of your screen. Sometimes the taskbar is configured to hide itself along an edge; if you can spot just a portion of it, try dragging it into view with your mouse. When the taskbar appears, it looks like the taskbar shown in Figure 3-6.

2 Click on a blank area of the taskbar (usually near the clock) with your right mouse button, and choose Cascade from the menu that appears.

Windows deals all the currently open windows across your desktop like playing cards, looking somewhat like Figure 3-7.

3 Click on the taskbar with your right mouse button again.

4 Click on the taskbar's Tile Horizontally button.

This time, Windows tiles the windows across the screen, giving each one equal space. They'll probably be a pretty awkward size, like the example in Figure 3-8. But hey, at least they're all out in front of you.

Ctrl+Esc displays taskbar

☑ Progress Check

If you can do the following you've mastered this lesson.

❑ Find your Desktop's currently running windows and programs.

❑ Move windows around on the desktop.

❑ Tile and cascade windows across the desktop.

Figure 3-8: Click either of the taskbar's Tile buttons, and Windows tiles all your open windows across the screen.

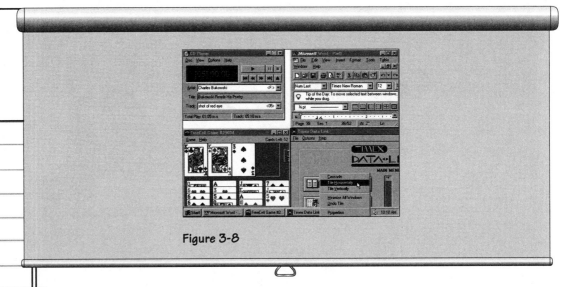

Figure 3-8

The taskbar's Tile and Cascade options work well for finding all your currently running programs and putting them on-screen in front of you. These commands work only on open *windows,* however; they don't affect programs that are minimized as icons along the bottom of the screen.

Lesson 3-4

Using a Window's Menus and Controls

The first few lessons in this unit showed you how to move a window around the screen until you positioned it within easy reach. When the window is sitting comfortably in front of you, you boss it around through *menus:* little buttons, sliding levers, and check boxes that control a program's behavior.

By pointing and clicking on a window's various menus, you can handle just about any program predicaments.

Choosing something from a drop-down menu

The most common menus live along a window's top, just beneath its title bar. In Figure 3-9, for example, notice the words Edit, View, and Help beneath the Calculator program's title bar. The next few steps show you why they're there.

1 **Load the Calculator program.**

Load Calculator the same way you loaded Solitaire in Unit 2: Click on the Start button, and then choose Programs from the pop-up menu. Choose Accessories from the top of the Program's menu, and then click on Calculator from the Accessories menu. (Unit 4 covers loading programs in much more detail.)

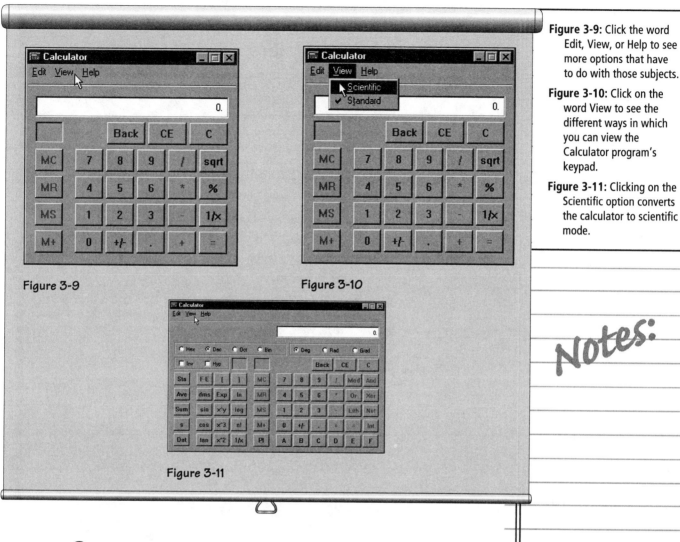

Figure 3-9

Figure 3-10

Figure 3-11

Figure 3-9: Click the word Edit, View, or Help to see more options that have to do with those subjects.

Figure 3-10: Click on the word View to see the different ways in which you can view the Calculator program's keypad.

Figure 3-11: Clicking on the Scientific option converts the calculator to scientific mode.

Notes:

2 **Click on <u>V</u>iew on Calculator's menu bar.**

A *drop-down menu* tumbles from the word View, as shown in Figure 3-10. The drop-down menu lists the two different ways in which you can view the Calculator program.

3 **Click on the word <u>S</u>cientific.**

The Calculator immediately turns into a scientific calculator, as shown in Figure 3-11.

4 **Click on <u>V</u>iew and choose S<u>t</u>andard.**

The Calculator goes back to its normal mode, known as *standard.*

Most of the menus you encounter in Windows drop down from keywords along the program's top. Click a keyword to see more options for that particular subject.

Sometimes choosing an option from a drop-down menu brings a box to the screen that's chock-full of more options. I cover those startling situations in Lesson 3-5.

on the test

Holding down the Alt key and pressing the underlined letter in a menu does the same thing as clicking on the word containing the underlined letter.

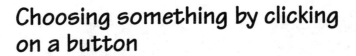

Choosing something by clicking on a button

This task is one of the easiest: Windows puts two or more buttons on-screen and asks you to choose the one you want. The solution? Just click on the button you're after. Here's an example:

1 Click on the Start button.

Press Ctrl+Esc if you can't find the Start button.

2 Choose Sh<u>u</u>t Down from the menu that appears.

Worried, Windows 95 sends a box to the screen, asking whether you're *sure* that you want to close it down.

3 Click on the <u>N</u>o button.

When you click on a button, Windows carries out the action written on the button's label. In this case, clicking on the <u>N</u>o button tells Windows that no, you didn't *really* want to shut it down.

Sliding and dragging a box

Remember the drag and drop concept that you learned earlier? Windows brings it up again in its menus. By sliding certain objects around inside a window with the mouse, you can control various parts of a program.

For example, here's how to *scroll* up and down a list of topics in the Windows Help program:

1 Load the Calculator and press F1.

Load the Calculator from the Start menu, just as you did earlier in this unit. Then press F1, the function key near your keyboard's upper-left corner. Calculator's Help program rises to the forefront.

2 Click on <u>H</u>elp from Calculator's top menu, and choose Help Topics from the menu that drops down.

3 Click on the tab marked Index along the Help program's top edge.

A window appears on-screen, as shown in Figure 3-12. Note the strange-looking edge along the window's right side.

4 Find the window's scroll bar and scroll box.

As shown in Figure 3-12, the *scroll bar* is that thick border along the window's right side; the *scroll box* is the box that lives inside the border.

5 Drag and drop the box about an inch down the scroll bar.

Moving the box up or down the shaft is like moving an elevator to change floors. In this case, dragging and dropping the box changes your view of the window: Your new view is about an inch farther down.

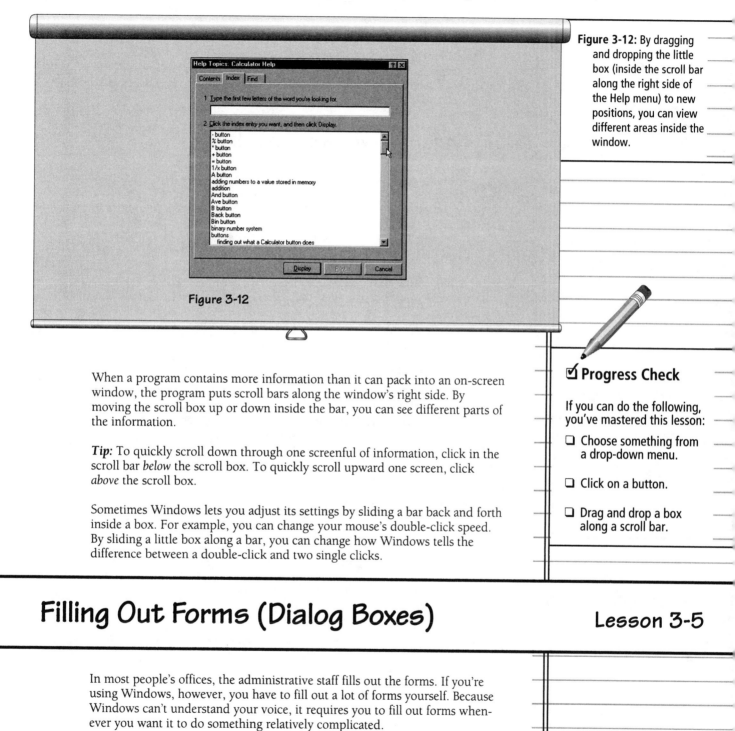

Figure 3-12

Figure 3-12: By dragging and dropping the little box (inside the scroll bar along the right side of the Help menu) to new positions, you can view different areas inside the window.

When a program contains more information than it can pack into an on-screen window, the program puts scroll bars along the window's right side. By moving the scroll box up or down inside the bar, you can see different parts of the information.

Tip: To quickly scroll down through one screenful of information, click in the scroll bar *below* the scroll box. To quickly scroll upward one screen, click *above* the scroll box.

Sometimes Windows lets you adjust its settings by sliding a bar back and forth inside a box. For example, you can change your mouse's double-click speed. By sliding a little box along a bar, you can change how Windows tells the difference between a double-click and two single clicks.

☑ Progress Check

If you can do the following, you've mastered this lesson:

❑ Choose something from a drop-down menu.

❑ Click on a button.

❑ Drag and drop a box along a scroll bar.

Filling Out Forms (Dialog Boxes)

Lesson 3-5

In most people's offices, the administrative staff fills out the forms. If you're using Windows, however, you have to fill out a lot of forms yourself. Because Windows can't understand your voice, it requires you to fill out forms whenever you want it to do something relatively complicated.

Want to highlight a word in a letter? Fill out a form to choose between bold and italics. (And don't forget type size.) Try to change the options during a game of Solitaire, and you're hit with a form: Timed game? Single draw? Triple draw? Standard, Vegas, or no scoring?

Notes:

You can't escape them, but the mouse makes the process of filling out forms faster than you may think. (You'll find a few keyboard shortcuts sprinkled in the lesson as well.) Forms come in several different parts, each discussed in the following sections.

Filling in words and numbers

This type of form is probably the most familiar — it's the old fill-in-the-blank stuff that you learned in grade school. Whenever Windows needs some words or numbers, it usually tosses a box in your face and asks you to type the text.

The Official Labelers at Microsoft refer to these types of forms as *text boxes*, and they work like this:

1 **Click on the Start button.**

2 **Click on Run from the Start menu.**

A box like the one shown in Figure 3-13 appears.

3 **Type the word** sesame**, as in Figure 3-14.**

4 **Click on the Cancel button.**

Normally, you click on the OK button after filling out a text box; doing so tells Windows to carry out its action by using the word or numbers that you typed in the box. But this is just an example, so click on Cancel. (The Open Sesame command rarely works in Windows, anyway.)

on the test

A text box can accept text, numbers, symbols, or blank spaces.

Choosing an item with a checkbox

Most people order more than one thing from a menu: an appetizer, a main course, and dessert, for example. When Windows offers you more than one choice on a menu, it often presents a checkbox. Here's how to change your game options in Solitaire by using a checkbox:

1 **Open the Solitaire program.**

You'll probably know how to load Solitaire by the end of Unit 3. (*Hint:* Start by clicking on the Start button and then move from Programs to Accessories to Games.)

2 **Click on Game.**

3 **Click on Options.**

A box with lots of options appears, as shown in Figure 3-15.

4 **Click in the three boxes next to Timed game, Status bar, and Outline dragging.**

As soon as you click in the box, you toggle its on or off position. If a check mark appears in the box, the option is activated. If no check mark is present, the option is turned off.

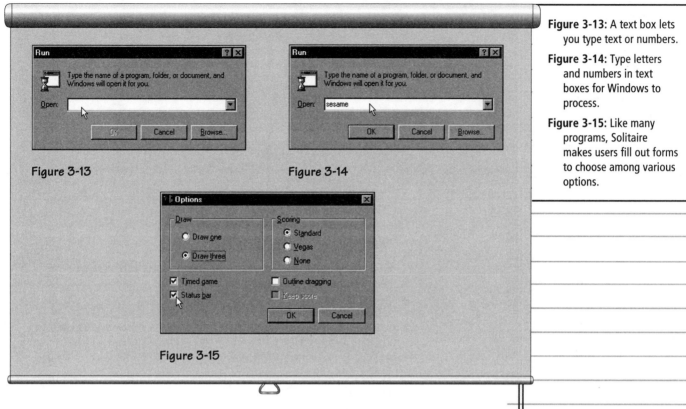

Figure 3-13: A text box lets you type text or numbers.

Figure 3-14: Type letters and numbers in text boxes for Windows to process.

Figure 3-15: Like many programs, Solitaire makes users fill out forms to choose among various options.

Figure 3-13

Figure 3-14

Figure 3-15

5 Press Esc.

Because you're here to learn about window mechanics, you're not supposed to be playing cards. Pressing Esc tells Windows to forget any changes you've made to the form and put the form away from harm.

Down the line, if you want to save changes that you make to a form, click on the OK button instead.

Tip: Keep the Timed game option turned on, or the little sun on the back of one of the decks of cards won't stick his tongue out every 60 seconds. (You won't see the flying bats, the energized robot, or the sneaky card dealer, either.)

Choosing an item from a list box

Lesson 3-4 showed you how some menus drop down from beneath words along the top of a window: Click on the word to see the menu, and then choose the option from the menu.

But Windows also packs menus into its forms. Known as a *list box,* it's a convenient way to stick a lot of options into a small box. The next few steps, for example, show you how to use a list box to see which programs you've loaded through the Start menu's Run box:

1 Click on the Start button.

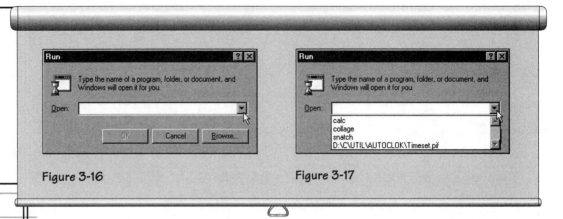

Figure 3-16: The Run box lets you type the name of a program for Windows 95 to run.

Figure 3-17: Clicking on the downward-pointing arrow reveals a drop-down list box with names of previously run programs.

Figure 3-16   Figure 3-17

✔Progress Check

If you can do the following, you've mastered this lesson:

❑ Fill out a text box.

❑ Choose items with a checkbox.

❑ Find and choose items from a list box.

2 Click on Run from the pop-up menu.

Discussed earlier and shown in Figure 3-16, the Run box lets you type the names of programs for Windows 95 to run.

3 Click on the downward-pointing arrow next to the Open text box.

See the little downward-pointing arrow at which the mouse pointer is aimed in Figure 3-16? When you click on the little arrow, a menu — shown in Figure 3-17 — that lists names of programs you've recently typed in the box drops down.

4 Click on the Cancel button.

If you had really wanted to load one of those programs, you would have clicked on its name from the menu and clicked on the OK button. But you're learning menus here, not running previously loaded programs, so click on Cancel.

Drop-down list boxes work just like drop-down menus; they come in handy because they can pack a lot of options into a small format.

Unit 3 Quiz

Circle the letter of the correct answer or answers to each of the following questions. Some questions have more than one correct answer, so don't be too hasty.

1. **The little bar along a window's top that lists a program's name is called:**

    A. Little top bar.

    B. Name bar.

    C. Title bar.

    D. Joe's Bar.

2. **Double-clicking on the bar along a window's top, where the program's name is printed, does the following:**

   A. Makes a window-sized program completely fill the screen.

   B. Makes a full-screen program shrink itself into a window.

   C. Closes a window.

   D. Minimizes a program into an icon.

3. **When a window is maximized, the following things happen:**

   A. The window fills the screen.

   B. The window's borders disappear.

   C. The window's corner borders disappear.

   D. The window stops working.

4. **You can type text, numbers, symbols, or spaces in a text box.**

   A. True.

   B. False.

5. **What happens when you double-click on an icon in the Start menu, even when that icon is currently listed in the taskbar along the bottom of the screen?**

   A. The icon explodes.

   B. Windows loads a second copy of the program that's currently running.

   C. Windows ignores your action and safely brings your currently running program to the forefront.

6. **How can you tell where you're moving a window as you drag and drop it on-screen?**

   A. The entire window moves with the mouse.

   B. A faint border of the window moves with the mouse.

7. **If you don't have a mouse, can you still use the Windows menus?**

   A. Not at all.

   B. Yes, by holding down the Alt key and pressing the underlined letter within a menu's options.

Notes:

Unit 3 Exercise

Notes:

1. Click on the Start button and move to the Program menu's Accessories area.

2. Load the Calculator program.

3. Close Calculator.

4. Load Solitaire.

5. Maximize the Solitaire window.

6. Turn the Solitaire program back into a window.

7. Minimize Solitaire.

8. Turn Solitaire back into a window.

9. Make the Solitaire window a few inches smaller.

10. Move the Solitaire window a few inches over on your desktop.

11. Tile your windows across the screen with the taskbar.

12. Cascade your windows across the screen with the taskbar.

13. Choose a new deck of cards in Solitaire.

Part I Review

Unit 1 Summary

▶ **The mouse:** Windows lets you control your computer by pushing around a mouse that maneuvers a little arrow on your computer screen. By pointing the arrow at different on-screen locations and pushing buttons on the mouse, you can make Windows perform various tasks.

DOS, by contrast — an older method of controlling computers — makes you direct your computer by typing code words with your keyboard.

▶ **Making Windows 95 appear:** If Windows doesn't automatically appear when you turn on your monitor, type **exit** at the DOS prompt and press the Enter key.

▶ **Start button:** Whenever Windows is running on your screen, so is a program called the taskbar, which contains the Start button. To close down Windows, click on the Start button and choose Shut Down from the menu.

▶ **Closing a Windows program:** To close down a Windows program, click with the left mouse button on the little X in the window's upper-right corner.

▶ **Turning off your computer:** Some people leave their computers turned on all the time; others turn them off at the day's end. (Both methods have their advantages.) Everybody turns off the monitor after they finish working, though.

Unit 2 Summary

▶ **Clicking:** To *click* something in Windows, move your mouse across the desktop until its arrow points to the on-screen object. Then press and release your left mouse button.

▶ **Right-clicking:** Clicking on something with your left mouse button usually makes Windows 95 select it. Clicking on something with your right mouse button usually makes Windows 95 bring up a menu or more information about that item.

▶ **Double-clicking:** A *double-click* works the same as a click with one exception: You press and release your left mouse button *twice in rapid succession*. (If you're not quick enough, Windows thinks that you're making two single clicks.)

▶ **Dragging and dropping:** To *drag and drop* something in Windows, point the mouse's arrow at the object you want to move — a window or box on-screen, for example. Then *hold down* the mouse button while sliding the mouse across your desktop. When the arrow hovers over the place you'd like to drop the object, let go of the mouse button, and you've "dropped" the object there.

▶ **IntelliMouse:** The new Microsoft IntelliMouse comes with a wheel positioned between its two buttons. Spinning the wheel brings more control to the program: You can quickly see more pages in Microsoft Word, for example. The IntelliMouse only works with programs that specially support it, however, like Microsoft Office 97 and a few others.

▶ **Getting more information about an icon:** To find out more information about an icon, rest the mouse pointer over it or click on it with the right mouse button.

▶ **The function keys:** A keyboard's function keys — usually located along the keyboard's top or side edge — quickly perform actions when you press them. Pressing F1 usually brings up the Windows Help program, for example.

▶ **The Alt and Ctrl keys:** The Alt and Ctrl keys work in tandem with other keys. For example, pressing Alt and the Backspace keys simultaneously (known as Alt+Backspace) undoes your most recent keystrokes.

▶ **The Esc key:** Pressing the Esc (Escape) key tells Windows to cancel what it's doing: put away an unneeded form, for example, or make a menu disappear.

Part I Review

▶ **The arrow keys:** The keyboard's arrow keys move your cursor around, letting you type words and numbers in various places within a form or program.

Unit 3 Summary

▶ **Loading a program:** To load a program, click on its icon or name from the Start menu.

▶ **Closing a program:** To close a program, click on the little icon in the program's upper-right corner. (The icon contains a big X.)

▶ **Making a program fill the screen:** To toggle a program into filling the whole screen, click on the middle-most little icon in the window's upper-right corner. (The icon contains a big square.)

▶ **Shrinking a full-screen program:** To toggle a full-screen program back into a window, click on the middle-most icon in the window's upper-right corner. (The icon contains two little overlapping squares.)

▶ **Minimizing a program to an icon on the taskbar:** To minimize a currently running program into an icon along the taskbar, click on the left-most little icon in the program's upper-right corner. (The icon contains a little line inside a square.)

▶ **Restoring a minimized program:** Double-clicking on an icon on the taskbar turns it back into a program.

▶ **Adjusting a window's size:** By dragging and dropping a window's borders and edges, you can carefully adjust the window's size.

▶ **Finding a program's window:** To find misplaced windows, press Alt+Tab. Doing so summons a window listing all your currently running programs.

▶ **Moving a window:** Dragging and dropping a window by its title bar is the quickest way to move it across the screen.

▶ **The taskbar:** Click the Windows taskbar with your right mouse button for a menu that lets you deal your open windows across the screen like cards or tile them across the screen like a shower floor.

▶ **Revealing more menu options:** Clicking on a word listed along a program's top edge usually reveals a drop-down menu with more options.

▶ **Choosing an item:** To choose an item from a menu, button, or checkbox, click on it.

Part I Test

The questions on this test cover all the material presented in Part I, Units 1 through 3.

True False

T   F   1. Windows always loads itself automatically when you turn on the computer.

T   F   2. Windows always closes down automatically when you click on Shut Down from the Start menu.

T   F   3. Computer monitors should never be turned off.

T   F   4. You need a mouse to use Windows.

T   F   5. An icon listed on the taskbar is the same as an icon listed on the Start menu.

T   F   6. Open windows can't be moved to different positions on-screen.

T   F   7. You can run only one program at a time.

T   F   8. Windows 95 uses both the left and right mouse buttons.

T   F   9. The Windows taskbar serves as an executive's To Do List.

T   F   10. All windows come with the same parts that work pretty much the same way.

Multiple Choice

For each of the following questions, circle the correct answer or answers. Remember, each question may have more than one right answer.

11. **Windows lets you use a mouse for the following tasks:**

    A. Changing a window's size and location.

    B. Loading a program.

    C. Doing laboratory experiments.

    D. Telling Windows what to do.

12. **The Windows Start menu performs the following function:**

    A. Loads your programs.

    B. Mangles your programs.

    C. Hides your programs.

    D. Shuts down Windows.

13. **Save your work at these times:**

    A. Before exiting a program.

    B. Before exiting Windows.

    C. Whenever you finish writing a paragraph.

    D. Whenever you think about it.

14. **Windows lets you drag and drop the following items:**

    A. Icons across the desktop.

    B. On-screen windows.

    C. The edges and borders of windows.

    D. Cards in Solitaire.

Part I Test

15. What is a Windows dialog box?

A. A way for people to communicate on the Information Superhighway.

B. A fancy form for giving information to Windows programs.

C. Software that comes free with a mail-in card.

D. The psychologist program that's built into Windows 95.

16. A Windows menu comes with the following:

A. Fortune cookies.

B. Gum beneath the tables.

C. Options to make a program do something.

D. Red wine stains.

17. The following steps can help find a lost or covered-up Windows program:

A. Press Alt+Tab and look for the program's name on the pop-up list.

B. Look for the program's name on the taskbar along the bottom of the desktop.

C. Click on any visible part of the window.

D. Call the computer salesperson.

18. If Solitaire's running under the Timed game option, the following animation appears on the deck:

A. The robot with the ticking clock.

B. The hand with the card popping out of its sleeve.

C. The bats with the flapping wings.

D. The beach with the floppy-tongued sun.

Matching

19. Match up the following keystrokes with the corresponding action:

A. F1   1. Bring up the Start menu to load programs.

B. Ctrl+ Esc   2. Undo your last command.

C. Alt+ Back-space   3. Make unwanted menus and forms disappear.

D. Esc   4. Bring up the Windows Help program.

E. Alt+ F4   5. Close down the currently active program.

20. Match up the following window parts with their function:

A.   1. Double-click to close a window.

B.   2. Click to minimize a window.

C.   3. Click to maximize a window.

D.   4. Click to turn a maximized program back into a window.

E.   5. Drag in or out to change the window's size.

Part I Test

21. Match up the action on the right with the click location on the left.

A. 1. Scroll the view down, one page at a time.

B. 2. Scroll the view up, one page at a time.

C. 3. Drag the view to a new place.

D.  4. Move the view up, one line at a time.

E. 5. Move the view down, one line at a time.

Part I Lab Assignment

This is the first of several lab assignments at the end of each part of this book. The lab assignments are designed to provide realistic ways to apply the information that you learned in the part's preceding units.

As opposed to the exercises at the end of each unit, the lab work is more open. That means that you're free to experiment a little bit. It also means that you'll have to figure out more of it for yourself.

In this first lab assignment, you'll start a Windows session, load programs, move windows around with the mouse and keyboard, and close down the session.

Step 1: Load Windows and find the Start button and Start menu

Turn on your computer and find the Start menu.

Step 2: Load programs

Load the Solitaire and Calculator programs.

Step 3: Arrange the programs

Arrange your open programs in the following ways:

1. Use the taskbar to tile and cascade the windows across the screen.

2. Use the program's minimize, maximize, and restore buttons to make the windows jump to new sizes.

3. Drag the windows' borders to change their sizes.

4. Drag the windows' title bars to change their locations.

5. Close all the windows.

Step 4: Close down Windows

Although you haven't done any work in this particular lab assignment, you'll find yourself creating things in other lab assignments throughout the book. So before shutting down Windows, be sure to save your work first.

You got off lucky this time. Part I just teaches Windows basics, so this lab assignment doesn't include anything specific. The following ones will make up for it, though.

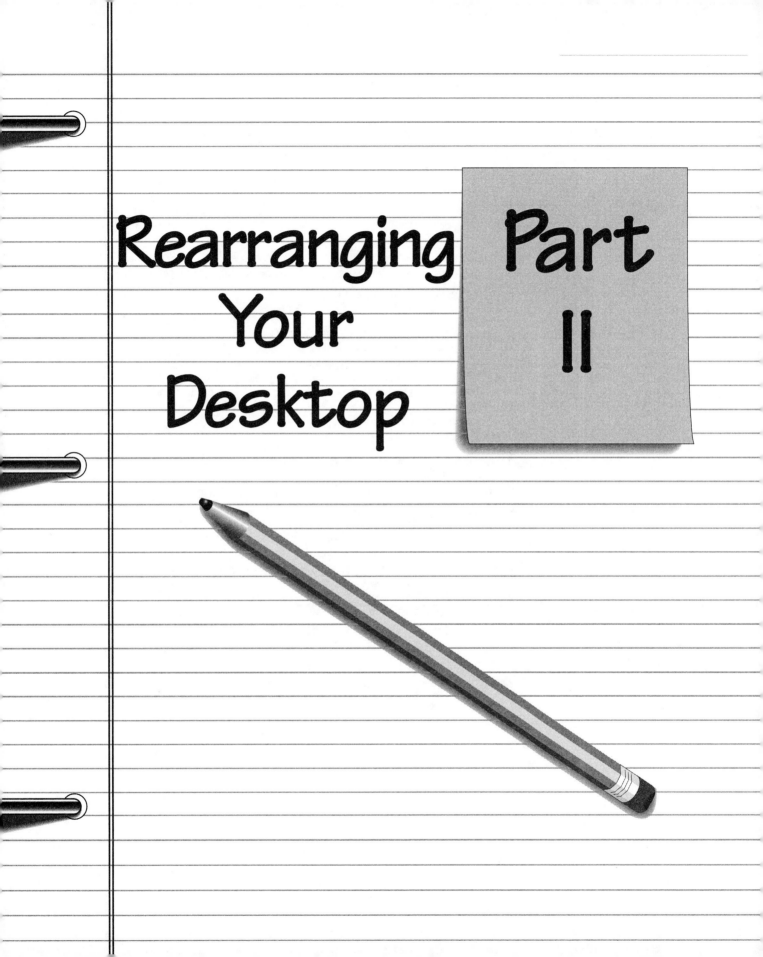

Rearranging Your Desktop

Part II

In this part . . .

Windows 95 completely computerizes your once-messy desktop. Your manila folders, an In basket, random scraps of paper, a CD player — even a trendy recycling bin — now live on your computer screen.

In some ways, this new computerized version of a desktop is easier to use. Pencils no longer roll into the black void behind the desk. Desktop need dusting? A wipe of a shirt sleeve across the monitor quickly clears things up.

But in other ways, the Windows 95 desktop is more complicated than the traditional mahogany version. Annoying menus pop up with every action. On particularly bad days, your folders will seemingly vanish. You'll often know what *you* want to do — the hard part is making *Windows 95* know what you want to do.

This part of the book teaches you how to move your desktop to your computer screen with a minimum of fuss. You'll learn how to start your work by choosing a program from the Start button — and if your favorite programs don't appear on the Start menu, you'll learn how to put them there.

You'll learn about the icons that sit on your desktop — My Computer, InBox, and Recycle Bin. Plus, you'll learn about the folders and files scattered throughout your computer's innards.

You won't be using all your Windows programs every day or even once a week. But you will find yourself using the information covered in this part of the book several times each day. Don't be afraid to jot lots of notes in the margins in these next two units.

Working with the Desktop, Start Menu, and Taskbar

Prerequisites
- Pointing and clicking the mouse (Lesson 2-1)
- Moving and sizing windows (Lessons 3-2 and 3-3)
- Filling out forms (Lesson 3-5)

Objectives for This Unit

✓ Finding and using the taskbar

✓ Loading programs from the Start menu

✓ Customizing the Start menu

✓ Finding lost programs and files with the Start menu

✓ Making shortcuts to programs and files on the desktop

✓ Using the Recycle Bin

✓ Using the InBox

Whenever Windows takes the screen, your computer's hard drive makes whirling noises, and lots of pretty icons jump onto the screen. But then all the action stops, and Windows 95 simply sits there, a bureaucrat at heart.

See, Windows 95 doesn't manage programs; it merely starts them — and that's if you know the right places to click the mouse. This unit teaches you how to fight back against this lazy nonsense. You'll learn how to find and push the icon that starts your program. Plus, you'll learn the ways in which the Start button organizes its icons on the Start menu. You'll also pick up some techniques for changing the way the Start menu loads programs.

If the Start menu doesn't list your favorite programs and files, you'd better grab a screwdriver. An Extra Credit assignment teaches you how to put an icon there yourself.

Finally, you'll learn about a few other ever-present icons and programs — the taskbar, Recycle Bin, InBox, and My Computer icons.

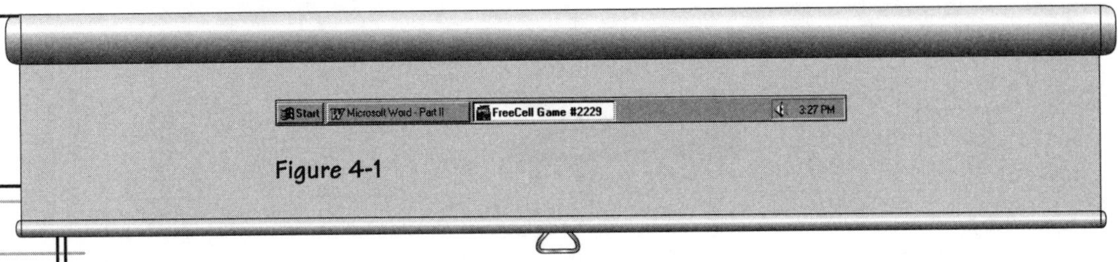

Figure 4-1: The taskbar normally rests along the bottom of your screen.

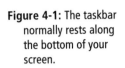

Figure 4-1

Lesson 4-1

Using the Taskbar

Because the taskbar is almost always on-screen, it's a handy base of operations. The taskbar lets you load programs, close programs, and change your computer's settings, and it can even tell you the time of day. This lesson shows you how to get the most out of the taskbar with minimal effort.

Finding the taskbar

The taskbar, shown in Figure 4-1, can be a handy Windows 95 tool — if only finding the darn thing wasn't so hard sometimes.

Normally, the taskbar rests along the bottom of your screen. But if it isn't in plain sight, the following steps usually bring it out into the open:

1 Look for the taskbar along the bottom of the screen.

Most of the time, you'll see the taskbar resting there. It contains the Start button and an icon for each currently running program, as well as a few push-buttons for starting some other programs. Not there? Wait a second to see whether it pops up — it may be running in hidden mode. If nothing happens, move on to Step 2.

2 Look for a little gray border along the bottom of the screen.

Sometimes the taskbar has been dragged off the edge of the screen until it's barely visible. If you spot its edge, point at it with the mouse: The mouse arrow grows two heads, and you can drag and drop the taskbar until it's more visible.

3 Point the mouse at all four edges of the screen, pausing for a few seconds at each edge.

In its fervent desire to let users customize their desktops, Windows 95 lets people run their taskbars on the bottom, top, left, or right edge of the screen.

By pointing the mouse at all four edges — or dragging and dropping the taskbar into view if necessary — you can start to make the taskbar do the useful things described in the rest of this lesson.

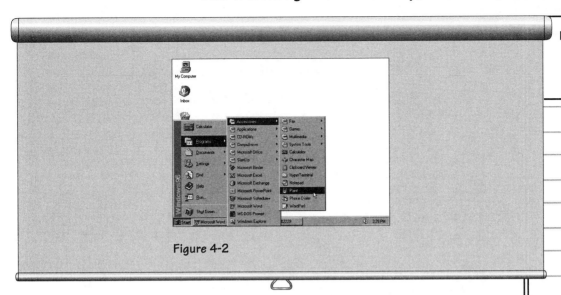

Figure 4-2

Figure 4-2: Click on a program's name or icon from the Start menu to load that program.

Loading a program with the taskbar's Start button

The Windows 95 Start menu, found on the edge of the taskbar, would drive diners in a restaurant crazy. Instead of packing all the choices onto a single page, the Start menu constantly shoots additional menus out its edges. If you're lucky, the menu-within-a-menu system works great, letting you steadily whittle down your choices until you find the right program. If you're not lucky, you're stuck rummaging through annoying menus that list every program but the one you want.

For example, the next steps show you how to load the Paint drawing program — if everything works out the easy way:

1 Click on the taskbar's Start button to make the Start menu appear.

You learned how to find the taskbar in the preceding section.

2 Click on the Programs option.

The Start menu's list of program categories appears.

3 Click on the Accessories option.

The Start menu lists the available Accessories programs.

4 Click on Paint in the Accessories menu (see Figure 4-2).

The Paint program comes to the screen.

5 Close the Paint program.

Unit 3 shows you how to close a program — by clicking on the X in the program's upper-right corner.

So what's the hard part? Well, sometimes the icon you're after is nowhere in sight. That's because some rude programs don't put themselves on the Start menu when you first install them, and you have to find the programs yourself.

Notes:

Luckily, the Start menu comes with a Find program that can sniff through your hard drive for lost programs and files. The Find command — and other ways to find and start programs — get coverage in the more extensive Start menu section found later in this unit. (You'll also learn how you can customize the Start menu, putting your favorite programs onto it with a quick drag and drop.)

The Start menu's Programs menu is merely a list of programs that you can load. By clicking on a program's name or icon in the menu, you start the program.

See the little black triangles on the right side of some of the Start menu items in Figure 4-2? Holding the mouse pointer over those items makes another, more detailed menu appear.

Most Windows programs add themselves to the Start menu's Programs menu when you first install them.

Using the taskbar to switch between loaded programs

Whenever Windows 95 loads a program, an icon for that program appears on the taskbar. Because programs often cover themselves up when running on your crowded computer-sized desktop, the taskbar is an easy way to pluck the program you want from the mix. These steps show you how to move among several programs on your desktop by clicking on their icons on the taskbar:

1 **Click on the Start button and load the Paint program.**

You learned how to do so in the preceding section. Notice how the Paint program's icon appears on the taskbar.

2 **Load the Calculator program.**

This program is on the same menu as the Paint program. And when it's loaded, Calculator's icon appears on the taskbar as well.

3 **Load the Notepad program.**

Its icon appears, too, making the taskbar look like Figure 4-3.

4 **Click on the Paint program's icon on the taskbar.**

See how the taskbar immediately brings the Paint program to the forefront?

5 **Click on the Calculator program's icon on the taskbar.**

Windows brings Calculator to the top.

The taskbar not only lists all your currently running programs, but it also lets you switch between them.

Tip: To close a Windows program, click on its icon on the taskbar with your right mouse button. When the menu appears, select Close. The taskbar shuts down the program, first asking whether you'd like to save any unsaved work.

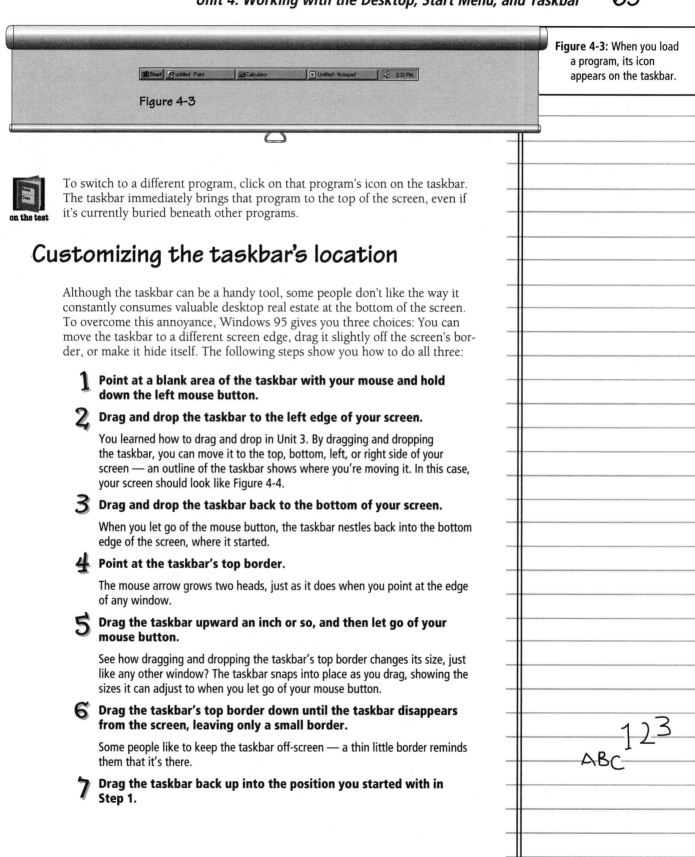

Figure 4-3

Figure 4-3: When you load a program, its icon appears on the taskbar.

To switch to a different program, click on that program's icon on the taskbar. The taskbar immediately brings that program to the top of the screen, even if it's currently buried beneath other programs.

Customizing the taskbar's location

Although the taskbar can be a handy tool, some people don't like the way it constantly consumes valuable desktop real estate at the bottom of the screen. To overcome this annoyance, Windows 95 gives you three choices: You can move the taskbar to a different screen edge, drag it slightly off the screen's border, or make it hide itself. The following steps show you how to do all three:

1 Point at a blank area of the taskbar with your mouse and hold down the left mouse button.

2 Drag and drop the taskbar to the left edge of your screen.

You learned how to drag and drop in Unit 3. By dragging and dropping the taskbar, you can move it to the top, bottom, left, or right side of your screen — an outline of the taskbar shows where you're moving it. In this case, your screen should look like Figure 4-4.

3 Drag and drop the taskbar back to the bottom of your screen.

When you let go of the mouse button, the taskbar nestles back into the bottom edge of the screen, where it started.

4 Point at the taskbar's top border.

The mouse arrow grows two heads, just as it does when you point at the edge of any window.

5 Drag the taskbar upward an inch or so, and then let go of your mouse button.

See how dragging and dropping the taskbar's top border changes its size, just like any other window? The taskbar snaps into place as you drag, showing the sizes it can adjust to when you let go of your mouse button.

6 Drag the taskbar's top border down until the taskbar disappears from the screen, leaving only a small border.

Some people like to keep the taskbar off-screen — a thin little border reminds them that it's there.

7 Drag the taskbar back up into the position you started with in Step 1.

Figure 4-4: You can move the taskbar to any edge of your screen by using the drag and drop technique.

Figure 4-5: The taskbar's Properties menu lets you change the taskbar's appearance and behavior.

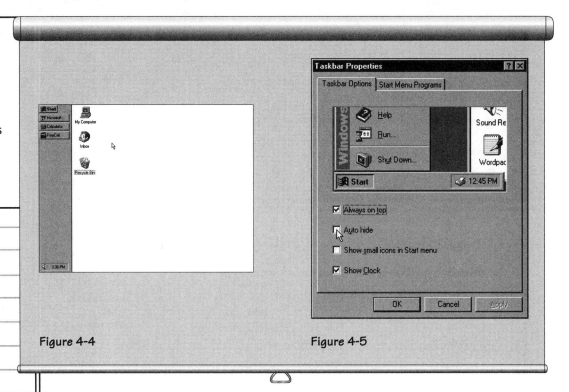

Figure 4-4

Figure 4-5

Notes:

8 **Click on a blank area of the taskbar with your right mouse button.**

Don't click on an icon; click on a blank portion of the taskbar, and a menu appears.

9 **Choose Properties from the taskbar's menu.**

Another menu appears, as shown in Figure 4-5.

10 **Click on the A̲uto hide option, and then click on the OK button.**

A check mark appears in the Auto hide box, meaning that you've selected that option. When you click on the OK button at the bottom of the menu, the menu disappears. And when the menu disappears, notice that the taskbar has hidden itself from the desktop as well.

11 **Position the mouse pointer over the bottom edge of the screen.**

The taskbar magically appears whenever you hover the mouse pointer at the edge of the screen containing the taskbar — and that's usually the bottom edge, unless you've moved the taskbar to a different part of your screen, as shown in Step 2.

12 **Repeat steps 8 and 9, and then disable the A̲uto hide option.**

Tip: Running a lot of programs simultaneously? Then drag the taskbar's edge to make it a little wider. Doing so allows more room for all your icons and makes it easier to spot the one you're after.

on the test

The taskbar can be on the top, bottom, right, or left edge of your screen.

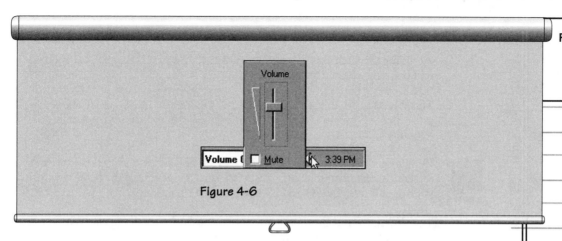

Figure 4-6

Figure 4-6: Slide the little bar up to increase the volume or down to decrease the volume.

Turning the volume up or down

This feature may be the best thing Windows 95 has to offer: an easily accessible switch to turn your computer's sound up or down. Here's how it works:

1 **Click on the taskbar's little speaker, located next to the clock.**

A strange-looking menu appears, as shown in Figure 4-6.

2 **With the mouse, drag and drop the little box up and down the shaft.**

When you drop the little box, Windows 95 makes a little "ping" sound to show the current volume. Moving the little box up the shaft increases the sound; moving it down the shaft quiets things down.

click on Mute box on volume control to turn off sound temporarily

extra credit

What are the other options in the taskbar's Properties menu?

The taskbar's Properties menu, shown in Figure 4-5, offers several options, all explained here:

Always on top: A check mark in this box means that the taskbar is always on top of the screen, no matter how many windows are piled on top of it. If no check mark is present, the taskbar lets itself be buried beneath other open windows. (Pressing Ctrl+Esc always brings the taskbar into view, though.)

Auto hide: As explained earlier in this section, this option makes the taskbar hide itself from view until a mouse pointer rests on it. (Forgotten where you hid your taskbar? Try all four sides, and one will work.)

Show small icons in Start menu: A check mark in this box shrinks the size of the icons in the Start menu. That can be handy if your computer has a lot of programs and the Start menu is getting crowded.

Show Clock: The taskbar normally shows a small digital clock on the edge opposite the Start menu. If no check mark is in this box, you won't see the clock.

Start Menu Programs tab: Click on this tab for options pertaining to your Start menu. These options let you add or remove programs from the Start menu and clear the list of recently opened documents from the Start menu's Documents menu.

☑ **Progress Check**

If you can do the following, you've mastered this lesson:

❑ Load a program from the Start menu.

❑ Switch between running programs with the taskbar.

❑ Move the taskbar to a different part of the screen.

❑ Make the taskbar hide itself automatically.

❑ Use the taskbar to change the computer's volume.

Notes:

By sliding the shaft up or down — and listening to the little ping — you can find the right volume for your current setup.

Tip: Want to turn down that B.B. King CD in a hurry to catch that phone call? Click on the Mute box on the Volume control to turn off the sound temporarily.

Don't forget that the taskbar can also cascade and tile windows across your screen. As described in Unit 3, just click on a blank area of the taskbar with your right mouse button and choose between the two options.

Tip: When you rest the mouse arrow over the clock on the taskbar, Windows 95 displays the current day and date.

Lesson 4-2

Using the Start Menu

In its efforts to please, Microsoft tried to make using computers as easy as possible. So Microsoft wants you to click on the Start button to start working in Windows 95; a click of the button brings up the Start menu, which lists everything you might possibly want to do with your computer.

Or does it? What happens if the program you're after isn't listed on the menu? And what are all those other options supposed to do, anyway? This lesson teaches you how to make the Start menu start working for you instead of the other way around.

Finding lost programs and files with the Start menu

Computers are just as good at losing things as they are at creating them. So Windows 95 comes with a great Find program that can snoop through all the parts of your computer, looking for lost files. The Find command on the Start menu lets you search for files in several different ways. First, you can simply search for a file based on its name.

Can't remember the name? Find can search for all the files you created yesterday or on any particular time and day.

Don't remember what you called the file or when you created it? Well, the ever-helpful Find program can even search for files containing specific words. By following the next few steps, you should be prepared to find even the most evasive files and programs:

1 Choose <u>F</u>ind from the Start menu, and then choose Files or Folders.

The Find program appears, as shown in Figure 4-7.

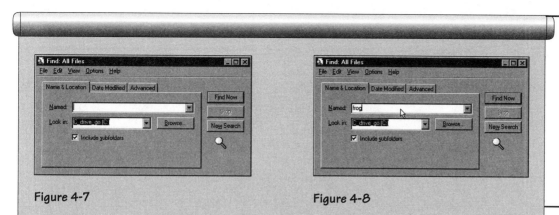

Figure 4-7

Figure 4-8

Figure 4-7: The Find program can seek out and retrieve lost files on your computer.

Figure 4-8: Type the name of a missing file — or a portion of the file's name — in the Named box, and Windows 95 searches for it on your hard drive.

2 **Type** frog **in the Named box, as shown in Figure 4-8, and click on the Find Now button.**

Windows 95 searches through your computer's hard drive and brings up a list of all the files with the word frog in their names. If you have more than one hard drive, Windows 95 searches the C drive.

3 **When you spot your file on the list, double-click on it.**

Windows 95 loads the program that created your file, loads the file into the program, and brings them both to the screen. Pretty slick, eh?

If you remember the date on which you created the file but not its name, don't click in the Named box like you did in Step 2. Instead, click on the Date Modified tab. From there, you can tell Windows 95 to bring up a list of all files created within a certain number of days or created between certain dates. (Click on the Find Now button to make the Find program start the search.)

To make Windows 95 search your computer for files containing certain words, click on the Advanced tab. Type the word or words you're looking for in the Containing Text box, and then click on the Find Now button.

Tip: Before using the Find program, look to see whether your missing file is in the Start menu's Documents list. If you've used the file recently, it's probably listed there, and a double-click on the file's name brings it back into action.

heads up

When using the Find program's Advanced search feature, be sure that you're searching for the exact sequence of words contained in the file. For example, if your missing file contains the phrase *squash and parsnips* and you tell Windows to search for a file containing *squash parsnips,* the Find program won't find your file because you left out the word *and.*

Tip: The Find program normally just searches the hard drive on which Windows 95 resides. To make Windows 95 search your entire computer — including your hard drives, your CD-ROM drive, and any disks currently in your floppy drives — click on the little arrow in the Find program's Look in box, and then choose My Computer from the list that drops down.

☑ Progress Check

If you can do the following, you've mastered this lesson:

❑ Load a program from the Programs menu.

❑ Load a recently used file from the Documents list.

❑ Find a file by using the Find program.

Notes:

Quick, what do all those Start menu options stand for?

Most of the time, you use the Start menu for starting programs. But occasionally, you'll want to dip into some of the other menu's options. Although these areas are covered later in this unit and throughout the book, they're described here to cut down the confusion to a more manageable level.

Programs: As you learned earlier in this unit, clicking here lets you start Windows programs by clicking on their names from the menus.

Documents: This one's a real time-saver because it lists the last ten files you've worked on. So the next time you sit down at your computer, choose Documents and then click on the name of the file. Windows 95 loads the program that created the file, grabs the file, and puts them both on-screen for immediate access.

Settings: This option lets you change your computer's settings. Choose Taskbar,

for example, to customize the taskbar, just as if you'd chosen the taskbar's Properties command, as described in Lesson 4-1. You can also change your printer's settings as well as access the Control Panel. The Control Panel lets you customize just about every aspect of your computer.

Find: This command gets its own section in this lesson. It lets you search through your computer to find misplaced files and programs.

Help: Choosing this option is the same as clicking on your desktop and pressing F1. It simply brings the Windows Help system to the screen, ready to answer your questions. (Unit 18 covers the Windows Help system more completely.)

Run: Type a program's name here and press Enter, and Windows runs the program. You'll find a few catches, though, and they're covered in Unit 6.

Lesson 4-3 Using the Desktop

Windows 95 offers you plenty of ways to do the same thing. That flexibility often makes Windows 95 easier to use, because it increases your chance of stumbling across the right way to do something. But it often complicates matters because you have so many things to remember.

The trick? Don't try to remember them all. Just pick out a method that works right for you, and stick with it. The next few sections show you some of the easier ways for working with the Windows 95 desktop — the backdrop on the computer screen on which all your windows live. These lessons show you the basics; Unit 16 shows you how to use these tools to customize your desktop and make your work life a little easier.

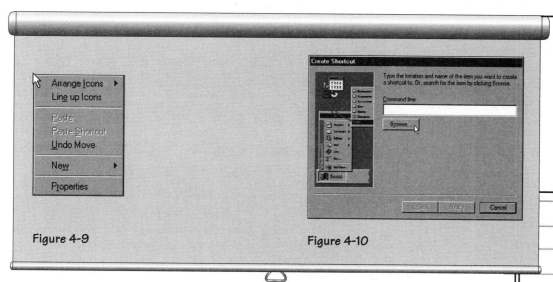

Figure 4-9   Figure 4-10

Figure 4-9: Click on a blank area of the desktop with the right mouse button to see a list of options.

Figure 4-10: Click on the Browse button to select a program to which the shortcut should lead.

Notes:

Making shortcuts to programs and files on the desktop

Everybody likes a good shortcut; that's why Microsoft stuck so many of them into Windows 95. A shortcut is a quick and easy path to get somewhere fast. Because nobody likes wading through menus in order to load their favorite programs and files, Microsoft made it easy to install shortcuts to those places.

You can even create shortcuts to your favorite folders — areas in which Windows 95 stores files. (You'll learn much more about folders in the next unit.)

If you find yourself using the Windows 95 Calculator program a lot, for example, you can install a shortcut to the Calculator on your desktop so that it's easier to reach. Here's how:

1 Click on the desktop with your right mouse button.

A menu pops up, as shown in Figure 4-9.

2 Choose New from the menu.

Another menu juts out from the word New.

3 Choose Shortcut from the New menu.

The Create Shortcut menu appears, as shown in Figure 4-10.

4 Click on the Browse button, and then double-click on the little Windows folder.

The Browse window subsequently shows you the programs living in the Windows folder. To see more programs, click on the little scroll bars — those elevator-mimicking buttons that you learned about in Unit 3.

5 Double-click on the Calculator icon.

The program is named Calc, and the icon is just to the left of the name.

6 **Click on the Next button.**

7 **Type** Calculator **in the name box, and then click on the Finish button.**

A shortcut to the Calculator program now appears on your desktop, where you can drag and drop it to any convenient location.

When sitting on the desktop, a shortcut looks just like the program it leads to, but there is a big difference. A shortcut is only a push-button that starts a program — it's not the program itself. So when you create or delete a shortcut, you don't affect the program at all. You're simply adding or removing a button that summons that program.

Here's something to think about as well: Remember how the Find command in the last section came up with a list of files matching certain criteria? Well, you can create shortcuts to those files, too. Just point at the file you want, and then drag and drop it onto the desktop. A shortcut to that file immediately appears on the desktop.

Tip: To quickly organize your desktop icons into neat, orderly rows, click on the desktop with the right mouse button and choose the Line up Icons command.

Adding folders to the desktop

The more shortcuts you add to the desktop, the harder spotting the one you want will be. To keep your shortcuts organized, Windows 95 lets you create desktop folders. Just drag and drop your icons into the folders. It works like this:

1 **Create a shortcut for the Calculator program.**

The preceding section showed you how to do so. In fact, you can skip this step if your Calculator shortcut is still on your desktop.

2 **Click on the desktop with the right mouse button and choose Folder from the New menu.**

An empty manila folder appears on-screen where you clicked in Step 2.

3 **Type** Junk **and press Enter.**

The new folder appears, waiting for you to type a name. If you don't type anything, Windows 95 simply calls the folder New Folder.

4 **Drag and drop the Calculator shortcut icon into your new Junk folder.**

The Calculator shortcut disappears from the desktop.

5 **Double-click on the Junk folder.**

The folder opens up to display a window containing its contents — in this case, the Calculator shortcut.

Notes:

recognize shortcuts by little arrow in bottom-left corner of icon

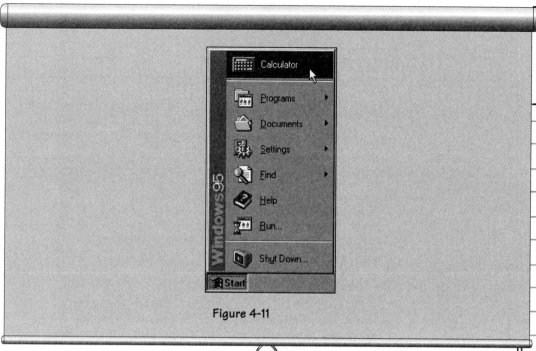

Figure 4-11

Figure 4-11: By dragging and dropping shortcuts onto the Start button, you can place them on the Start menu.

put shortcuts to folders, programs, or data files on Start menu by dragging and dropping them onto Start button

These steps may seem relatively pointless right now, but give them some thought. By creating shortcuts to your favorite programs, files, and storage areas — and storing them in neatly organized folders on-screen — you'll be able to find your work much more quickly and easily.

And if you're lucky, you won't have to use the Start menu's Find command so much, because nothing will get lost!

Unit 16 shows you how to organize your desktop in several different ways by using shortcuts and folders.

Tip: If you're unsure about what dragging and dropping a file or folder will do, drag and drop with the *right* mouse button. A menu appears, letting you choose whether to move, copy, or create a shortcut to that file or folder.

Customizing the Start menu

This one's pretty simple, actually. The Start menu contains a list of shortcuts that start programs. So to put new programs or files on the Start menu, simply drag and drop shortcuts for those programs and files onto the Start menu. It works like this:

1 Create a shortcut on your desktop for the Calculator program.

If you already have a shortcut for the Calculator program, you can skip this step.

2 Drag and drop the Calculator shortcut icon onto the Start button.

That's it. You've placed the Calculator on the Start menu, as shown in Figure 4-11.

☑ **Progress Check**

If you can do the following, you've mastered this lesson:

❑ Understand the Start menu options.

❑ Find lost programs and files with the Find command.

❑ Make shortcuts to programs and files on the desktop.

❑ Add folders to the desktop.

❑ Put shortcuts in desktop folders.

❑ Add shortcuts to the Start menu.

Lesson 4-4

Retrieving Deleted Files from the Recycle Bin

Drop an old letter into a wastebasket, and you have until the next trash day to pick it out again. But computers aren't nearly as forgiving: One press of the Delete key can wipe out a year's worth of work, with no chance of retrieval.

Computer engineers finally listened to the wails of anguished users, and now Windows 95 comes with a Recycle Bin. Shown in Figure 4-12, the Recycle Bin is an ingenious way to find deleted files. The following steps show you how to pluck an accidentally deleted file from the Recycle Bin:

1 **Create a shortcut to the Calculator program on your desktop.**

You learned how to do so in the first section of Lesson 4-3.

2 **Drag and drop the Calculator shortcut into the Recycle Bin.**

You can also click on the Calculator shortcut icon with your right mouse button and choose Delete from the pop-up menu. Or you can click on the icon with your left mouse button and press the Delete key. All three methods delete the shortcut from the desktop.

3 **Double-click on the Recycle Bin icon.**

The Recycle Bin window opens, listing all your most recently deleted files, as shown in Figure 4-13.

extra credit

Why do they call it the Recycle Bin?

The name Recycle Bin is a misnomer; Windows 95 doesn't really recycle your deleted stuff. It simply moves the deleted files to a secret folder on your hard drive called Recycled. When you open the Recycle Bin, Windows 95 is really showing you the contents of the secret Recycled folder.

Pull a file out of the Recycle Bin, and Windows 95 pulls the file out of the secret Recycled folder.

Unfortunately, the Recycle Bin can't hold on to deleted files forever, or your hard drive would fill up. So Windows 95 stakes out 10 percent of your hard drive and uses that space for its secret Recycled folder. For example, if you have a 500MB hard drive, Windows 95 uses 50MB of that space to store your deleted files. When the

Recycle Bin reaches that 50MB limit, Windows 95 really starts to delete files. It simply deletes the oldest files in the bin.

Think of the Recycle Bin as a box for you to toss scrap paper into. You can reach into the box and retrieve mistakenly pitched items. But when the box is full, you need to delete things permanently to make room for the new stuff. Because the oldest stuff is in the bottom of the box, that stuff is thrown out first, leaving the freshest — and usually most important — stuff lying on top.

Windows 95 handles all this stuff automatically, but you can fiddle with the Recycle Bin's options if you want. Just click on the Recycle Bin icon with your right mouse button and choose Properties from the pop-up menu.

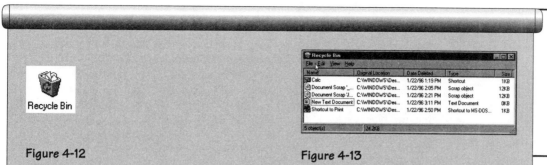

Figure 4-12

Figure 4-13

Figure 4-12: The Recycle Bin.

Figure 4-13: To protect against accidents, the Recycle Bin stores recently deleted files in case you need to salvage them.

 Drag and drop the Calculator shortcut icon back onto the desktop.

You can also undelete the file by clicking on its name with the right mouse button and choosing R̲estore.

When the Recycle Bin contains no deleted files, its icon contains no pieces of paper. After the Recycle Bin starts storing deleted files, however, little pieces of paper appear inside its wastepaper-basket icon.

Tip: Finding deleted files is sometimes easier if they're listed by the date on which they were deleted. To list them that way, choose Arrange I̲cons from the Recycle Bin window's V̲iew menu and select by D̲elete Date.

extra credit

What's the InBox?

The Microsoft InBox uses *telecommunications* — a fancy word that describes the notoriously difficult world of connecting computers to phone lines and making them talk to each other. Before computers can use phones, however, they need modems — little gadgets that translate computer language into sound.

The Windows 95 InBox comes set up to use The Microsoft Network, and for good reason: Microsoft owns The Microsoft Network. Unfortunately, very few people use The Microsoft Network because, frankly, it pales in comparison to the competition.

Luckily, the InBox is part of Microsoft Exchange, which lets your computer connect to other online services like CompuServe, America Online, and Prodigy.

Because Windows 95 comes with files only for The Microsoft Network, you have to contact your online service and ask for an installation disk that lets it work with Microsoft Exchange.

By running the installation program (installing new programs is covered in Unit 19), you'll be able to use the Microsoft Exchange InBox with your preferred online service. After everything is set up correctly, Microsoft Exchange lets you send and receive e-mail automatically. It can even dial automatically, grab your messages, and hang up.

Unfortunately, the program is too complex to be covered in this book. The adventurous will find excellent information in Brian Livingston's *Windows 95 SECRETS* (IDG Books Worldwide, Inc.).

choose Arrange
Icons from View
menu and select
by Delete Date to
list files by date
they were
deleted

☑ **Progress Check**

If you can do the following, you've mastered this lesson:

❑ Delete a file.

❑ Retrieve a deleted file from the Recycle Bin.

on the test

Deleting a shortcut deletes only the push-button that leads to a program, file, or folder; it doesn't delete the program, file, or folder itself.

Tip: Running out of space on the hard disk? Click on the Recycle Bin icon with your right mouse button and choose Empty Recycle Bin from the pop-up menu. The Recycle Bin lets go of all your old, deleted files, creating more space on the hard disk. (The Recycle Bin continues to save files that you delete in the future; it just won't have room to save as many deleted files before letting them go for good.)

Unit 4 Quiz

Circle the letter of the correct answer or answers to each of the following questions. (A few questions have more than one answer, just to keep things lively.)

1. **The Start menu's main job is the following:**

   A. Starting programs.

   B. Losing programs.

   C. Helping you find lost programs.

   D. Starting and closing Windows.

2. **How do you control the windows and folders on your desktop?**

   A. The same way you control other Windows programs and windows.

   B. With a mouse and keyboard.

   C. With the taskbar's Tile and Cascade options.

   D. With joysticks.

3. **Most Windows programs add themselves to the Start menu's Programs menu when you first install them.**

   A. True.

   B. False.

4. **Pointing the mouse arrow at a menu item containing a little black triangle makes even more menu items jump to the screen.**

   A. True.

   B. False.

5. **Deleting a shortcut from the desktop does the following:**

    A. Deletes the shortcut from your computer's hard drive.

    B. Deletes the shortcut and its program, folder, or file from your hard drive.

    C. Deletes the shortcut, its program, folder, or file, and all your other programs from your hard drive.

    D. Removes only the icon from your desktop.

6. **Which of these methods deletes a file?**

    A. Dragging and dropping the file into the Recycle Bin.

    B. Clicking on the file's name and pressing the Delete key.

    C. Clicking on the file's name with the right mouse button and selecting Delete.

7. **You can't add or remove programs from the Start menu.**

    A. True.

    B. False.

8. **You can move the taskbar to any edge of your screen.**

    A. True.

    B. False.

9. **To make a hidden taskbar appear, you press these keys simultaneously:**

    A. Alt+Esc.

    B. Ctrl+Esc.

    C. Alt+Tab.

    D. Alt+Ctrl.

Unit 4 Exercise

1. Create a new folder called Favorite Programs on your desktop.

2. Put copies of Solitaire (called SOL) and Calculator into the Favorite Programs folder.

3. Delete the folder.

4. Retrieve the shortcuts from the Recycle Bin.

5. Find all the files on your hard drive that contain the word distance, and then create shortcuts to them on your desktop. (Hint: Use the Start menu's Find command.)

6. Create a new folder on your desktop named Long, and drag and drop all your new distance file shortcuts into it.

7. Delete your Long folder and all the shortcuts that it contains.

Working with Files and Folders in My Computer and Explorer

Prerequisites

▶ Opening a program (Lesson 4-2)

▶ Choosing an item from a menu (Lesson 3-4)

▶ Pointing and clicking with a mouse (Lesson 2-1)

▶ Opening, closing, and moving windows (Lessons 3-1, 3-2, and 3-3)

▶ Dragging and dropping with a mouse (Lesson 2-1)

Objectives for This Unit

✓ Understanding files, folders, disks, and drives

✓ Viewing files, folders, disks, and drives

✓ Understanding the My Computer program

✓ Understanding the Explorer program

✓ Creating folders

✓ Opening files and folders

✓ Copying and moving files and folders

✓ Copying floppy disks and folders

✓ Deleting files and folders

✓ Formatting a floppy disk

✓ Moving a file from one folder to another

✓ Using Explorer

▶ Angry Diatribe

on the disk

After you work with Windows for a while, your files will pile up, just like they do on any other desktop. In a good-faith effort to help you organize your work, Windows offers you a computerized file cabinet system for storing the important stuff.

In its overly helpful way, Windows 95 offers two completely different computerized file cabinets; one's called My Computer, and the other's called Explorer. The two systems' intricacies and obstinacy can be frustrating; they are probably the most complicated parts of Windows 95. But if you don't learn how to use these computerized file cabinets, you won't be able to find your work when you need it.

Lesson 5-1

Understanding File Management

Notes:

To create and store files, you need to understand four basic areas of computer life: *files, folders, disk drives,* and *disks* (both floppy disks and hard disks). Think of your computer as a big file cabinet with several drawers, and all this stuff becomes a little easier to understand.

Just as you need to organize a file cabinet, moving related items into clearly labeled folders, you need to organize your computer's files. And that's where the My Computer and Explorer programs come in: They let you create folders, label them, and move your files into them.

Both the My Computer and Explorer programs put buttons, windows, and folders across your screen so that you can access your computer's files, folders, disks, and drives — all described in this lesson. Figure 5-1 shows the My Computer program with its parts labeled; Figure 5-2 shows the Explorer program. Both programs display your computer's innards, but they do so in very different ways. You'll want to refer to both figures as you read the next few sections.

This particular lesson doesn't have much hands-on stuff, but don't worry — after you learn the stuff in this lesson, the *real* hands-on stuff will come up quickly.

Understanding files

In keeping with the file cabinet metaphor, a *file* is a batch of information stored in a file cabinet's file folder.

Files contain computerized information: burp sounds, love letters, music videos, programs, or pictures of toasters — anything that you can store on a computer is stored in a file. Whenever you want to store information — or use information that's already been saved — you need to use a file. Files come in all sizes, from empty to pathetically swollen, depending on the amount and type of information stored in them.

Windows 95 itself dumps more than 400 files onto your computer; as time goes by, you'll probably add a few hundred yourself.

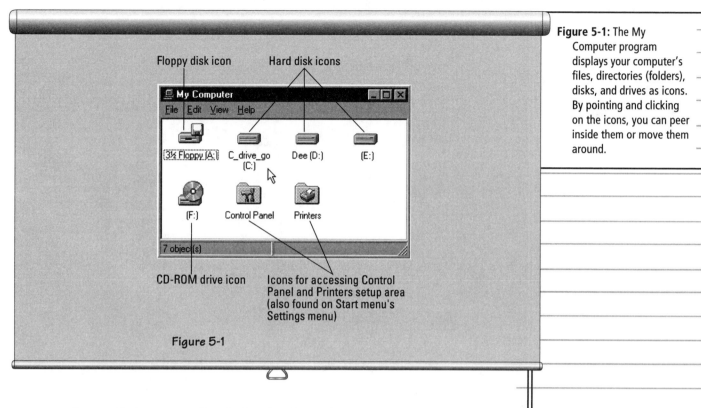

Floppy disk icon   Hard disk icons

CD-ROM drive icon   Icons for accessing Control
Panel and Printers setup area
(also found on Start menu's
Settings menu)

Figure 5-1

Figure 5-1: The My Computer program displays your computer's files, directories (folders), disks, and drives as icons. By pointing and clicking on the icons, you can peer inside them or move them around.

Figure 5-2 shows some files displayed in the Explorer program; when you click on a folder on the left side of the Explorer window, a description of that folder's contents spill onto the Explorer window's right side.

Understanding folders and directories

After the files start adding up, you'll want to keep them stored neatly away inside *folders*. In computerland, folders are usually called *directories;* Windows 95 breaks tradition by sticking with the term *folders*. Folders let you store related files for easy access.

To keep things orderly, folders store files that have related information. You can store all your files relating to organic carrots, lettuce, and peas in a Vegetables folder, for example. Install a program, and that program will probably create a new folder in which it stores all its files, too.

Although the computer's pretty good about keeping its related files in organized directories, many users tend to scatter their new files around their hard drive. ***Remember:*** The more careful you are about keeping your files organized, the easier it is to find those files when you need them.

Just as you can place "real" manila file folders inside each other, you can create Windows 95 folders inside other folders to further organize your information. Create a Food folder, for example, and create two more food folders — Meat and Junk — to live inside it. Plus, you can put your Vegetables folder inside your Food folder as well.

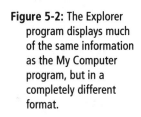

Figure 5-2: The Explorer program displays much of the same information as the My Computer program, but in a completely different format.

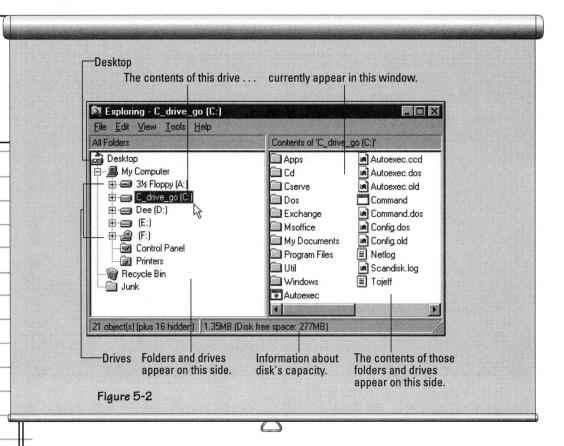

Figure 5-2

Note: Don't be afraid to create new folders for new programs or incoming files; doing so makes it easier to find the files later.

extra credit

What's a root folder?

Figure 5-3 shows a typical directory "tree" with folders sprouting from each other; the files grow more closely related as the branches extend outward. With real trees, everything grows outward from the roots: A trunk leads to branches, which lead to clusters of leaves. In keeping with this tree business, the Official Computer Name for the computer's first folder — the folder that everything branches from — is the drive's *root folder*. (I'm not making this up.)

When you double-click on your drive C icon in the My Computer program, My Computer brings a new window showing the contents of drive C to the screen. That window shows the root folder of drive C.

Of course, this stuff is pretty technical. But if a program ever bugs you about the *root folder*, now you'll know where to find it: It's the first window that appears when you double-click on a drive's icon in My Computer.

easily created and easily deleted, folders make finding files easier later on

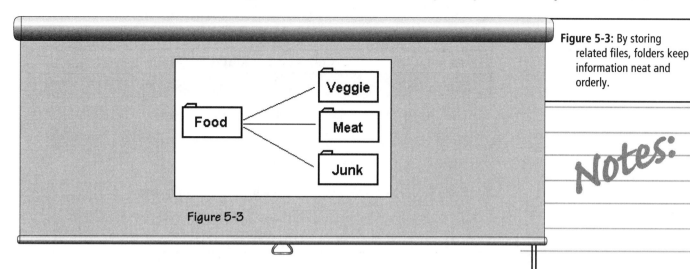

Figure 5-3

Notes:

Understanding disks

A file cabinet stores its folders and files in big drawers. A computer, by contrast, stores its folders and files on *disks*.

For the most part, computers store their information on three types of disks: *floppy disks, hard disks,* and *compact discs,* often referred to as *CD-ROMs.* Floppy disks are those square, plastic things that look like coasters (one is included in the back of this book). Compact discs look just like the ones you use in your stereo. And hard disks live permanently inside computers where nobody can see them.

Yawn. At least you have to learn this stuff only once. And mainly, just remember this about floppy disks: Keep them away from magnets and moisture. (Both are disk killers.)

Also, disks come in different sizes, shapes, and capacities. Table 5-1 gives the rundown.

keep floppy disks away from magnets and moisture

Q/A Session

Question: What do K and MB stand for?

Answer: Computers store their information in nuggets called *bytes.* A byte is pretty much like a character or letter in a word. For example, the words *pig's eye* contain nine bytes. (The space and the apostrophe count as one byte each, too.) Computers use the metric system, so bytes are measured in kilos (1,000), megas (1,000,000), and gigas (incredibly large).

Table 5-1	Common Computer Disks		
Drive Letter	**Type**	**Content**	**Popularity**
Usually A or B	5¹/₄ Floppy	360K	Obsolete
Usually A or B	5¹/₄ Floppy	1.2MB	Very rare
Usually A or B	3¹/₂ Floppy	720K	Very rare
Usually A	3¹/₂ Floppy	1.44MB	Very common
C or above	Hard	From 40MB	Very common to 1,000MB
D or above	Compact	Up to 600MB	Increasingly popular

Remember: Keep track of how much free space you have on your disks; sometimes they won't have enough room to store all the information you'd like.

Understanding drives

Drives are the parts of computers that read or write information onto disks. The floppy drive, for example, is that slot into which you insert a floppy disk. CD-ROM drives suck in compact discs like a home stereo does. And hard drives sit inside your computer, out of sight.

All drives do their work in the background, so just remember a few things:

- Floppy drives can't store much information on disks. Although the disks don't hold much information, they're cheap and portable, making them ideal for moving information to other computers.

- Hard drives can read and write a lot of information quickly, so they're used most often. (In fact, whenever you save a file, your computer writes that file's contents to your hard drive.) Hard drives can't be moved to other computers easily, though.

- CD-ROM drives can read a lot of information, but more slowly than hard drives. Most CD-ROM drives can't write information onto compact discs (although the more expensive ones now can), so don't try to store any files there. No, you'll probably be storing all your information on your hard drive.

Most new computers come with at least one floppy drive and one hard drive. Any additional drives depend on the size of the computer owner's pocketbook.

Finally, files and folders all have similar names that consist of up to 255 characters; drives use a single letter. For example, your floppy drive is probably called *drive A*, and your hard drive is probably called *drive C*.

to see available disk space, click on drive with right mouse button in My Computer and choose Properties from menu

☑ Progress Check

If you can do the following, you've mastered this lesson:

❏ Understand how Windows 95 stores files.

❏ Understand different kinds of disks and disk drives.

extra credit

Q/A Session

Question: Why does my computer use up to 255 characters in its file and folder names, but my friend's computer can use only eight characters?

Answer: For years, most IBM-compatible computers could store only files with names using eight or fewer letters or numbers. Windows 95, by contrast, can use up to 255. Although those extra characters make thinking up descriptive filenames a lot easier, they can cause problems when you swap files with friends who don't use Windows 95.

For example, if you give your friend a disk containing a file named Incredible Thoughts, that file will appear to be named INCRED~1 on a computer that uses Windows 3.1.

Then, if your friend copies the file to her hard drive, adds some incredible thoughts of her own, and copies the file back to the floppy, be prepared for a surprise when you get the file back: It will still be named INCRED~1.

Lesson 8-2 contains more information about naming and saving files.

Notes:

Working with Drives   Lesson 5-2

If you were looking to retrieve a particular piece of paper that you'd filed away somewhere, you would walk to the file cabinet, grab the handle of the appropriate drawer, and give it a pull.

Retrieving information in Windows 95 works pretty much the same way. By opening the right drive, you can access the folders and files stored on that drive.

Drives come in several varieties and sizes, but this lesson includes some hands-on work with your floppy drive so that you can see what's stored on the floppy disk that comes with the book.

Finding out what's stored on a drive

Windows 95 tries to make it easy to peer inside your computer and look at files. To see what's inside your computer, you use the My Computer icon, shown in Figure 5-4.

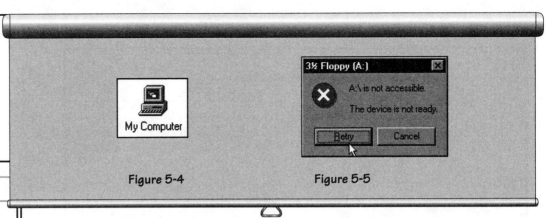

Figure 5-4: Double-click on the My Computer icon to see what's inside your computer.

Figure 5-5: This message usually means that you didn't insert a disk into a disk drive.

Figure 5-4   Figure 5-5

The following steps teach you how to use My Computer to see the files and folders on your computer's drives:

1 Open My Computer.

Double-click on the My Computer icon — that picture of a computer shown in Figure 5-4 — and the My Computer window appears on-screen (refer to Figure 5-1). Each gray icon in the My Computer window represents a disk drive on your computer; the three folders contain other information. In Figure 5-1, the computer has one floppy drive (A), three hard drives (C, D, and E), and a compact disc drive (F). Notice how each type of drive has a different type of icon?

2 Put this book's floppy disk in your disk drive.

Your floppy drive is one of the slots in the front of your computer; push the disk into the drive with the disk label facing up.

3 Double-click on the appropriate disk drive icon.

For example, if you put your disk into drive A, move the mouse until its arrow hovers over the A icon, as shown in Figure 5-1, and then double-click on the left mouse button.

My Computer opens a new window that shows you the disk's contents.

If you didn't put a disk in there, just to see what would happen, Windows reprimands you with a message like the one in Figure 5-5. Put the disk in the drive and then click on the Retry button, and the computer tries again.

4 Double-click on the C drive icon.

Notice how the My Computer program brings up another window, this time showing the contents of drive C — your hard drive?

5 Click on the remaining icons to see all the drives in your computer.

Notice how My Computer uses something that should be awfully familiar now: windows. See the telltale little icons in the windows' corners? See the scroll bar and title bar that you were introduced to in Unit 3?

The windows in My Computer work just like all the other windows you've read about in this book. You can have several open at once, for example, displaying the contents of several drives simultaneously. Or you can minimize or maximize them for better views of other windows. (You'll get to practice that stuff later in this unit, so don't get carried away now.)

double-click on any folder in My Computer to see its contents

You can even drag and drop files and folders from window to window in order to copy or move things around. (You'll hear plenty more about that later in this unit, too.)

One last thing: Opening all those folders probably left a lot of open windows cluttering your desktop. You can close those extra windows the same way you close any other window: click on the little X in their upper-right corner.

extra credit

How can I get more information about a disk or drive?

Sometimes you need to know more information about a drive than its current inventory. How much information can the drive hold, for example? And more important, how much space does the drive have left for storing your information?

You find out this information with a trick that should be getting familiar by now: Click on the drive's icon with your right mouse button and choose Properties from the pop-up menu. A window pops up, as

shown in Figure 5-6, listing the drive's total storage capacity, the amount of space that's currently being used, and the amount of space left over.

The Label box lets you name your drive as well. Plus, if the drive is acting funny, the window's Tools tab lets you check the box for errors. Close the window like any other, by clicking on the X in its upper-right corner.

on the test

Remember: When you put a new floppy disk in a drive, My Computer often forgets to update its view. Yep, it still shows you the files that were stored on the old disk. To make it update its view, press F5. In fact, make it a habit to press F5 every time you view a floppy by using My Computer, and you'll be safe.

on the test

To make My Computer display files and folders on a particular drive, double-click on that drive's icon in the My Computer window.

Deleting a drive

heads up

Deleting a computer's drive is impossible unless you have a screwdriver and some patience. You can't drag a drive's icon to the Recycle Bin. If you click on the drive icon with the right mouse button, the word Delete doesn't appear, either. (You can delete a drive's contents, though, so be careful when pointing and clicking at folders and files.)

---

dragging and dropping disk drive icons from My Computer onto desktop makes easily accessible shortcuts to them

to tell how much space a drive has left on its current disk, click on it with right mouse button and choose Properties from menu

Figure 5-6: Click on a drive or disk with your right mouse button and choose Properties to see how much space is left on it.

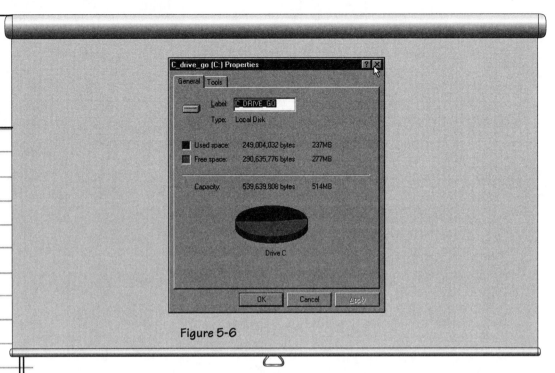

Figure 5-6

Lesson 5-3   Working with Folders

Folders let you store files in easily relocated places. Whenever you open a drive and peek inside, My Computer displays the folders stored on that particular drive. The next few sections teach you how to open (known in technical terms as "peek inside"), create, copy, move, and delete folders.

Looking inside a folder

on the test

If you want to see what's inside a different folder, just double-click on it. Here's an example for practice:

1 **Open My Computer.**

2 **Double-click on the C drive icon.**

My Computer brings a window to the screen, showing the files and folders stored on your C drive.

3 **Double-click on the folder labeled Windows.**

The files and folders contained in your computer's Windows folder appear on the right side of the screen. If you can't find your Windows folder, try clicking on the scroll bar in the C drive window until the Windows folder appears. (Lesson 3-4 covers scroll bars.)

Notes:

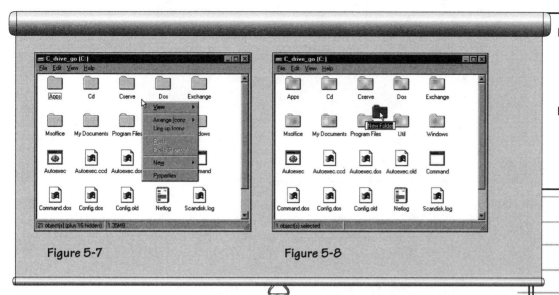

Figure 5-7: Click in a folder with your right mouse button to see a list of things that you can do with that folder.

Figure 5-8: When choosing a name for your new folder, use only letters, numbers, and the most common symbols for best results.

Figure 5-7   Figure 5-8

Tip: When you double-click on a folder, My Computer normally opens a separate window to show that folder's contents. Digging deep into several folders results in a string of open windows across your screen, each displaying a folder's contents. To make My Computer use the same window that changes each time you double-click on one of its folders, hold down Ctrl while double-clicking.

Creating a folder

Sooner or later, your life will branch off; you'll create some new files, and you'll need a new folder to hold them all. The following steps show you how to create a new folder on your C drive:

1 **Open My Computer.**

2 **Click on the C drive icon.**

A window appears, displaying all the files and folders on the C drive.

3 **With the right mouse button, click anywhere in the background of the newly opened C drive window.**

A menu pops up, as shown in Figure 5-7.

4 **Choose Folder from the New menu.**

A new folder appears, as shown in Figure 5-8.

5 **Type** Temporary Trash **as the name for your new folder, and then press Enter.**

Why Temporary Trash? Because that way, you'll have a folder to store files temporarily until you decide where to file them. (Remember: Folders, like files, can't have names longer than 255 characters.)

When you press Enter, your new folder appears on-screen.

Figure 5-9: If you're sure
that you want to delete
the folder, click on the
Yes button.

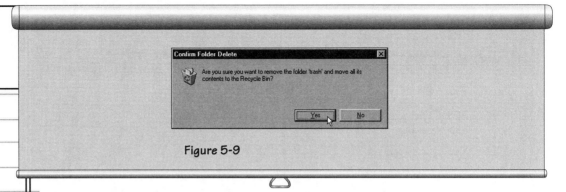

Figure 5-9

*to be safe, always
drag and drop with
right mouse button
to make Windows
95 bring up menu of
choices*

You can put a new folder inside any of your existing folders in the same way:
Simply open a folder, click on it with the right mouse button, and choose
Folder from the New menu.

Copying or moving a folder

You won't want to copy or move a folder very often, but the procedure is simple
because it uses one of the most basic Windows tricks: the drag and drop.

Follow these steps to create a folder and then move that folder to the Temporary Trash folder that you created in the preceding set of steps:

1 Create a folder called Junk on your C drive.

2 Drag and drop the Junk folder to the Temporary Trash folder.

You learned how to drag and drop in Lesson 2-1, but if you need a refresher,
here goes: Point at the Junk folder and, while holding down your left mouse
button, point at the Temporary Trash folder. Then let go of the mouse button.

Windows 95 does something pretty dumb to confuse people, though. It makes
you follow different rules when copying or moving folders — nothing wrong
with that. But it *reverses* those rules when you're copying or moving folders to
different disk drives. Table 5-2 helps you keep track.

Note: Windows 95 won't let you put two folders with the same name into one
folder. For example, you can't have two folders called Pig's Breath in one
Barnyard Hygiene folder. If you try, Windows 95 gently stops you, saying that
you already have a file named Pig's Breath in that folder, and you have to
change the name Pig's Breath to something else.

Table 5-2	Moving Files and Folders Around
To Do This . . .	*Do This . . .*
Copy a file or folder to another location on the same disk drive	Hold down Ctrl and drag it there.
Copy a file or folder to a different drive	Drag it there.
Move a file or folder to another location on the same drive	Drag it there.
Move a file or folder to a different drive	Hold down Alt and drag it there.

extra credit

Q/A Session

Question: How can I copy a folder to a different drive?

Answer: Just drag and drop it there. For example, open My Computer and find the folder you want to copy. Then find the icon for the drive onto which you want to copy the folder. You may need to put each folder in its own window and drag the windows around on-screen until they're both clearly visible. And remember, if you drag and drop something with your right mouse button, Windows 95 puts a menu listing your movement choices on-screen.

When you can see the folder's target, drag it there and let go.

Deleting a folder

heads up

This one's easy — so easy, in fact, that it can be dangerous. Before deleting a folder, give it a good ogle with both eyes open to make sure that you're not deleting anything important inside it.

1 Create a folder on your desktop called Trash.

You need something unimportant to delete.

2 Click on the Trash folder's name in My Computer.

My Computer highlights the folder's name.

3 Press the Delete key.

Depending on your computer's setup, My Computer does one of two things. It may just delete the folder immediately. Or it may toss a warning message like the one in Figure 5-9 in your face.

If you prefer less long-winded deletion methods, skip Step 2. Instead, just drag and drop the Trash folder to the Recycle Bin.

Changing a folder's name

1 Click on the folder you'd like to rename — perhaps the Temporary Trash folder that you created earlier in this unit.

2 Click on the folder's name to highlight it.

3 Type the new name and press Enter.

The new name replaces the old name.

Pretty easy, eh?

Lesson 5-4	# Working with Files

Notes:

In Lesson 5-1, you learned why your computer uses files, folders, disks, and drives for storing information. For the most part, you'll be using files, so be sure to pay careful attention to this lesson.

Opening a file

Opening a file in Windows 95 is pretty easy — if you can find the file you're after. As you learned earlier, you not only need to know the file's name, but you also need to know its *location:* the name of the folder in which the file's sitting and the name of the drive on which that particular folder lives.

After you find the file, you can open it by double-clicking on its name. The following steps show you how to open the letter called Angry Diatribe that was written in WordPad and supplied on the floppy disk that came with this book.

on the disk

1 **Open My Computer.**

2 **Click on the drive C icon to switch the view to drive C.**

3 **Click on the Dummies 101\Windows 95 folder.**

4 **Double-click on the Angry Diatribe file.**

Windows looks at the Angry Diatribe file and figures out that it was created in WordPad. So it loads WordPad and loads the file into that program.

Tip: For a quick look inside a file, click on it with the right mouse button and choose Quick View from the menu. Windows 95 shows you the file's contents, whether they were created by a word processor, spreadsheet, or other type of program. (Unfortunately, Quick View works better with Microsoft products than with those created by other companies.)

Copying or moving a file

This procedure works just like copying or moving a folder, described in Lesson 5-3. Nonetheless, here's a quick refresher to make sure that you've got it down pat:

1 **Create a folder called Temporary Junk on your desktop.**

2 **Open My Computer and double-click on the drive C icon.**

3 **Open the Windows folder.**

4 **Choose the Clouds and Bubbles files.**

on the test

Hold down Ctrl while clicking on the names of the two files. By holding Ctrl while you click, you enable My Computer to highlight more than one file. (If you mess up and click on the wrong file, click on the file again to "unhighlight" it.)

5 **With your right mouse button, drag and drop the files onto the Temporary Junk folder.**

6 **Choose <u>C</u>opy Here from the menu.**

By dragging and dropping with your right mouse button, you can choose between copying or moving files each time you drag them. Or if you have a good memory, memorize Table 5-2, which lets you know when dragging and dropping a file copies it and when dragging and dropping a file moves it. (You'll find an irritating difference.)

extra credit

Q/A Session

Question: How come Windows automatically loads some files when you double-click on them, but it doesn't load others?

Answer: When a Windows program creates a file, it usually tacks three hidden letters onto the end of its name. Save a file in Paint called Pistachio, for example, and Paint puts the letters *BMP* on the end of the filename. WordPad uses the letters *WRI,* and Notepad uses *TXT.* With these three-letter code words, Windows 95 can register files with the programs that created them.

That means two things: First, Windows 95 can use the right icon when displaying the file in My Computer. For instance, any file created with Notepad uses the Notepad icon. Second, Windows 95 can look at the hidden three letters, decide which program created the file, and — when you double-click on the file — bring the file to the screen inside the program that created it.

If Windows 95 doesn't recognize the three-letter association, however, it uses a boring, generic icon and subsequently gives you an error message when you double-click on the file.

Deleting a file

No longer using a file? Then delete it — in the same way you delete folders:

on the disk

1 **Click on Angry Diatribe to highlight the file's name.**

2 **Press the Delete key.**

Poof. My Computer wipes the file off your hard drive or floppy drive and puts it in your Recycle Bin (from which you can salvage it if you deleted it by mistake). You can't delete files and folders from compact discs, however; those CDs just won't let go.

3 **Open the Recycle Bin, click on Angry Diatribe with the right mouse button, and select <u>R</u>estore.**

Doing so brings the file out of the trash and puts it back on your hard drive. (You'll need the file for later lessons.)

extra credit

Q/A Session

Question: I want to copy some files from one floppy to another, but I have only one floppy drive.

Answer: If you want to copy a few files or folders from one floppy disk to another, just create a new folder called Junk on your desktop; then copy the floppy's files to that Junk folder. When you're done copying the files to your desktop, remove the first floppy disk, insert the second one, and move the files from the Junk folder to the second floppy.

Remember, you can hold down Ctrl while clicking on the names of files, and My Computer will select more than one file. That way, you can delete, copy, or move a whole bunch of files at once.

You can delete program files as well as files you've created, but doing so often causes problems. Programs rarely come in neat packages, and they tend to spread themselves across your hard drive. You should probably invest in an *Uninstaller* program that handles all the background issues involved in removing a Windows program from your computer. (In fact, Windows 95 comes with a built-in Uninstaller, which is covered in Unit 19. And the disk that comes with this book includes an uninstall program as well.)

Changing a file's name

You change the name of a file in the same way you change a folder's name: click on the file, click on the file's name, type the new name, and press Enter.

heads up

Just watch out; don't move too fast, or Windows 95 will mistake your two single clicks for one double-click and try to load your file.

Lesson 5-5   Working with Floppies and CDs

Like spouses and Kahlua cheesecakes, floppies and CDs require special care. This lesson shows you how to keep them happy and functioning well.

Formatting a floppy disk

When you first take them from the box, floppy disks may not be ready to be used. You need to *format* them first — a process that gets them ready for storing data. How do you know whether a disk needs to be formatted? Well, if you try to use the floppy and see the message shown in Figure 5-10, you know that you're dealing with an unformatted disk.

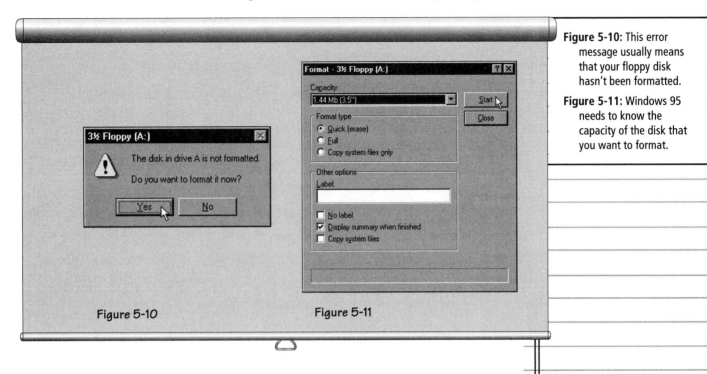

Figure 5-10

Figure 5-11

Figure 5-10: This error message usually means that your floppy disk hasn't been formatted.

Figure 5-11: Windows 95 needs to know the capacity of the disk that you want to format.

Follow these steps to format a floppy disk:

heads up

1 Slide the floppy disk into the floppy disk drive.

Formatting a floppy disk erases all the information it contains. Look at the disk's contents in My Computer to make sure that it doesn't hold anything important before you proceed.

2 With the right mouse button, click on the floppy disk drive's icon in My Computer and select Format.

A box appears, as Figure 5-11 shows.

3 Choose the capacity of the disk from the Capacity box.

Floppy disks can hold different capacities, as described back in Table 5-1. If you have a newer computer, you're probably using the high-capacity, 3½ inch disks. (That's the size and capacity of the disk bound into the back of this book.)

4 Click on the Start button.

Note: When you buy a box of new floppy disks, take the time to format them all. That way, you won't be stuck with an unformatted floppy when you're in a hurry to copy some important information.

Making a copy of a floppy

Sometimes you'll want to make an exact duplicate of a floppy disk. Some computers come with different sizes of drives, complicating matters.

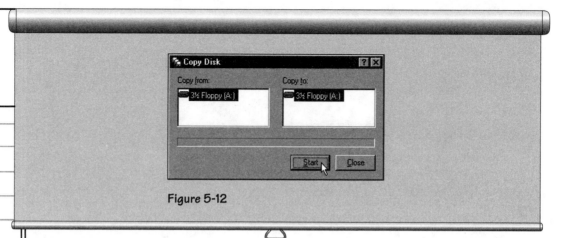

Figure 5-12: Windows can make a direct copy of a floppy disk, even if you have only one floppy drive.

Figure 5-12

Notes:

If you have two floppy drives that are the same size and capacity, stick your original floppy in one drive and your second floppy in the second drive. Then use what you learned in Lesson 5-4 to copy the files from one disk to the other.

Note: Making a backup copy of the disk that comes with this book is a good idea, just in case the first one falls behind the bookshelves or something.

But if you have only one floppy drive — or just one floppy drive that can handle your type of floppy disk — you have to follow these steps. (And actually, they're a little easier than those in Lesson 5-4, anyway.)

1 **Open My Computer and click on the floppy disk's icon with your right mouse button.**

2 **Choose Copy Disk from the pop-up menu.**

A window like the one in Figure 5-12 appears, letting Windows 95 know what disk you want to copy and what disk you want to copy the information to.

heads up

In the process of making an exact duplicate of a disk, Windows 95 formats the second disk, so make sure that your second disk doesn't contain any valuable information. Luckily, Windows warns you that you'll erase all information on the second disk.

3 **Make sure that Windows 95 displays your original disk on the left side of the window and the duplicate on the right side of the window.**

Windows 95 can make a duplicate of a floppy disk even if you have only one floppy drive, so both sides of the window can be your A floppy drive. (You just have to switch the original floppy with the duplicate a few times while Windows 95 is making the copy.)

4 **Click on the Start button.**

Windows 95 starts reading all the information from the disk.

5 **When instructed, insert the second disk and press Enter.**

6 **Follow the instructions on-screen.**

Windows 95 may make you swap the two disks once or twice until it's through copying all the information from one to the other. That's why keeping track of which disk is the original and which is the duplicate is important.

The Copy Disk command wipes out any information stored on the floppy disk to which you copy information.

on the test

Formatting a hard disk

heads up

Please don't do it. Formatting a hard disk wipes out any and all information stored on it.

Get a second opinion before even thinking about formatting your hard disk. (Then have the person who gave you the second opinion do the actual dirty work if a reformat is truly necessary.)

What am I trying to say here? Only that hard disks usually need to be formatted only once, and that's when you first stick them inside the computer. Almost any other time, you're asking for trouble.

Working with Explorer   Lesson 5-6

By now, you've learned what files and folders are supposed to do and which buttons you need to push to move them around. You learned how the My Computer program lets you peer inside your computer's hard drives, where you can see your folders and the files stored inside them.

But just as some people like pineapple on their pizza and others don't, Windows 95 comes with an alternative program for people who don't like My Computer. Called *Explorer,* the program lets you look at your files, folders, and disk drives in a different way.

This lesson shows you how to make Explorer do the same things as My Computer; by the end of the unit, choose to use the program you find less confusing.

Looking in folders and files with Explorer

Explorer and My Computer do the same things, but in different ways. Because the two programs are so similar, you shouldn't find it too surprising that you can launch Explorer directly from the My Computer program. The following section shows you how to load Explorer and perform some of the tasks described earlier in this unit.

☑ **Progress Check**

If you can do the following, you've mastered this lesson and are ready to move on to the Unit 5 quiz:

❑ Find information about your drives, disks, folders, and files.

❑ Copy and move files to different drives and folders.

❑ Create, copy, move, and delete folders.

❑ Format floppy disks.

❑ Make copies of floppy disks.

❑ Use Explorer's Find feature to find lost files.

to see file's size and creation date, choose Details from folders View menu for quick look at file's contents, click on file with right mouse button, and choose Quick View

Don't think that you can skip this stuff because you already know how to use My Computer. Explorer and My Computer use the same commands, so about everything you learn in this lesson applies to the My Computer program, too.

on the test

1 Click on My Computer with your right mouse button, and then choose Explore from the menu.

Or you can choose Windows Explorer from the Start menu's Programs menu. Or you can right-click on any folder and then choose Explore. Any of these three actions brings Explorer to the screen, as shown in Figure 5-13.

2 Click on the C drive icon in Explorer's left window.

Explorer changes its view and displays the contents of your C drive in its right window, as shown in Figure 5-14. The folders and files in the right window should look familiar; they're the same ones you see when you first open the My Computer program. However, the icons are smaller.

3 Choose Large Icons from Explorer's View menu.

Windows folders can display their contents by using large icons, small icons, a list of small icons, or a detailed list of file information — the file's size, type, and creation date. My Computer starts out by displaying large icons, just as Explorer is doing now.

4 Double-click on the Windows folder.

The right side of Explorer displays the contents of your C drive's Windows folder.

5 Choose List from Explorer's View menu.

List view often makes dealing with large groups of files easier.

6 Click on the file named Forest with the right mouse button and choose Quick View from the File menu.

Explorer displays the contents of the Forest file.

7 Close your open windows.

Like other windows, you close the Explorer and Quick View windows by clicking on the X in their upper-right corner.

Although the Explorer program, the My Computer program, and the folders on your desktop look very different, they share an almost identical menu for displaying files and folders. For example, all three use the same View menu for changing the size of the icons they display. They all let you sort the display by the icons' name, size, type, or creation date through the View menu's Arrange Icons command.

And most important, they all let you copy, move, or delete folders and icons by dragging and dropping them to different locations on the desktop: Dragging and dropping to other folders moves or copies objects, and dragging and dropping objects to the Recycle Bin deletes them. You can even drag and drop files and folders from My Computer to Explorer and vice versa.

Tip: Can't find a file? Choose Find from Explorer's Tools menu. Doing so brings up the same Find program that you learned about in the Start menu.

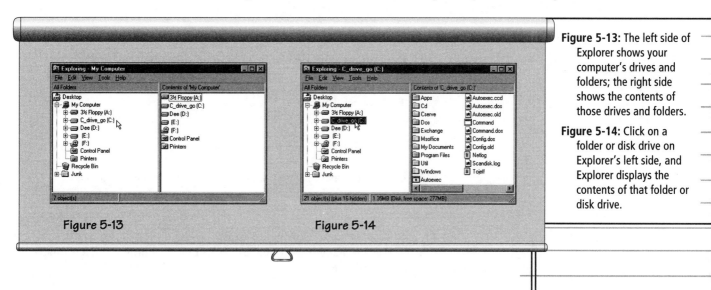

Figure 5-13

Figure 5-14

Figure 5-13: The left side of Explorer shows your computer's drives and folders; the right side shows the contents of those drives and folders.

Figure 5-14: Click on a folder or disk drive on Explorer's left side, and Explorer displays the contents of that folder or disk drive.

Unit 5 Quiz

Circle the letter of the correct answer or answers to each of the following questions. (Just like before, some questions have more than one answer to keep things from being too easy.)

1. **Computers use this name for their file folders full of information:**

   A. File folders.

   B. Manila danglers.

   C. Folders.

   D. Directories.

2. **Your computer's folders do this:**

   A. Store files for easy access.

   B. Organize related files.

   C. Lose files.

   D. Create films.

3. **Files and folder names can't exceed this number of characters:**

   A. 8.

   B. 11.

   C. 255.

   D. 64.

Notes:

Notes:

4. **Computers store their information on these types of disks:**

    A. Floppy disks.

    B. Compact discs.

    C. Hard disks.

    D. Frisbee-brand flying disks.

5. **Computers use drives to read and write information to disks.**

    A. True.

    B. False.

6. **Drives are named with one letter, and most computers have a hard drive called** *drive C.*

    A. True.

    B. False.

7. **My Computer displays this folder when you first open it:**

    A. Root folder.

    B. Branch folder.

    C. Currant folder.

    D. Current folder.

8. **Do this to make My Computer bring a new window to the screen, displaying files and folders on a certain drive:**

    A. Click on that drive's icon with your right mouse button.

    B. Wipe off your monitor with your sleeve.

    C. Beg.

    D. Double-click on that drive's icon with your left mouse button.

9. **Do this to make My Computer display a certain drive's files and folders in its currently open window:**

    A. Double-click on that drive's icon.

    B. Wipe off your monitor with your sleeve.

    C. Beg.

    D. Hold down Ctrl while double-clicking on that drive's icon.

10. **To make sure that My Computer is displaying the current contents of your floppy disk, you press this key:**

    A. Alt.

    B. Del.

    C. F1.

    D. F5.

11. **Do this to see a folder's contents:**

    A. Double-click on its folder in Explorer.

    B. Double-click on its folder in My Computer.

    C. Double-click on its folder on the desktop.

    D. Click on the folder with the right mouse button and choose Open from the menu.

12. **Do this to *move* a folder to a new location on the same drive:**

    A. Drag and drop its folder.

    B. Hold down Ctrl while dragging and dropping its folder.

    C. Pick it up and carry it.

    D. Toss it across the room.

13. **Do this to *copy* a folder to a new location on the same drive:**

    A. Drag and drop its folder.

    B. Hold down Ctrl while dragging and dropping its folder.

    C. Pick it up and carry it.

    D. Toss it across the room.

14. **To select more than one file at a time, hold down Shift while clicking on the files' names.**

    A. True.

    B. False.

15. **My Computer's Copy Disk command wipes out any information stored on the floppy disk to which you copy information.**

    A. True.

    B. False.

Unit 5 Exercise

1. Load My Computer.
2. Put a disk in drive A and view its folders.
3. Create a folder on the disk in drive A.
4. Move the newly created folder to drive C.
5. Delete the newly created folder from both drives.
6. Format a blank floppy disk.

7. Close My Computer and all its open windows.

8. Open Explorer and view the contents of the C drive's Windows folder.

9. Using the View menu's Arrange Icons command, sort the files alphabetically and find all the files in your Windows folder that begin with the letter C.

10. Using Quick View, view the Clouds file in your Windows folder.

11. Close Explorer and open My Computer.

12. Drag and drop each drive onto your desktop to create shortcuts.

Part II Review

Unit 4 Summary

▶ **The taskbar:** The taskbar is a strip that runs across the edge of your screen. It lists currently running programs, making them easy to find: Click on a program's icon, and its window rises to the top of the screen. The taskbar can be dragged and dropped to any side of the screen, although it's usually found along the bottom.

▶ **Start menu:** Clicking on the Start button (found on the taskbar) brings the Start menu to the screen. The Start menu lets you load programs, find misplaced files, change your computer's settings, open recently used documents, and perform other computer chores.

▶ **Loading programs:** Most programs automatically list themselves by name in the Start menu's Programs area. Click on a program's name, and Windows 95 brings that program to the screen.

▶ **The desktop:** All your work in Windows 95 takes place on your desktop — the background of your screen. Windows on the desktop can be *maximized,* where they fill the screen, or *minimized,* where they appear as icons along the taskbar. Almost all windows have scroll bars and menus, which lets you move and resize them all by using the same methods.

▶ **Shortcuts:** Sometimes digging through menus for frequently used items can be frustrating. To speed things up, Windows 95 lets you create shortcuts to those items. By double-clicking on the shortcut's icon, Windows 95 behaves just as if you'd double-clicked the frequently used item itself. You can create shortcuts to programs, files, and folders.

▶ **Deleting a shortcut:** Deleting a shortcut doesn't delete the shortcut's target — it just deletes the push-button that takes you to that target, be it a file, program, or folder. The file, program, or folder itself stays on your computer's hard drive.

▶ **Recycle Bin:** To delete a file or folder, drag and drop it on the Recycle Bin — that little trash can on your desktop. If you accidentally delete something, double-click on the Recycle Bin. You can usually salvage recently deleted files by dragging them out of the Recycle Bin and onto the desktop or into another folder.

Unit 5 Summary

▶ **The computer's four main tools:** When handling information, your computer uses four main tools: *files, folders* (also known as *directories*), *disk drives,* and *disks.* The My Computer and Explorer programs let you manipulate all four of these tools.

▶ **Files:** Windows 95 stores its information in files. Files are stored in folders, so they're easy to find later. Files and folders are stored on disks. Drives read and write files to those disks.

▶ **Windows:** The My Computer program displays its information by using windows — just like any other Windows program. Each window shows the files and folders that live on a particular folder on a particular drive.

▶ **Copying and moving files and folders:** You can move and copy files and folders to different places on your hard drive by dragging and dropping them. They can be dragged and dropped among My Computer, Explorer, and your desktop.

▶ **My Computer and Explorer are like file cabinets:** My Computer and Explorer work like big file cabinets, where information is packed into folders; the folders are packed onto disks, which can hold hundreds of folders. Also, you can put folders inside each other, further organizing your information.

▶ **Naming files and folders:** Files and folders have specific rules about their names: The names can use only letters, numbers, and certain symbols; plus, they can't be longer than 255 characters. Older versions of Windows can use only 8 characters, often causing problems if you swap files with friends who don't have Windows 95.

Part II Test

The questions on this test cover all the material presented in Part II, Units 4 and 5.

True   False

T   F   1. A drive can always read and write information to a disk.

T   F   2. After you delete a file, you can never retrieve it.

T   F   3. You can control the folders and windows in My Explorer just like you do the windows on your desktop.

T   F   4. Double-clicking on an program's name on the Start menu starts that program.

T   F   5. Programs usually put their names on the Start menu so that you can launch them easily.

T   F   6. You can use Windows 95 without a mouse.

T   F   7. Deleting a shortcut from the desktop deletes that shortcut's target, be it a file, program, or folder.

T   F   8. My Computer and Explorer perform the same functions, but in slightly different ways.

T   F   9. Many floppy disks must be *formatted* before you can use them.

T   F   10. You can move or copy files and folders by *dragging and dropping* them into other places in My Computer or Explorer.

Multiple Choice

For each of the following questions, circle the correct answer or answers. Remember, each question may have more than one right answer.

11. The My Computer program is often compared to this common object:

A. A trash can.

B. A nail file.

C. A file cabinet.

D. A television set.

12. My Computer lets you drag and drop the following items:

A. Files, folders, and drives onto the desktop.

B. Folders into other folders.

C. Files onto floppy disks.

D. Carrot peelings into the trash.

13. Both My Computer and Explorer can do the following tasks:

A. Load your programs.

B. Delete your programs.

C. Create folders.

D. Create icons.

14. What is a root folder?

A. A big folder on a disk that contains all the other folders.

B. A folder that's usually named after the drive it lives on.

C. A book that's popular with farmers.

D. The first folder that appears when you open My Computer.

Part II Test

15. **These disks can hold the most computer information:**

    A. Floppy disks.

    B. Hard disks.

    C. Compact discs.

    D. Vinyl disks.

16. **These things can damage floppy disks:**

    A. Sticky fingers.

    B. Magnets.

    C. Foul smells.

    D. Moisture.

17. **The following step(s) can help find a lost or covered-up window on the desktop:**

    A. Click the taskbar with the right mouse button and choose Cascade or one of the Tile commands.

    B. Press Alt+Tab.

    C. Click on any visible part of the window.

    D. Call home.

18. **My Computer lets you use a mouse for the following tasks:**

    A. Changing a window's size and location.

    B. Loading programs.

    C. Feeding cats.

    D. Deleting icons.

Matching

19. **Match up the following keystrokes with the corresponding action:**

    A. F1   1. Brings up a list of currently running programs.

    B. F5   2. Cancels an action.

    C. Alt+Tab   3. Brings up the Windows Help program.

    D. Esc   4. Makes My Computer and Explorer take another look at a newly inserted floppy.

    E. Enter   5. Opens or loads the highlighted item.

20. **Match up the icon for the drive with the drive's type.**

    A.   1. CD-ROM drive

    B.   2. Floppydisk drive

    C.   3. Hard drive

Part II Lab Assignment

This lab assignment gets to the nitty-gritty of Windows 95 — the sort of stuff that you'll find yourself doing on a day-to-day basis. You'll start a Windows session, create folders, copy files, load programs, and close down the session.

Step 1: Create a folder for a project

Create a new folder called Today's Work on the desktop.

Step 2: Create a shortcut to your book's disk folder

Make a shortcut on your desktop that leads to the folder where this book's disk is installed.

(**Hint**: The folder is called Windows 95, which lives in a folder called Dummies 101, which lives on your C drive. So using your right mouse button, drag and drop the Windows 95 folder out of My Computer's Dummies 101 folder and onto your desktop. Then select Create Shortcut Here from the menu.)

Step 3: Close all your desktop's open windows

Step 4: Double-click on the Dummies 101 shortcut

The folder containing your book's disk files opens up on-screen.

Step 5: Copy a file into your desktop's folder

Find the Eau de Froggie file, and then copy that file into your new Today's Work folder.

Step 6: Load and close a program

Double-click on the Eau de Froggie icon in the Today's Work folder, and then close Paint.

Step 7: Delete a file, shortcut, and folder

Delete the Eau de Froggie file from the Today's Work folder. Then close the Dummies 101 window and delete its shortcut from the desktop. Finally, close the Today's Work window and delete its folder from the desktop.

Step 8: Retrieve a deleted file from the Recycle Bin

Double-click on the Recycle Bin and drag the Eau de Froggie file back onto the desktop.

Getting into Windows

Part III

In this part . . .

The first half of this book taught the basics of Windows 95: moving a mouse, moving boxes around on-screen, and pushing the correct keys and buttons at the right times. Plus, you learned how to make the My Computer and Explorer programs do your bidding.

Congratulations! You're over the hill, so to speak, and the rest of this book has all the easy stuff. Because you've learned the basics, it's time to break things down into specifics. The next few units teach you how to start a program and load a file into it. After you fiddle with the file for a while, you'll learn how to save your work. Finally, you'll learn how to print the thing — if you decide that it's worth putting on paper.

Starting a Program

Objectives for This Unit

✓ Starting a program from the Start menu

✓ Starting a program from the desktop

✓ Starting a program in My Computer

✓ Starting a program in Explorer

✓ Starting a program in a Run box

on the disk

♦ Angry Diatribe

♦ Eau de Froggie

Windows may be a computerized desktop, but it starts out as an awfully empty one. Just as you need to pull the stapler out of the drawer before you can start stapling papers, you need to load programs before you can start working in Windows.

This unit shows you how to reach into the right drawers for grabbing programs out of your computer. Several main ways are available, but you'll use the method in the first lesson the most often. (The others are listed for those people who like to know *everything*.)

Lesson 6-1
Opening a Program from the Start Menu

By the time you've reached this part of the book, you're probably already familiar with loading programs through the Start menu. But in case you need a refresher — and because it's nice to have all the program-loading methods in one place — here's what to do. The following steps load the Paint program:

1 Click on the Start button and choose Programs from the Start menu.

A list of programs squirts out the side of the menu.

2 Choose Accessories from the menu.

3 Choose Paint from the Accessories menu.

Paint comes to the screen.

When installed, most programs automatically add their names to the Start menu, so this method is usually the easiest way to load a program.

Lesson 6-2
Opening a Program from the Desktop

The desktop lets you open programs in three main ways:

▶ First, you can double-click on any icon — like the Recycle Bin — and the desktop opens it.

▶ Second, you can create a shortcut to a program and double-click on it. (Creating a shortcut leaves a handy push-button for opening that program in the future.)

▶ Last, you can click on the desktop with the right mouse button and choose from the programs listed on the menu. The next few steps teach all three methods.

Loading a program from a desktop icon

1 Double-click on the My Computer icon.

Windows 95 opens the My Computer program.

2 Close the My Computer program.

See how easy things can be if your program already has an icon on the desktop? That's why shortcuts, described in the very next section, come in so handy. By creating shortcuts to your most frequently used programs and files, you can access them almost instantly.

Creating a desktop shortcut and loading a program

If your program already has a shortcut on the desktop, you can load that program quickly and easily. If you'll be loading the program only once, don't bother creating a shortcut; load it by using one of the other methods described in this unit. But if you'll be accessing the program a lot, the shortcut will save you some time. Follow these steps:

1 **Click on the desktop with your right mouse button.**

2 **Choose Shortcut from the New menu.**

3 **Click on the Browse button.**

A box that vaguely resembles Windows 95 Explorer appears. Just as with Explorer, the Browse box lets you double-click on folders to open them. And to look at other drives, click on the Look in box near the top of the box.

4 **Double-click on the Windows folder.**

I'll use the Windows folder as an example because it contains a lot of programs.

5 **Double-click on the Calc file.**

6 **Click on the Next button.**

7 **Type Calculator in the box, and then click on the Finish button.**

A handy shortcut for the Calculator program appears on your desktop. Double-click on the shortcut, and the Calculator program comes to the screen. Feel free to move the shortcut to any convenient place on-screen. You can even create a folder full of shortcuts that lead to your favorite files and programs.

Loading a program from the desktop menu

Some programs put themselves on the desktop's secret menu — the one that appears from nowhere when you click your right mouse button on a blank area of the desktop. Here's how the process works:

1 **Click on the desktop with your right mouse button.**

The secret menu appears. (It's not really a secret, though, because you saw the same menu in the preceding section.)

2 **Choose New from the menu.**

Windows 95 gives you a choice of new things to create, as shown in Figure 6-1.

3 **Select Text Document from the menu.**

Windows 95 immediately brings the Notepad program to the screen, ready for you to start typing some quick words.

Many programs add themselves to the desktop's right-click menu, which provides an easy way to summon them quickly.

Notes:

dragging and dropping programs from My Computer or Explorer onto desktop creates quick and easy shortcuts

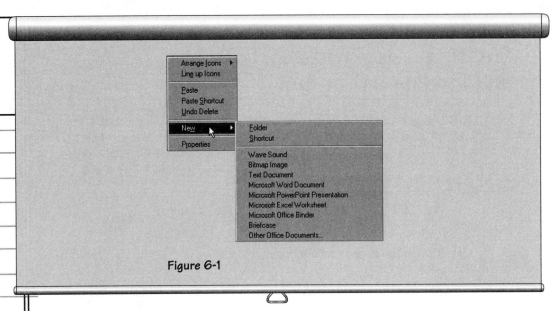

Figure 6-1: Clicking on the desktop with the right mouse button gives you access to a number of options.

Figure 6-1

Lesson 6-3 — Opening a Program in My Computer

holding down Ctrl
while double-
clicking folders in
My Computer keeps
all activity in
current window —
My Computer won't
open new window
for each opened
folder

Opening a program in My Computer is pretty easy; the hard part is finding the program. If you know which folder the program lives in, here's how to launch the program:

1 **Double-click on the My Computer program.**

The program opens on-screen, displaying your computer's disk drives.

2 **Double-click on the C drive icon.**

3 **Double-click on the Windows folder.**

4 **Double-click on the Calc icon.**

The Calculator program loads itself and comes to the screen. If you don't know which folder your program lives in, however, the program may be hard to find. In fact, your best bet may be to use the Find program, covered in Unit 4.

Lesson 6-4 — Opening a Program in Explorer

Opening a program in Explorer is almost identical to opening a program in My Computer. That means that they're both difficult to use if you don't know the folder in which the program lives. Explorer can be a little quicker, however, and it has a key feature: It doesn't leave trails of windows across your screen as it moves from folder to folder.

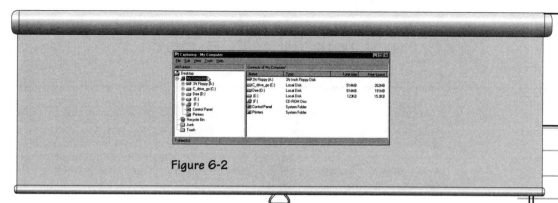

Figure 6-2

Figure 6-2: The files and
folders on Explorer's
right side live in
the folder that's
highlighted on
Explorer's left side.

If you know the name of a program's folder, here's how to bring the program to the screen:

1 Click on the My Computer program with your right mouse button.

2 Choose Explorer from the menu.

The Explorer program leaps to the screen, as shown in Figure 6-2.

3 Click on the C drive icon on the Explorer window's left side.

Explorer shows the contents of the C drive on the right side.

4 Double-click on the Windows folder on the right side.

Explorer lists the contents of the Windows folder on the right side. You'll probably have to slide the window's scroll bars to see all the folders and files inside the Windows folder. (The Scroll Bar Sliding Class took place in Unit 3.)

5 Double-click on the Calc icon.

The Calculator program loads itself and comes to the screen. Just as with My Computer, loading programs can be difficult in Explorer if you don't know the program's folder.

6 Close the Calculator program.

7 Double-click on the C drive's Dummies 101 folder.

The Dummies 101 folder's contents — in this case, the Windows 95 folder — spills out into the window's right side.

8 Double-click on the Windows 95 folder.

9 Double-click on the Eau de Froggie file.

on the disk

Doing so shows you a second way of opening programs that works throughout Windows 95: Double-click on a file, and Windows 95 loads the program that created the file and brings them both to the screen.

on the test

A program's name and its filename are two different things. The program's *name* — Calculator, for example — is designed for people to use. The program's *filename* — Calc, for instance — is for the computer to use.

click on My
Computer with
right mouse button
and choose <u>F</u>ind to
load Start menu's
<u>F</u>ind command

choose Tools from
Explorer's menu
and click on <u>F</u>ind
to load Start
menu's <u>F</u>ind
command

Lesson 6-5

Typing a Name in a Run Box

You probably won't have to deal with this one, but I'm sticking it in just in case. It's sort of a throwback to that DOS stuff that the computer oldsters rave about. See, back in the old days, people didn't just point and click at pictures to run their programs. Instead, they typed the program's name and pressed Enter. Windows 95 lets the old-school folks type a program's name in a Run box when loading programs in the Run section of the Start menu. The following steps show you how, if you're still interested:

1 **Click on the Start button.**

2 **Choose Run from the menu.**

A box similar to the one shown in Figure 6-3 appears.

3 **Type the program's filename and path in the box and click on OK.**

Here's where this task gets complicated. You not only need to know the program's filename, as described earlier, but you also need to know its path. Its *path* is its location on your hard drive, and it works as a road map that helps the computer find the file.

First, a path contains the letter of the disk drive, followed by a colon. Next, the path lists which folders the computer must look through to find the file. For example, say you're looking for the Peeler program that's in your Carrot directory. The Carrot directory lives in the Veggie directory, which is in your Food directory. And all this stuff is on your C drive.

Whew. One more thing, though: All the folders and names need to be separated by the \ character.

So the path for your Peeler program would be C:\Food\Veggie\Carrot\Peeler, and that's what you'd type in the box in Figure 6-3.

When you click on OK, the Start menu uses that path as a road map to find the Peeler program. When the Start menu finds the program, it loads that program and brings it to the screen.

You'll rarely use the Run boxes in Windows 95, but they're there. And now you know what a path does.

Oh, one last thing: If the computer doesn't find your program — make just one mistake in the path, and the computer gets confused — it comes back with an error message like the one shown in Figure 6-4.

Browse boxes, like the one used in Lesson 6-2, also let you type in a path to avoid wading through a bunch of menus to find your file or program.

☑ Progress Check

If you can do the following, you've mastered this unit:

❑ Load a program from the Start button menu.

❑ Load a program from the desktop.

❑ Load a program from My Computer.

❑ Load a program from Explorer.

❑ Load a program from a Run box.

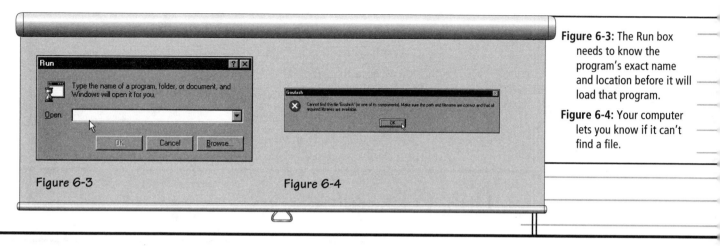

Figure 6-3: The Run box
needs to know the
program's exact name
and location before it will
load that program.

Figure 6-4: Your computer
lets you know if it can't
find a file.

Figure 6-3   Figure 6-4

Unit 6 Quiz

Circle the letter of the correct answer or answers to each of the following
questions. (Remember that some questions have more than one right answer to
keep things from being too easy.)

1. **How do a program's name and its filename differ?**

   A. One is for people to use; the other is for the computer to use.

   B. One can be longer than 255 characters; the other can't.

   C. One is a trademark; the other isn't.

   D. One got teased in school; the other didn't.

2. **Loading programs is easiest to do by using this program:**

   A. Start menu.

   B. Explorer.

   C. My Computer.

   D. UNIX.

3. **Windows 95 can create shortcuts to these items:**

   A. Programs.

   B. Folders.

   C. Files.

   D. Success.

4. **When you double-click on a file's name, Windows does this:**

   A. Sends an error message.

   B. Loads the file.

   C. Loads the file if it can figure out which program created the file.

   D. Writhes in agony.

5. **A path serves this purpose:**

    A. Holds cookie crumbs.

    B. Gives the computer directions to a file's location.

    C. Lists a file's current folder.

    D. Lists a file's current drive.

Unit 6 Exercise

By completing this exercise, you practice loading the WordPad program in each possible way. Close WordPad after each step so that you can bring it to the screen again in the next step.

1. Double-click on the WordPad icon from the Accessories area of the Start menu's Programs area.

2. Type C:\Windows\Write in the Run box and press Enter.

3. While in My Computer, double-click on the Write file located in your Windows directory.

4. While in Explorer, double-click on the Write file located in your Windows directory.

on the disk

5. Double-click on the Angry Diatribe file in the C:\Dummies 101\ Windows 95 folder.

6. Create a shortcut on the desktop to Angry Diatribe in your C:\ Dummies 101\Windows 95 folder. (Hint: You can type **C:\Dummies 101\Windows 95** in the Browse box instead of choosing Browse and pointing and clicking through the folders.)

Unit 7

Opening or Creating a File

Objectives for This Unit

✓ Loading a file into a program

✓ Loading a file by using My Computer or Explorer

✓ Creating a file from the desktop

Prerequisites

▶ Using a mouse (Lesson 2-1)

▶ Moving and controlling on-screen windows (Unit 3)

▶ Opening My Computer and Explorer (Unit 5)

▶ Loading WordPad (Lesson 4-2)

on the disk

▶ Angry Diatribe

▶ Eau de Froggie

When a painter finishes creating a painting, the painting is done. There's no need to mess with it anymore — the paint's dry and the work's complete. Computers aren't nearly as static as a painting hanging in a gallery. After you finish creating a file and save it to disk, you'll probably want to open it again someday. You may want to print the file's contents again. Or you may want to modify an angry letter to your credit card company and turn it into a hateful form letter to send to your latest long-distance company.

This unit shows you how to load files into programs, something you'll find yourself doing over and over again.

Loading a File into a Program

Lesson 7-1

on the disk

Feeling like a poodle? Here are the hoops that WordPad makes you leap through before it lets you play with a file. Luckily, most programs use an identical scheme. In this case, you'll open a letter file called Angry Diatribe from the folder created by the disk in the back of this book.

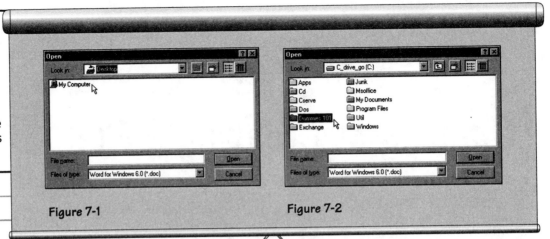

Figure 7-1: When Windows programs open files, they let you choose the file's drive, folder, type, and name.

Figure 7-2: Double-clicking on the C drive reveals the folders and WordPad files living on that drive.

Figure 7-1   Figure 7-2

Notes:

1 Click on the Start button.

2 Load WordPad from the Accessories area of the Programs menu.

Click on the WordPad icon — the one that looks like a little quill pen hovering over a notepad.

3 Choose Open from WordPad's File menu.

A box somewhat like the one in Figure 7-1 appears. Notice how it has four main areas: folders and drives are listed in the big area of the window, while two little boxes along the bottom let you specify filenames and types. Because different computers are set up differently, your screen may look slightly different than the one in Figure 7-1.

The Files of type area is WordPad's way of filtering out all files that it didn't create. See, whenever WordPad creates a file, it secretly tacks on the letters *DOC* to the end of the file's name; that lets WordPad locate the file more easily later.

Windows 95 hides those DOC letters, known as a *file extension,* because normal, healthy-minded people don't need to know about them. Only WordPad (and a few computer engineers) really care about the whole concept.

4 Click on the Look in box.

This lets you choose the drives and folders for WordPad to peer into.

5 Click on the C drive icon from the Look in box.

Because you're after a file that lives on the C:\ drive, select that drive, as shown in Figure 7-2. WordPad displays the files and folders on drive C.

6 Choose the Dummies 101 folder.

The box changes views to show the files and folders living in the Dummies 101 folder, as shown in Figure 7-3.

7 Choose the Windows 95 folder.

Doing so moves to the folder containing the disk files that came with this book.

8 Double-click on the Angry Diatribe file.

That double-click tells WordPad to load the file.

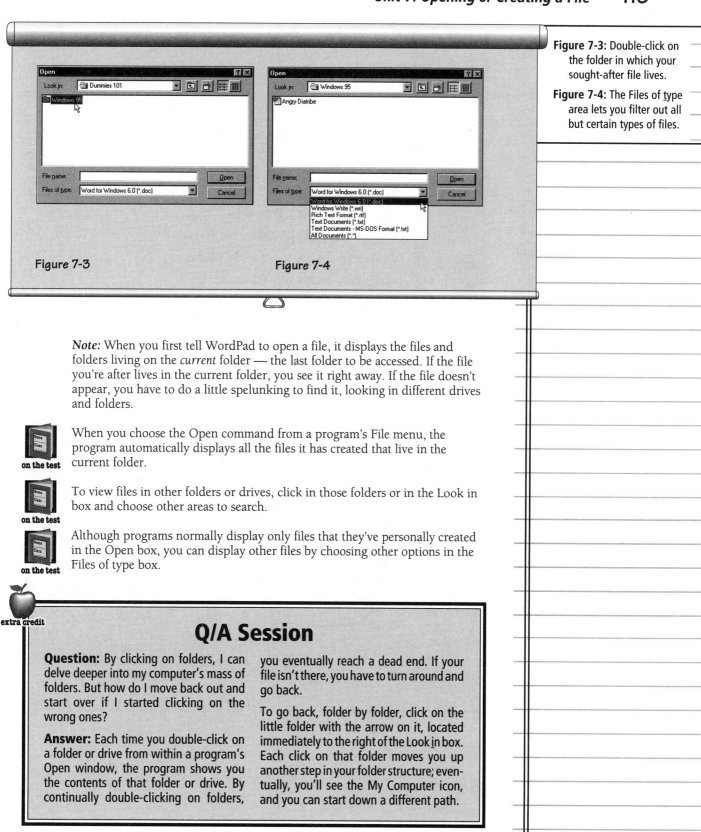

Figure 7-3: Double-click on the folder in which your sought-after file lives.

Figure 7-4: The Files of type area lets you filter out all but certain types of files.

Figure 7-3   Figure 7-4

Note: When you first tell WordPad to open a file, it displays the files and folders living on the *current* folder — the last folder to be accessed. If the file you're after lives in the current folder, you see it right away. If the file doesn't appear, you have to do a little spelunking to find it, looking in different drives and folders.

When you choose the Open command from a program's File menu, the program automatically displays all the files it has created that live in the current folder.

To view files in other folders or drives, click in those folders or in the Look in box and choose other areas to search.

Although programs normally display only files that they've personally created in the Open box, you can display other files by choosing other options in the Files of type box.

Q/A Session

Question: By clicking on folders, I can delve deeper into my computer's mass of folders. But how do I move back out and start over if I started clicking on the wrong ones?

Answer: Each time you double-click on a folder or drive from within a program's Open window, the program shows you the contents of that folder or drive. By continually double-clicking on folders,

you eventually reach a dead end. If your file isn't there, you have to turn around and go back.

To go back, folder by folder, click on the little folder with the arrow on it, located immediately to the right of the Look in box. Each click on that folder moves you up another step in your folder structure; eventually, you'll see the My Computer icon, and you can start down a different path.

Lesson 7-2

Loading a File from within My Computer or Explorer

you can start program by clicking on names of files that program has created

Hey, I'm not going to punish you twice; you already learned this trick back in Lesson 5-4. If you were out sick that day and want to try and fake it, however, here's a rough sketch. Use this lesson to do what you did in Lesson 7-1: load the Angry Diatribe file into WordPad.

1 **Load My Computer or Explorer.**

2 **Double-click on the C drive icon.**

3 **Double-click on the Dummies 101 folder.**

4 **Double-click on the Windows 95 folder.**

on the disk

5 **Double-click on the Angry Diatribe file.**

Windows 95 recognizes the secret file extension, loads WordPad, and tosses the Angry Diatribe file into WordPad for your use.

If this method seems a little weird, head back to Lesson 5-4.

extra credit

Q/A Session

Question: How do I load a file into WordPad if its filename doesn't end in DOC?

Answer: When you tell a program to load a file, that program automatically displays the files that it knows it has personally created. For example, WordPad always tacks the letters DOC onto the end of its files' names, so it automatically displays files ending in DOC. But what if you're trying to load a file into WordPad and WordPad *didn't* create it? For example, the file FLAPPER.TXT won't show up in the box because it ends in the letters TXT. The fix? Use the Files of type area in the Open box. Click on the little downward-pointing arrow and choose among the other types;

as shown in Figure 7-4, each line lets you filter out all but a certain type of file.

If you want to see *all* the files in a certain folder, choose the *.* option. Be careful, though. Because different programs tend to save their files in different formats, you usually can't open other types of files in your program.

One last caveat: Microsoft likes to link its programs so integrally that people wouldn't even think about buying something from another company. So Microsoft Word for Windows and WordPad both use DOC as their identifying file extension. Don't be surprised to see Word come up when you want WordPad or vice versa.

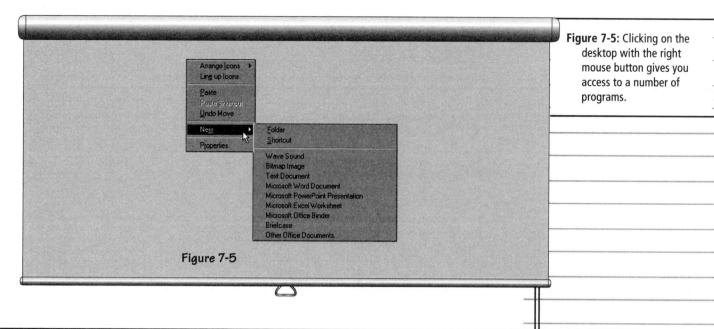

Figure 7-5

Creating a File from the Desktop Menu

Lesson 7-3

You're really getting off easy with this unit, because you've already learned how to do this task, too. Back in Unit 6, you learned how to load a program straight off the desktop. That trick works when creating files, too, and the following steps show you how:

1 Click on the desktop with your right mouse button.

The secret menu appears. (By now, it shouldn't be a secret; it's an integral part of Windows 95.)

2 Choose New from the menu.

Windows 95 gives you an option of new files to create, as shown in Figure 7-5.

3 Choose Text Document from the menu.

Windows 95 immediately brings the Notepad program to the screen, ready for you to start typing some quick words.

Many programs add themselves to the desktop's right-click menu, which provides you with an easy way to summon them quickly.

Tip: To create a text file, record a sound, draw a picture, or access some of your other programs, click on the desktop with your right mouse button and choose New from the pop-up menu.

☑ Progress Check

If you can do the following, you've mastered this unit:

❏ Open a file from within a program.

❏ Load a file into a program from within My Computer and Explorer.

❏ Create a file by right-clicking on the desktop.

Unit 7 Quiz

For each question, circle the letter of the correct answer or answers. Remember, each question may have more than one right answer.

1. **The Open command from a program's File menu displays this:**

   A. All the files on your computer.

   B. All the files the program has created.

   C. All the files stored in the program's currently open folder.

   D. Nothing.

2. **Double-clicking on the folders or drives in a program's Open files window lets you view these:**

   A. The files and folders inside those folders.

   B. The files and folders inside those drives.

   C. The contents of files.

   D. Files the computer didn't create.

3. **Choose this option in the Files of type box to make a program display all the files in the current folder:**

   A. Show All.

   B. Documents.

   C. $.$.

   D. All files (*.*).

Unit 7 Exercise

on the disk

In this exercise, you open the Eau de Froggie file in the Paint program by using the methods you learned in this unit.

1. Open the Start menu.

2. Load Paint.

3. Load Eau de Froggie into Paint from the Windows 95 folder (which lives in the Dummies 101 folder on your C drive).

4. Close Paint.

5. Load Eau de Froggie by double-clicking on its name in My Computer.

6. Close Paint.

7. Load Eau de Froggie by double-clicking on its name in Explorer.

8. Close Paint.

Saving a File

Objectives for This Unit

✓ Learning where to save your work

✓ Saving your work

✓ Saving in different formats

Prerequisites

◗ Pointing and clicking a mouse (Lesson 2-1)

◗ Manipulating windows (Unit 3)

◗ Opening folders (Lesson 5-3)

◗ Opening a Windows program (Lesson 4-2)

◗ Loading a file (Lesson 7-1)

Y ou know how your most important thoughts can drift away if you don't write them down. Computers do the same thing.

When a computer saves a file, it writes the information onto a disk so that it can grab the information later. And if the information doesn't get written down, it drifts away like the smell of perfume from a passing Nordstrom shopper.

heads up

The problem is that most computer programs don't save your work automatically — you have to give them a nudge every so often. How often? The answer's easy: *Save your work whenever you think of it.* You never know when the power might go out, somebody might accidentally kick the power cord, or your computer might simply expire.

So if you're word processing, try to save your work after every paragraph. If you've just come up with a killer sentence, save your work. And of course, be sure to save your work after you finish writing the document.

Windows usually reminds you to save your work before it lets you exit your program, so you get off easy there. Nevertheless, this unit teaches you how and where to save your work in Windows 95.

Lesson 8-1

Knowing Where to Save Your Work

Notes:

You learned this trick back in Lesson 5-1, but here it is again: When storing files on a computer, store them in related folders. For example, keep all your correspondence in a Letters folder. And if you start getting a lot of business letters and personal letters, make two additional folders in your Letters folder, one for business letters and the other for personal letters. Then divide up the files, putting each one in its appropriate folder.

Still too much correspondence? Then start making even *more* folders and start dividing them by date. Believe me, doing so will make finding that letter you wrote back in June 1992 (the one asking the phone company to explain that $324 charge for a phone call to Bulgaria) a lot easier.

The following steps show you how to create a system of folders that I just discussed:

1 Open My Computer.

Double-clicking on the My Computer icon opens it up for viewing.

2 Open the C drive.

Again, a double-click does the trick.

3 Click on a blank area of the C drive folder with the right mouse button.

A familiar-looking menu appears.

4 Choose <u>F</u>older from the Ne<u>w</u> menu.

A new folder appears, waiting for you to type in a name.

5 Type Letters **and press Enter.**

6 Double-click on the new Letters folder.

The Letters folder opens up.

7 Click inside the new Letters folder with your right mouse button and choose <u>F</u>older from the Ne<u>w</u> menu.

8 Name the new folder Business Letters.

9 Repeat Step 7, but name the folder Personal Letters.

By following those steps, you have a Letters folder on your C drive, and the Letters folder contains two additional folders, one for personal letters and the other for business letters. After you get the hang of creating folders, it's not as hard as it appears.

folders can be
dragged and
dropped inside
each other even
when you're saving
a file

extra credit

Q/A Session

Question: Why can't I just keep all my folders on the desktop?

Answer: The desktop itself is a tempting place to put new folders, but it's not the best place. No, reserve the desktop for shortcut icons that point to the folder's *real* location on your hard drive. Doing so keeps your desktop free of clutter and lets you "nest" folders on your hard drive.

Feel free to create folders on the desktop, like the Letters example I just explained, which you broke down into Business Letters and Personal Letters folders. But after you create the Letters folder on your desktop, create a folder on your C drive called Words and move the Letters folder into it.

Saving Your Work
Lesson 8-2

All Windows programs work the same way when it comes to saving a file. The following steps save a file in WordPad, but you follow the same steps for any Windows program:

1 Load WordPad from the Start menu.

WordPad is in the Start menu's Accessories area (which is located in the Programs area).

2 Type a sentence in WordPad.

You can use your imagination here. Type the words **Aphids suck plant juice** if you're having trouble thinking of something. You just need something to save.

3 Choose Save from WordPad's File menu.

If you had saved that file previously, the program would simply save the file using all the information you gave it before. But because you're saving this file for the first time, a questionnaire appears in a box, as shown in Figure 8-1.

4 Choose your C drive from the Save in box.

As Figure 8-1 shows, the Save in box that runs along the top of the window explains where WordPad will stuff your file if you don't choose anything else. But because you want the C drive, click on the little black triangle at the end of the Save in box, and choose the C drive from the list of drives and folders that appears.

(You can save your work on any drive, but for this example you're using drive C.)

The Save As box changes its view to display all the folders living on your C drive, as shown in Figure 8-2.

Figure 8-1: You fill out this form when saving a file for the first time.

Figure 8-2: Choosing the C drive from the Save in box reveals the folders living on that drive.

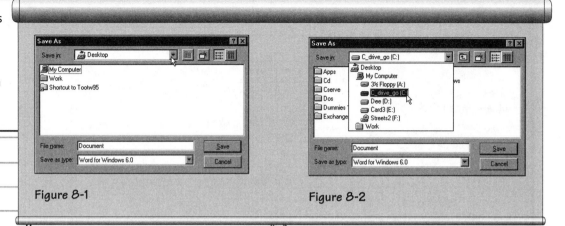

Figure 8-1

Figure 8-2

Notes:

5 **Double-click on the Dummies 101 folder.**

See the Dummies 101 folder listed in the box? Double-click on that folder to choose it. Windows 95 opens the folder and shows what's inside.

6 **Double-click on the Windows 95 folder.**

That opens up the Windows 95 folder, which lives inside the Dummies 101 folder. As before, Windows 95 opens the folder and shows what's inside.

extra credit

Q/A Session

Question: The Save File window doesn't let me create a new folder for storing my new file!

Answer: For years, Windows programs didn't let you create new folders while you were trying to save your file. For example, say you just drew a picture of a cigar in Paint and want to save it in your age-old Cigar folder. But you've drawn a picture of a *Cuban* cigar, so you want to save it in a new folder called Cuban. How can you create a Cuban folder inside your Cigar folder at the same time you save your new file?

Windows 95 lets you create new folders on the fly when you're saving a file for the first time. First, open the Save File window and move to your Cigar folder. Then, with the Save As window on-screen, as shown in Figure 8-1, click on the little folder icon with the little shining explosion on its upper-right corner. (Can't tell which folder icon has the explosion? Hold your mouse pointer over each folder icon until a little box that says Create New Folder appears.) A new folder appears in the window and asks you for a name. After you name the new folder, double-click on it to open it up and save your program inside.

Tip: Lost? Clicked too far into some of your folders and need a way out? Click on the little folder along the top with the arrow in it — the folder closest to the Save in box — to make Windows 95 back out of your current folder. Keep clicking that little folder with the arrow, and you'll eventually see all your listed drives; then you can start over.

7 **Ignore the Save as type box.**

Because you're saving the file in the WordPad program, WordPad automatically saves the file in its special *WordPad* format (and that's why it tacks on the letters *WRI* to the end of the file). WordPad, as well as some other Windows programs, can get sneaky and save files in other formats, but I'll cover those later.

8 **Type** Study in Aphid Sucking **in the File name box, replacing the word** *Document.*

Here's some good news about the file's name. For years, IBM-compatible PCs could use only eight characters when naming their files. That meant that people had to use names like REPORT12 and 950122.

Windows 95 lets you use 255 characters, so you can name your file Study in Aphid Sucking because you've written about aphids sucking plant juice.

9 **Click on the Save button.**

The computer saves the Study in Aphid Sucking file in the Dummies 101\ Windows 95 folder on your computer's C drive.

Now, because you've assigned a name, folder, and drive to that particular file, you'll only have to perform Step 3 when saving that file in the future: just choose Save from WordPad's File menu, and WordPad automatically saves your file using the same name and location that you used before.

on the test

Filenames can be 255 characters long and can contain letters, numbers, and some common symbols. You can't use the following symbols in filenames: . , " / \ [ ] : * | < > + = ;

extra credit

> *to save files quickly, press Alt+F+S*

Q/A Session

Question: What if I don't choose a drive, folder, or name when saving my file?

Answer: If you don't choose a drive or folder when saving a file, the program simply saves the file in the *current folder*, or the drive that happens to be open at the time. Usually, this means that the program saves the file in the same drive and folder that the program itself lives on, which makes the file harder to find in the future.

Programs almost always make you choose a name when saving a file for the first time, however. If you don't choose a name, they'll make up a name like Unnamed File or New Text Document.

Lesson 8-3

Saving in Different Formats (the Save As Command)

Notes:

People in different countries often speak different languages; foreigners don't know what they're saying. So it's only natural that computer programs do the same thing when storing files: They store them in different formats that other programs can't read.

But just as some people can understand more than one language, some Windows programs can read and write in other computer program's formats. Plus, some wise computer engineers came up with a computerized *Esperanto* — a file format that a whole bunch of computer programs can understand. (The language is called *ASCII* — pronounced *ASK-ee* — if you ever see that word and wonder what it means.)

You save files in different formats with the Save as type command. To teach you how the process works, this lesson shows you how to create a file in WordPad and store it in a format that Notepad, another Windows program, can read. First, you see what happens when you try to open a WordPad file in Notepad:

1 Load Notepad.

The Notepad icon is that little green spiral-bound notebook in the Accessories menu of the Start menu's Program area.

2 Choose <u>O</u>pen from Notepad's <u>F</u>ile menu.

A box appears, as shown in Figure 8-3.

3 Choose drive C from the Look <u>i</u>n box.

The window shows you the files and folders on your C drive.

4 Choose the Dummies 101 folder, and then open the Windows 95 folder that lives inside it.

Now, Notepad lists the files in that folder *if* they are stored in the proper Notepad format. However, you stored Study in Aphid Sucking in WordPad format, so that file won't be listed in the box.

5 Choose Cancel and close Notepad.

Now, reload the Study in Aphid Sucking file into WordPad and save it in a format that Notepad can understand:

1 Load WordPad.

2 Choose <u>O</u>pen from WordPad's <u>F</u>ile menu and load Study in Aphid Sucking.

Loading a file is covered in Lesson 7-1; the file is in the Windows 95 folder, which lives in your C drive's Dummies 101 folder.

3 Choose Save <u>A</u>s from WordPad's <u>F</u>ile menu.

A box appears that lets you save the Study in Aphid Sucking file in a different format (see Figure 8-4).

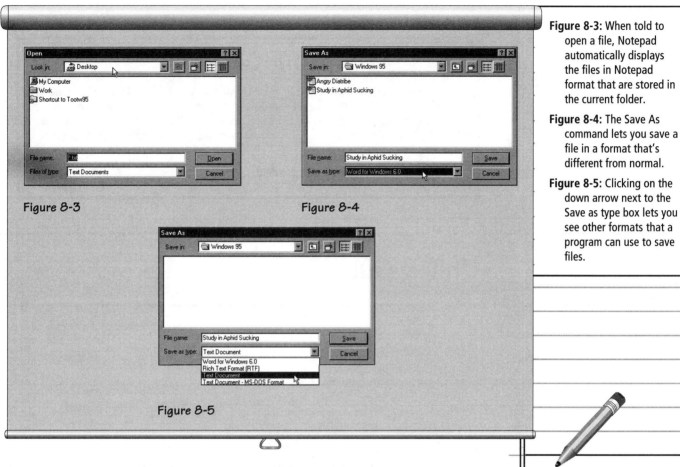

Figure 8-3

Figure 8-4

Figure 8-5

Figure 8-3: When told to open a file, Notepad automatically displays the files in Notepad format that are stored in the current folder.

Figure 8-4: The Save As command lets you save a file in a format that's different from normal.

Figure 8-5: Clicking on the down arrow next to the Save as type box lets you see other formats that a program can use to save files.

4 Choose Text Document from the Save as type menu.

Click on the Save as type box to see the other formats WordPad can handle, as shown in Figure 8-5. Then choose the Text Document option to save the Study in Aphid Sucking file as an ASCII file — a text file that Notepad can read — rather than as a WordPad file, which Notepad can't handle.

5 Change the Study in Aphid Sucking file's name to Study in Aphid Sucking.txt.

That way, Notepad can recognize the file as being readable. See, Notepad's not smart enough to look at the file before deciding whether or not it can read it. It looks only at the last three letters of the file's name — which Windows 95 normally hides. So by tacking the letters TXT to the end of the file's name, you tell Notepad to make an effort to read it.

6 Load Notepad.

7 Load Study in Aphid Sucking into Notepad.

Now, because you've saved the file as a text file and added the letters TXT to the end of its filename, Notepad recognizes the file as something it can handle. So it lists Study in Aphid Sucking as a file it can open — something it couldn't do back in Step 4 of this lesson's first section.

☑ Progress Check

If you can do the following, you've mastered this lesson:

❏ Know when to save a file.

❏ Save a file.

❏ Save a file in a different format.

Save as command comes in handy for saving files in formats that other programs can read

Notes:

extra credit

Q/A Session

Question: Couldn't I save some time by renaming Study in Aphid Sucking to Study in Aphid Sucking.txt and then loading the file into Notepad that way?

Answer: No. Simply renaming the file by choosing the Rename command would allow it to appear on Notepad's menu of readable files, and Notepad would make an effort to load it. But it would spit the file back out as indigestible when it discovered that it wasn't stored in true Notepad format.

Unit 8 Quiz

Circle the letter of the correct answer or answers to each of the following questions. (A few questions may have more than one right answer.)

1. **Save your work at these intervals:**

    A. When you've completed work on a project.

    B. After you write a page.

    C. After you write a unit.

    D. Whenever you think about it.

2. **Windows programs let you create a new folder at the same time you save a file.**

    A. True.

    B. False.

    C. Sometimes.

    D. Never.

3. **Filenames can contain up to this number of characters:**

    A. 8.

    B. 16.

    C. 64.

    D. 255.

4. **Filenames can't contain these symbols:**

    A. , " / \

    B. [ ] : * |

    C. < > + = ;

    D. @ ! # $ %

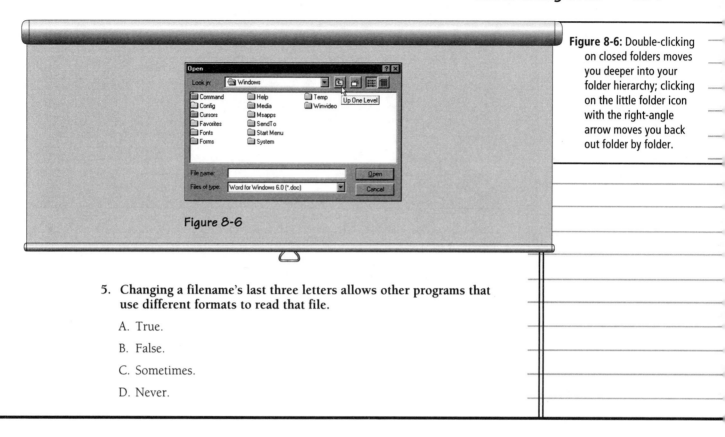

Figure 8-6

Figure 8-6: Double-clicking on closed folders moves you deeper into your folder hierarchy; clicking on the little folder icon with the right-angle arrow moves you back out folder by folder.

5. **Changing a filename's last three letters allows other programs that use different formats to read that file.**

   A. True.

   B. False.

   C. Sometimes.

   D. Never.

Unit 8 Exercise

1. Create a file in WordPad and save it in Rich Text Format.

   (Rich Text Format is like the "Rich Man's ASCII" format. Many programs can read it, and unlike ordinary ASCII, Rich Text Format preserves much of a document's formatting, including bold, italics, margin settings, and other features.)

2. Choose Open from WordPad's File menu. When the Open box appears (refer to Figure 8-3), practice double-clicking on all the folders in the Open box — both the open ones and the closed ones — until you've looked inside every folder on your hard drive.

   To move deeper into your folder hierarchy, double-click on the folders again. To move out, click on the little folder icon with the "right-angle" arrow on it, as shown in Figure 8-6.

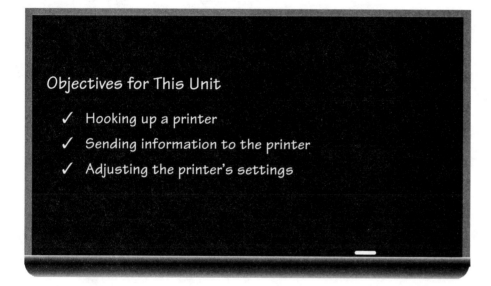

Unit 9

• • • • • • • • • •

Printing a File

Objectives for This Unit

✓ Hooking up a printer

✓ Sending information to the printer

✓ Adjusting the printer's settings

Prerequisites

▶ Loading a Windows 95 Program (Unit 6)

▶ Opening a Windows 95 file (Unit 7)

▶ Navigating windows with a mouse (Lesson 2-1)

on the disk

▶ Angry Diatribe

▶ Eau de Froggie

Windows makes printing pretty easy, unless the paper gets jammed. (And if the paper does get jammed a lot, take the beast to the repair shop for a thorough cleaning. Believe me, doing so will save you a lot of aggravation.)

This unit takes you through the process of transporting your thoughts from the computer's monitor onto paper so that you can pass them around, post them, or if you really messed up, make paper airplanes out of them.

If you don't have a printer or won't be doing any printing yourself, you can jump ahead to Unit 10. This book's not like college, which forces people to take courses in Medieval Literature even though they just want to be tax attorneys.

Hooking Up a New Printer

Lesson 9-1

Follow these steps if you've brought home a new printer and are hooking it up for the first time.

Figure 9-1: Double-click on the Printers folder in My Explorer to find the Add Printer icon.

Figure 9-2: The Add Printer Wizard takes you through the steps of installing a new printer in Windows 95.

Notes:

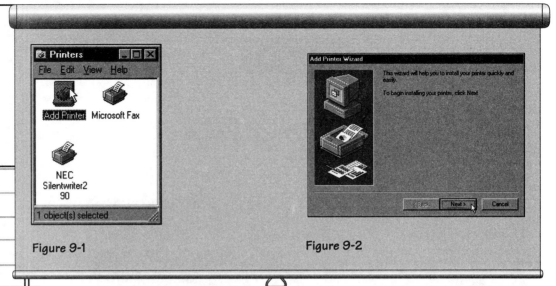

Figure 9-1   Figure 9-2

heads up

Before plugging anything into your computer, be sure to save any current work in progress, shut down Windows 95, and turn off your computer.

1 Put the printer on a desk near your computer.

It doesn't have to be on the same desk; just make sure that it's close enough for the printer cable to reach your computer. (The cables are usually less than six feet long.)

2 Plug the printer cable from the printer into your computer's parallel port.

The parallel port is in the back of your computer; it's usually the biggest port back there, and it has 25 pin-sized holes. (Count 'em if you don't trust me.)

3 Double-click on the Printers folder from the My Computer program.

Or click on Printers from the Start menu's Settings menu; both actions bring up the Printers window, shown in Figure 9-1.

4 Double-click on the Add Printer icon.

The Add Printer Wizard pops into action, as Figure 9-2 shows. The mystical Wizard takes you through the printer installation steps, pitching in some tips when things go wrong.

5 Click on the Next button.

The Printer Wizard brings a huge menu to the screen, listing printer manufacturers on the left and printer model names on the right.

6 Click on the manufacturer of your new printer, and then choose the model from the right side of the box.

You may need to scroll up or down the list of manufacturers by using the scroll bar along the list's right side. (Scroll bars were covered in Lesson 3-4, if you skipped that one.) When you find the manufacturer's name, click on it — and choose your printer's model from the list that appears in the window's right side.

7 **Click on the Next button.**

Windows asks the most confusing question of the entire process: What port do you want to use? Stick with the one that's already highlighted — the one called LPT1: Printer Port.

8 **Make sure that the <u>Y</u>es button is highlighted, and then click on the Next button.**

Because you want Windows 95 to use your new printer as the *default printer* — the printer that Windows 95 automatically chooses if you don't choose something else — choose the Yes button. Choose the No button if you'll be using several printers and plan to switch among them manually each time you print.

9 **Plug the printer into the wall.**

10 **Turn on the printer.**

It should whir to life, ready to spit out pages containing your work.

11 **Make sure that the <u>Y</u>es button is highlighted, and click the Finish button.**

That tells Windows to print a test page to your printer so that you can tell whether it gets along well with your computer.

extra credit

Q/A Session

Question: What if my new printer isn't listed on the Add list?

Answer: If Windows doesn't list your new printer on the list of printers, choose the Have Disk button. Then look in the new printer's package for a floppy disk. (Windows needs information from it in order to know how to speak to your computer.) Some printers come with installation programs that bypass this stuff altogether. I hate to say this, but you may have to read your printer's manual to figure this one out.

on the test

Before trying to use a printer, make sure that it's plugged in and turned on. Also, Windows 95 works with most printers on the market.

Sending Information to the Printer

Lesson 9-2

Sending information to a printer is one of the easiest Windows tasks, as you'll see by following these steps:

1 **Load WordPad.**

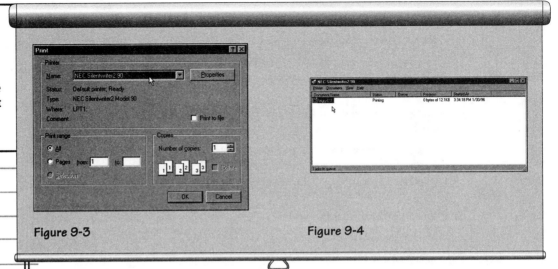

Figure 9-3: WordPad asks some questions before allowing you to print a file.

Figure 9-4: The print queue is a traffic controller that carefully routes files to the printer.

Figure 9-3   Figure 9-4

Notes:

on the disk

2 Open the Angry Diatribe file from the Windows 95 folder in your Dummies 101 folder.

3 Choose <u>P</u>rint from WordPad's <u>F</u>ile menu.

WordPad tosses a dialog box in your face, as shown in Figure 9-3.

Printing options differ in different programs. Some let you print out more than one page; others can tell the printer to use different colored paper for certain tasks. (Lesson 9-3 runs you through the most common printer settings.)

4 Choose OK.

When you choose OK, WordPad tosses your file to a place called the *print queue*, described in the Extra Credit section.

extra credit

What's the print queue?

The print queue, shown in Figure 9-4, is a traffic controller of sorts, keeping too many files from trying to worm their way into the printer at the same time. See, you can send files to the printer a lot faster than the printer can print them. To avoid traffic jams, the print queue stacks the files in order and sends them to the printer, one after the other.

The print queue works in the background, so you'll probably just notice it as a tiny printer icon that sits next to the digital clock along the bottom of your screen

while you're printing. But if you want to be tricky, you can tell the print queue to change the order of the files you're printing. Just double-click on the tiny icon to bring the print queue to the screen, then "drag and drop" a file from near the bottom of the queue's list to near the top of the list, and the print queue lets that file have cuts in line.

The print queue lets you cancel print jobs as well: Click on the listed file with your right mouse button and select Cancel Printing from the menu that pops up.

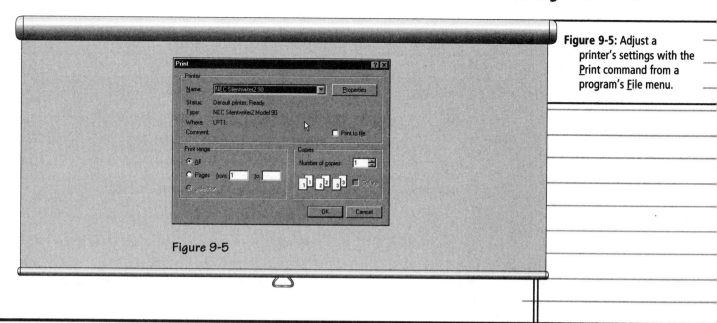

Figure 9-5

Figure 9-5: Adjust a
printer's settings with the
Print command from a
program's File menu.

Adjusting the Printer's Settings

Lesson 9-3

Sometimes you want something a little extra from your printer. For example,
maybe you have more than one printer hooked up to your system and want to
switch to a different printer.

Maybe you want to change paper sizes, print sideways, or take advantage of
some of your particular printer's other "sexy" features. That's all done through
the Print command, found in the File menu of most programs.

heads up

Here's a warning, however. Because different brands of printers work differently and have different features, your Print command will probably work
differently than the one I describe here.

Nevertheless, here's how to adjust the settings on an NEC Silentwriter laser
printer. Your printer's settings will probably be similar, yet a little different.

1 Load WordPad.

Any program will do, but use WordPad because you probably know how to load
it quickly.

2 Choose Print from the File menu.

A box like the one in Figure 9-5 appears.

3 Adjust your printer's settings and click on OK.

Table 9-1 shows you what some of these settings mean; some of the settings
are on the first window, others appear when you click on that page's Properties button.

Notes:

Table 9-1	Print Commands
This Setting	**Does This**
Name	People who have more than one printer connected to their computer can choose a particular printer here. The *default* printer is the one that Windows always uses unless you tell it otherwise.
Print range	Normally, you choose All so WordPad prints all your pages. But if you want to print only a few — pages 3 through 6, for example — you can set that up here.
Number of copies	Yep, this works just like a copy machine. Type in the number of copies you'd like here.
Print to file	Windows asks for a filename and then prints your page to a file. (Not used frequently.)
Options	If you have this button, click on it to take advantage of your particular program's advanced features.

Click on the Print menu's Properties button for these additional choices:

Paper size	Here, you can choose among the different sizes of paper that your printer can use.
Layout	Some printers can squeeze two or even four pages of text onto a single page. If your printer can handle it, you'll see the feature listed here.
Orientation	*Portrait* means to print on the paper normally — like a portrait of a person hanging on a wall. *Landscape* means to print on the paper horizontally, as if you were printing a wide picture of a landscape.
Paper source	Does your printer have a top tray? Bottom tray? Choose the one you want to use here.
Resolution	Found in the Graphics menu, this option adjusts the way your graphics appear on paper.

Printing a File in My Computer or Explorer

Lesson 9-4

You can print a file from the desktop or the My Computer or Explorer program, but you won't have a chance to change your printer settings, as you'll see in the following steps:

1 Load My Computer and find the Windows 95 folder in your Dummies 101 directory.

on the disk

2 **Click on the Angry Diatribe file with your right mouse button.**

3 **Choose Print from the menu.**

Windows immediately sends Angry Diatribe off to the printer without giving you a chance to examine and adjust any of your printer settings. You won't be able to choose the number of copies, for example, or choose among the printers you have connected to your computer.

If you think of any last-minute changes that you'd like to make, you're stuck; if you click on Cancel to cancel the print job, you aren't left in WordPad, where you can make your last-minute fixes. No, the print queue simply disappears, leaving you to load WordPad yourself and fix the changes there.

If you just want to dash off a quick copy of a letter, printing directly from the desktop or the My Computer or Explorer programs might be a decent alternative. But unless you're sure that everything's set up correctly, printing directly may be more of a hassle than it's worth.

Tip: Most Windows programs use WYSIWYG. Pronounced wizzy-wig, it stands for What You See Is What You Get, meaning that the images you see on-screen are the same as the images you see on the printer.

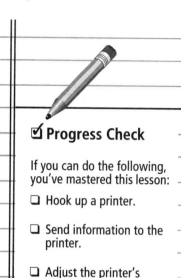

☑ Progress Check

If you can do the following, you've mastered this lesson:

❑ Hook up a printer.

❑ Send information to the printer.

❑ Adjust the printer's settings.

Unit 9 Quiz

Circle the letter of the correct answer or answers to each of the following questions. (A question may have more than one right answer.)

1. Do these things before using a printer:

A. Make sure that it's plugged in.

B. Make sure that it's turned on.

C. Make sure that your program is set up to print to the right brand of printer.

D. Wash your hands.

2. Windows works with most printers on the market.

A. True.

B. False.

C. Sometimes.

D. Only when the printer is plugged in, turned on, and set up properly.

3. **Windows can print files from the desktop and the My Computer and Explorer programs.**

   A. True.

   B. False.

   C. Sometimes.

   D. Yes, but it's rarely worth the effort.

Unit 9 Exercise

on the disk

1. Load Paint.

2. Open Eau de Froggie from the Windows 95 folder in your Dummies 101 folder.

3. Print Eau de Froggie.

4. Quit Paint.

5. Load My Computer.

6. Print Eau de Froggie from the My Computer program.

7. Load Explorer.

on the disk

8. Print Angry Diatribe from the Explorer program.

9. Close all open files.

Sharing Information (That "Cut and Paste" Stuff)

Prerequisites
▶ Loading programs (Unit 6)
▶ Loading files (Unit 7)
▶ Navigating windows with a mouse (Lesson 2-1)

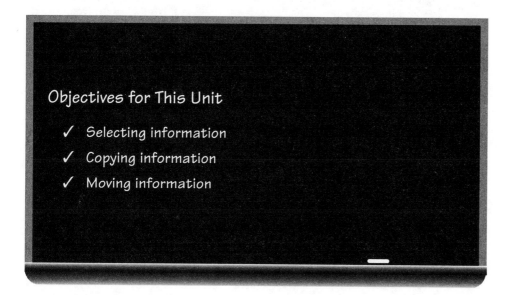

Objectives for This Unit

✓ Selecting information

✓ Copying information

✓ Moving information

on the disk
▶ Angry Diatribe
▶ Fax Cover
▶ Eau de Froggie

You know how big corporations despise each other? Oh, sure, competing CEOs will sit together in big rooms, smoke cigars, and share guffaws, but they're silently plotting to bat each other over the head with their humidors.

Computer programs used to be like that. Each software company thought that it had come up with the best way to save information. So when you tried to move information from one program to another, the receiving program choked. The programs wouldn't cooperate, and you had to suffer for it.

With Windows, however, everybody gets along. To move information from one program to another, you simply "cut and paste," just like a preschooler. Or if you're feeling less drastic, you can "copy and paste," creating a second copy of your information to spread around.

This unit shows you how to grab, cut, copy, move, and paste your work without any hard feelings.

Lesson 10-1

Selecting Information

In Windows, you can move just about all information from one program to another. You can copy words and paragraphs from one letter to another. You can create a "multimedia" postcard by pasting sounds, pictures, and movies into a letter. You can grab a chart from a spreadsheet, paste it into a report, and add a gasp sound as well.

But first, you have to *select* the information you'd like to grab. The process works slightly differently in different programs, but basically it involves *highlighting* the information with a mouse. The following steps show you how to select information in WordPad; after you select the information, you can cut or copy it to a new location, as the subsequent lessons show.

on the disk

1 Load WordPad.

2 Load Angry Diatribe from the Windows 95 folder in your Dummies 101 folder.

3 Point at the start of the first paragraph.

As Figure 10-1 shows, the mouse cursor is at the beginning of the first word of the first paragraph.

4 Hold down the mouse button and, while dragging the cursor down and across the screen, point at the end of the first paragraph.

See how the first paragraph is highlighted, as in Figure 10-2? That means you've selected it, and it's ready for further action.

Highlighting text by sliding the mouse cursor over it can be awkward at times, so Table 10-1 shows you a few shortcuts that some (but not all) Windows programs use.

Table 10-1	Shortcuts for Highlighting Information
To Do This	*Do This*
Highlight a word	Double-click on it
Highlight a paragraph	Double-click next to it in the left margin
Highlight a sentence	Hold down Ctrl and double-click on the sentence
Highlight an entire document	Hold down Ctrl and double-click in the left margin

heads up

Note: Be very careful when you've highlighted something, because you can accidentally delete it. Anything you type — even an accidental keystroke — replaces the highlighted information.

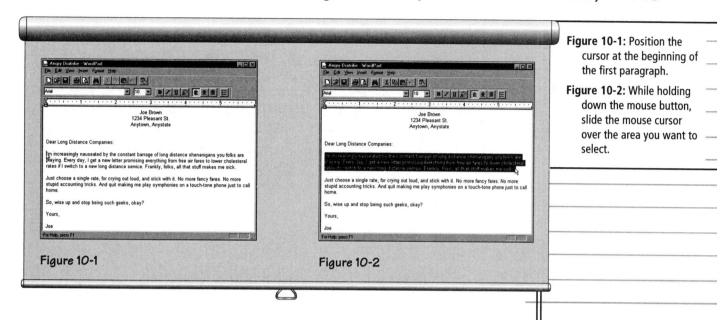

Figure 10-1

Figure 10-2

Figure 10-1: Position the cursor at the beginning of the first paragraph.

Figure 10-2: While holding down the mouse button, slide the mouse cursor over the area you want to select.

on the test

If you highlight some information and accidentally delete it, immediately press Alt+Backspace or Ctrl+Z to bring it back.

Note: If you want to delete a lot of information, select it and press the Delete key.

Selected information and *highlighted* information stand for the same thing: information that's been chosen for later action.

to delete information, select it and press Delete

Copying Information

Lesson 10-2

Copying information from one program to another is easy, once you get over the fact that everything happens in the background: You won't be able to see anything happen on-screen, but here's how the process works:

1 **Follow Steps 1 through 4 in Lesson 10-1.**

Following these steps highlights the first paragraph of the Angry Diatribe file in WordPad.

2 **Choose Copy from WordPad's Edit menu, as shown in Figure 10-3.**

Or if you don't like using the menus, press Ctrl+C to do the same thing. Pressing Ctrl+Insert has the same effect, too. Choose whichever method is easiest for you to remember.

Watch the screen carefully, and prepare yourself for a surprise: Nothing happens. At least, it doesn't *look* like anything happens. But Windows grabs your highlighted information and sticks it in a special place called the *Clipboard*, where it can be transported to wherever you'd like to put it. Trust me; the information has been copied.

Figure 10-3: Choose Copy from WordPad's Edit menu.

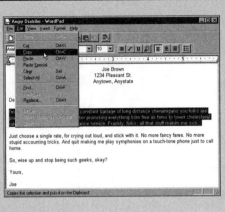

Figure 10-3

heads up

The Clipboard can hold only one chunk of information at a time; each new piece of cut or copied information replaces the previous piece.

extra credit

What, you don't trust me?

How do you know that the information *really* got copied to that special place called the Clipboard? After all, nothing visible happened on-screen. Well, you can peek at the information, just to make sure. Choose the Clipboard Viewer icon from the Start menu's Accessories area, and you should see your information sitting in the Viewer's window.

In fact, if I'm doing a lot of copying, I keep the Clipboard Viewer window open in the

bottom corner of my screen so that I can keep a cautious eye on what's going into and out of it.

If you can't find the Clipboard Viewer on your computer, Windows 95 may not have installed it in order to save hard disk space. Unit 19 shows you how to install parts of Windows 95 that never made it to your hard drive.

Lesson 10-3

Cutting Information

The Cut command isn't much different from the Copy command, actually. Both commands place your selected information on the Clipboard, from which you can paste the information into another program.

But here's the big difference: The Cut command deletes the highlighted information after copying the information to the Clipboard. That lets you move the information to another program.

For example, here's how to cut a word or two from WordPad for later pasting into another program:

on the disk

1 **Load WordPad.**

2 **Load Fax Cover from the Dummies 101\Windows 95 folder.**

3 **Select the word *Comments* from the Fax Cover document.**

Double-clicking on a word is a quick way to highlight it, as you learned from Table 10-1.

4 **Choose Cut from WordPad's Edit menu.**

Poof! The highlighted word, *Comments,* disappears immediately, having been yanked to the Windows Clipboard for later action.

on the test

Choose the Copy command to *copy* information to another location. Use the Cut command to *move* information to another location. Shortcut-lovers can press Ctrl+X or Shift+Delete to cut the highlighted information as well.

Pasting Information

Lesson 10-4

After you cut or copy information to the Clipboard, you can paste that information into another program. Basically, that process involves two steps: locating a spot to paste it and pushing the Paste button. You'll learn both steps in this lesson.

on the disk

1 **Load WordPad.**

2 **Load Angry Diatribe from the Windows 95 folder in your Dummies 101 folder.**

3 **Copy the first paragraph from the Angry Diatribe file.**

You did this exact step in Lesson 10-2.

4 **Open Notepad.**

5 **Choose the Paste command from the Edit menu.**

The paragraph you copied from WordPad magically appears in the Notepad file. Notice how the paragraph appears where the cursor happens to be in Notepad — in this case, at the very beginning of the file.

6 **Return to WordPad and select the second paragraph from the Angry Diatribe file.**

7 **Cut the paragraph.**

You learned how to complete Step 7 in Lesson 10-3.

Notes:

☑ Progress Check

If you can do the following, you've mastered this unit:

❑ Select information.

❑ Copy information and paste it into other places.

❑ Cut information and paste it into other places.

8 Return to Notepad and select the Paste command.

This time, the second paragraph appears in the Notepad file.

on the test

Two shortcut commands for the Paste command are Ctrl+V and Shift+Insert.

Unit 10 Quiz

Notes:

Circle the letter of the correct answer or answers for each question. (Just to keep things lively, some questions have more than one right answer.)

1. **Which action can't be seen on-screen?**

   A. Pasting.

   B. Selecting.

   C. Copying.

   D. Cutting.

2. **If you select some text and press the spacebar, what happens?**

   A. The text disappears.

   B. The text is replaced with a space.

   C. A spacebar replaces the text.

   D. The spacebar disappears.

3. **Selected information and highlighted information both mean this:**

   A. Information that's been professionally desktop published.

   B. Information that's been chosen for later action.

   C. Information that's of global importance.

   D. Information that stands out in a textbook.

4. **To retrieve information that you've accidentally cut, you do this:**

   A. Press Ctrl+V.

   B. Press Shift+Insert.

   C. Press Alt+Backspace.

   D. Grab a Band-Aid.

5. **To cut highlighted information and put it on the Clipboard, you do this:**

   A. Choose Cut from the Edit menu.

   B. Press Ctrl+X.

   C. Press Shift+Delete.

   D. Grab scissors.

6. **The Copy and Cut commands do the same thing except for this:**

   A. The Cut command deletes the highlighted information after copying it to the Clipboard.

   B. The Cut command is more sterile.

   C. The Copy command needs a printer ribbon.

   D. The Copy command puts a second copy of the information into your program.

7. **To paste information, you do this:**

   A. Choose Paste from the Edit menu.

   B. Press Ctrl+V.

   C. Press Shift+Insert.

   D. Lick the back of it.

Unit 10 Exercise

1. Open Paint.

2. Open Eau de Froggie and select a portion of it.

   Click on either of the top two "dotted line" icons at the top of Paint's toolbox. Then, while holding down your mouse button, run the mouse pointer over the portion of the picture you want to select.

3. Select Copy.

4. Open WordPad and select Paste.

on the disk

Part III Review

Unit 6 Summary

▶ **Starting a program by double-clicking:** Windows 95 lets you start a program in several ways. Double-clicking on the program's icon in the Start menu is the easiest way. Or if you know the program's filename, you can double-click on that name in the My Computer or Explorer program.

▶ **Starting a program from the desktop:** Clicking the right mouse button on a blank part of the desktop brings up a menu that lets you create new documents. Clicking on the New section, for example, brings up programs ready to create new text documents, WordPad documents, sounds, and other types of files.

▶ **Starting a program by using the Run box:** The least common method of starting a program is to type the program's filename in the Start menu's Run box.

▶ **Starting a program by double-clicking on a filename:** Finally, you can start a program by double-clicking on the name of a file that the program has created. Clicking on the name of a file created in WordPad, for example, tells Windows 95 to load WordPad and then load the file into WordPad.

Unit 7 Summary

▶ **Opening files from the File menu:** All Windows programs let you open files by following the same basic steps: Choose Open from the program's File menu, click on the file's name in the box that appears, and click on the OK button.

▶ **Opening files from My Computer and Explorer:** You can also open a file by double-clicking on its name from within My Computer or Explorer.

▶ **Opening files from shortcuts:** Finally, you can open a file by double-clicking on a shortcut that leads to that file.

Unit 8 Summary

▶ **Save in a location you can find later:** When saving a file, be sure to save it in a location that you'll be able to find later. For example, you may want to create a new folder on your hard drive, as Unit 5 discusses.

▶ **Saving a file: All Windows programs let you save a file by following the same basic steps:** Choose Save from the program's File menu. If you're saving the file for the first time, Windows asks you to choose a name and location for the file. The program automatically uses that name and location whenever you save the file again.

▶ **Saving a file with a new name or in a new location:** To save the file with a different name or in a different location, use the Save As command from the program's File menu. In some programs, the Save As command also lets you save the file in a different *format* — a way of saving information that lets other types of programs read it.

▶ **Filenames:** A filename can contain up to 255 characters. Windows 3.11 and DOS programs can only use 8-character filenames, so Windows 95 sometimes truncates filenames when you swap files with friends using older computers.

Unit 9 Summary

▶ **WYSIWYG:** Most Windows programs use *WYSIWYG*. Pronounced *wizzy-wig*, it stands for *What You See Is What You Get,* meaning that the images you see on-screen are the same as the images you see on the printer.

▶ **Printing a file:** Almost all Windows programs print the same way: You choose Print from the File menu. The program asks whether you'd like to change any of the settings on your particular brand of printer. Click on the OK button, and the program sends the information to the print queue, a special program that routes information to the printer. (That way, you can keep working while your computer prints in the background.)

Part III Review

Unit 10 Summary

♦ **Cutting, copying, and pasting:** Cutting, copying, and pasting information are primary ingredients in Windows 95. In Windows, all the programs are aware of each other, so you can easily move information from one program to another.

♦ **Selecting information:** The process starts when you *select* information — highlight it by dragging the mouse cursor over it while holding down the mouse button. Some programs also have Select options built into their Edit menus.

♦ **Choosing the Cut or Copy command:** Next, either cut or copy the information to the Windows Clipboard, a special holding tank for temporarily holding data. Cutting deletes the data from the program; copying sends a duplicate image to the Clipboard. Both the Cut and Copy commands are on the program's Edit menu.

♦ **Pasting information:** Finally, put the cursor in the program where you'd like the information to appear and choose Paste from the program's Edit menu. The program puts a copy of the information from the Clipboard into the program.

Part III Test

The questions on this test cover all the material presented in Part III, Units 6 through 10.

True False

T   F   1. Clicking on a program's icon in My Computer starts that program.

T   F   2. Although Explorer can copy files and programs, you can't use it to load programs.

T   F   3. Copying new information to the Clipboard erases any old information on the Clipboard.

T   F   4. Many printers let you choose among various options before printing.

T   F   5. You should not save files until you've finished working on them.

T   F   6. Programs can't always read files that other programs created.

T   F   7. You can copy information from one program's window into another program's window fairly easily.

T   F   8. Programs can store files in only one particular format.

T   F   9. The three letters that a program tacks onto the end of a filename are known as an *extension*.

T   F   10. Windows uses a file's extension to identify which program created which file.

Multiple Choice

For the following questions, circle the correct answer or answers. Remember, each question may have more than one right answer.

11. **What do the letters WRI, BMP, and TXT have in common?**

    A. They are all extensions used by Windows programs.

    B. They all let Windows identify the program that created a particular file.

    C. They all have three letters.

    D. They all appear on WordPad, Paint, or Notepad files.

12. **Windows can load programs from within these other programs:**

    A. My Computer.

    B. Explorer.

    C. The Clipboard.

13. **To open a file from within a program, you need this information:**

    A. The file's name.

    B. The file's current folder.

    C. The disk drive containing the file's current folder.

    D. The file's size.

14. **This is the proper pronunciation of the term ASCII:**

    A. *ASK-too.*

    B. *ask-TOO.*

    C. *ASK-EE.*

15. **Most word processing programs can read files saved in this format:**

    A. WordPad format.

    B. ASCII format.

    C. Notepad format.

    D. Paint format.

Part III Test

16. **You usually load programs through this program:**

    A. The Start menu.

    B. My Computer.

    C. Explorer.

17. **After you choose Copy from the Edit menu, how can you be sure that the information has been copied?**

    A. The selected information disappears.

    B. You can look inside the Clipboard Viewer program.

    C. You can paste the information and watch it appear.

Matching

18. **Match up the following keystrokes with the corresponding action:**

    A. Alt+F, S   1. Open a file.

    B. Alt+F, P   2. Create a new file.

    C. Alt+F, O   3. Print a file.

    D. Alt+F, N   4. Save a file.

    E. Alt+F, X   5. Exit the program.

19. **Match up the following tasks with the corresponding action:**

    A. To highlight a word.   1. Double-click next to it in the left margin.

    B. To highlight a paragraph.   2. Hold down Ctrl and click in the left margin.

    C. To highlight an entire document.   3. Double-click on it.

    D. To highlight text.   4. Hold down the mouse pointer while dragging the cursor over the text.

Part III Lab Assignment

In this lab assignment, pretend that a friend of yours wants a copy of your Eau de Froggie picture. He needs it stored in BMP format, however. By completing this assignment, you'll open a program, load and save the file, print it, and do a little cutting and pasting on the side.

Step 1: Open a program

Open the Start menu, and then load the Paint program.

Step 2: Load a file

Load the Eau de Froggie file from the Windows 95 folder in the Dummies 101 folder.

Step 3: Save a file in another format

Save the frog picture in BMP format onto one of your floppy disks.

Step 4: Print a file

Print Eau de Froggie, and then close the Paint program.

Step 5: Cut and paste

Load WordPad. Then write this two-paragraph note to your friend:

type your address here

type the date here

Jerry Tode
3423 Lagoon Ave.
Riverside, CA 92000

Hey, Jerry, here's that picture of the Frog Perfume that you wanted. It smells real good, and you might want to give some to your frog friends.

Say hello to the wife and kids for me.

Best,

type your name here

Cut the first paragraph from the letter; then paste the paragraph back into the letter. (It probably looked better that way, anyway.) Finally, print the letter.

The Free Programs

Part IV

In this part . . .

Everybody likes to get something for nothing. Microsoft's marketing mavens certainly know that, judging by the number of "freebie" programs tossed into the Windows software box. Sure, Windows comes with My Computer and Explorer — programs that can manage files and launch programs. But Windows also comes with a handful of desktop tools: Paint, WordPad, and Notepad, for example. Some of these little programs work better than others; some barely work at all. And others, like Internet Explorer, let your computer hop onto the Internet and surf the World Wide Web, swapping information with computers around the world.

This part of the book tackles the programs that Microsoft tossed into the Accessories area of the Start menu's Programs section. You discover which of the little programs are worth learning about, and which ones aren't worth the effort.

Finally, because you've completed half of the book, you should be relatively familiar with the Windows 95 "feel." You know how to move windows and files around on your computer. You know how to make the mouse's desktop dances turn into productive, "point-and-click" work on-screen.

The other parts of this book teach you how to use Windows, sometimes in hypothetical ways. This part of the book, by contrast, teaches you how to create something practical with each program. When you're through, you'll know how to create party flyers, write letters, watch computerized videos, and do other computer tasks that you've seen other people do on their computers. This part is probably where you'll have the most fun.

Paint
(Making a Party Flyer)

Objectives for This Unit

✓ Making a party flyer

✓ Creating graphics

✓ Mixing text with graphics

✓ Making circles and squares

✓ Copying graphics

Prerequisites
▶ Navigating windows with the mouse (Lesson 2-1)
▶ Opening programs (Unit 6)
▶ Opening and saving files (Units 7 and 8)
▶ Cutting and pasting (Unit 10)
▶ Printing a file (Unit 9)

This unit finally brings it all together. You'll be using almost all the skills you learned in the book's first ten units. First, you learn about Paint, the drawing program that comes with Windows 95. You learn how to create graphics and add text to your drawings. You learn how to cut and copy snippets of artwork from Paint so that you can save them for later use or paste them into other programs.

After all this work, you'll have something to show for it: a party flyer that you can either use or show off to your friends.

Just start with the first lesson in this unit and keep going — each step takes you closer and closer to the finished product.

Lesson 11-1

Using Paint's Tools

Notes:

Paint comes with lots of tools and colors for crafting artwork. Because you'll be using many of them throughout this unit, Table 11-1 explains them all — you can use it for reference.

Table 11-1	Paint Tools	
What It Looks Like	**What It's Called**	**What It Does**
	Free Form Select	Cuts or copies irregular chunks of the screen
	Select	Cuts or copies a rectangular chunk of the screen
	Eraser/Color Eraser	Rub over parts of your work you'd like to remove
	Fill with Color	Click in a certain area, and it fills up that area with color
	Pick Color	Grabs colors from one part of the drawing to use in another
	Magnifier	Enlarges portion of drawing for detail work
	Pencil	An awkward pencil for freehand drawing
	Brush	A thicker pencil with different brush shapes
	Airbrush	Works like a can of spray paint
	Text	Lets you add text in different fonts
	Line	Draws a straight line between two points (hold down the Shift key to make vertical or horizontal lines)
	Curve	Draws a line and lets you bend it twice (strange)
	Rectangle	Creates rectangles on-screen
	Polygon	Lets you draw a series of connected lines to create polygons
	Ellipse	Draws circles and egg shapes
	Rounded rectangle	Creates rectangles with rounded edges, which are handy for creating borders

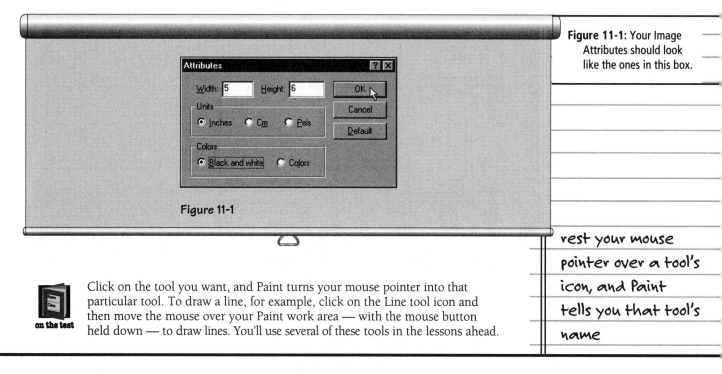

Figure 11-1: Your Image Attributes should look like the ones in this box.

Figure 11-1

Click on the tool you want, and Paint turns your mouse pointer into that particular tool. To draw a line, for example, click on the Line tool icon and then move the mouse over your Paint work area — with the mouse button held down — to draw lines. You'll use several of these tools in the lessons ahead.

on the test

rest your mouse pointer over a tool's icon, and Paint tells you that tool's name

Choosing a Size and Color

Lesson 11-2

Paint can create a file of just about any size. Because you'll be creating something specific in this unit, however, you'll set up Paint to create a file of a specific size. Follow these steps to create a file that's 5 inches wide by 6 inches long:

1 Load Paint from the Accessories area of the Start menu's Programs menu.

Feel free to make the Paint window a little larger if it doesn't fill the screen.

2 Choose Attributes from Paint's Image menu.

A little box appears.

3 Set the Width to 5 inches, the Height to 6 inches, and the Colors to Black and white.

The easiest way to obtain these settings is to start at the Units box and click in the circle marked Inches. Then type **5** in the Width box, **6** in the Height box, and click in the Black and white option under Colors.

The Attributes box should look like Figure 11-1.

4 Click on OK.

Paint cautiously resizes itself to your new specifications, first warning you that changing your image attributes can make permanent changes to images that are currently on-screen.

Figure 11-2: Paint can
create perfect rectangles.

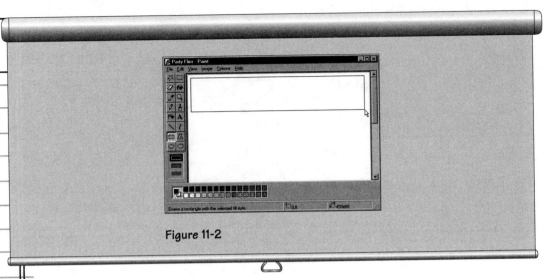

Figure 11-2

5 **Save your work.**

Save your work as Party Flyer in your Dummies 101\Windows 95 folder. Sure,
you don't have much artwork to save yet, but at least you're saving the future
image's shape and colors.

Note: If you have a color printer, go ahead and choose Colors from the Colors
box in Step 3. Paint can create images in both color and black and white. I'm
using black and white in this book because many people don't have color
printers.

on the test

Pressing Ctrl+Z immediately undoes any mistake you make in Paint and
almost any Windows 95 program.

Lesson 11-3   Making a Border

Now that you've created a workspace in Lesson 11-2, you can start creating
some artwork. Start by using some of Paint's many tools — those little icons
along the left side.

1 **Complete Lesson 11-2 and load the Party Flyer file.**

When you load your Party Flyer file, you have a blank, black-and-white work
area that's 5 inches wide and 6 inches tall. You may want to adjust the size of
the Paint program's window, as you learned in Lesson 3-2, so that it fits
comfortably on-screen.

2 **Click on the Rectangle tool.**

Pictured in Table 11-1, the Rectangle tool has solid lines. (The Select tool icon
looks similar but has dotted lines.) Confused? Remember this: Holding your
mouse pointer over a tool icon makes Paint tell you the tool's name.

Notes:

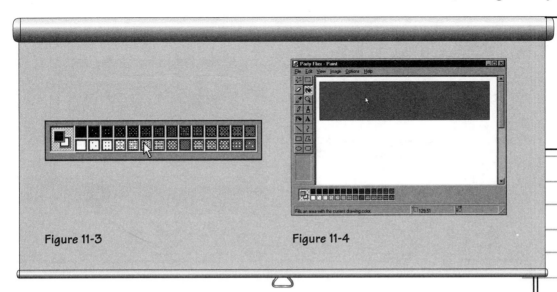

Figure 11-3

Figure 11-4

Figure 11-3: Click on this light shade of gray from the Color Box, and Paint begins using that for its current color.

Figure 11-4: The Fill tool fills a shape with a color.

3 Draw a rectangle.

Point the mouse near the top corner of your Paint work area, hold down the mouse button, and move the mouse until a large rectangle appears, like the one in Figure 11-2. Release the mouse button. Like what you've done? Then move on to step 4. If your rectangle doesn't look like the one in Figure 11-2, however, press Ctrl+Z to undo it and start over.

4 Save your work.

Whenever you complete something in Paint that you're happy with, be sure to save the file. That way, you won't have to start from scratch if you *really* mess up.

Although the icon only has a picture of a rectangle, you can use the tool to create squares, too.

choose Undo from the Edit menu (or press Ctrl+Z) to undo actions

Adding Color

Lesson 11-4

Now you're ready to add a little color to the rectangle you created in Lesson 11-3. Because you're not using *real* color in this example, you'll use the shades of gray provided along the bottom:

1 Click on the Fill with Color tool.

As shown in Table 11-1, the Fill with Color tool is the one that looks like a pouring bucket.

2 Click on the color you want to use from the Color Box along the bottom of Paint.

In this case, choose a light shade of gray, as shown in Figure 11-3.

3 Click inside the rectangle you drew in Lesson 11-3.

Paint immediately fills the rectangle with color, as shown in Figure 11-4.

4 Save your work.

Notes:

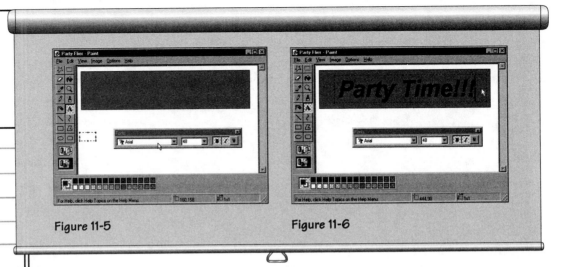

Figure 11-5: Paint lets you choose from a wide variety of fonts.

Figure 11-6: Type **Party Time!!!** in the banner until it looks like this.

Figure 11-5   Figure 11-6

Lesson 11-5   Adding Text

on the test

Although primarily a drawing program, Paint also lets you use a wide variety of fonts, sizes, and special effects. Now add some text to your banner by following these steps:

1 Choose black from the color box.

Remember how you chose gray in Lesson 11-4? Use what you learned in that lesson to choose black instead of gray. (That way, you can create black letters on your gray background.)

2 Click on the Text icon.

As shown in Table 11-1, the text icon has the letter *A* on it.

3 Click along the left edge of your page.

If a Text Toolbar box doesn't jump onto your screen, choose Text Toolbar from Paint's View menu. The Text Toolbar lets you choose from all Windows fonts; you can view them by clicking on the name of the font currently displayed in the Text Toolbar.

4 Choose Arial from the Font box. Then click on the B for Bold and the I for Italic. Finally, choose 48 from the size box.

The page should look like Figure 11-5.

5 Click twice — slowly — in the top-left corner of the colored rectangle that you created in the preceding lesson.

Paint prepares to create text inside your border. You may need to drag and drop the Text Toolbar out of the way so that it doesn't block your view.

6 **Drag and drop the incoming text box's right edge until it meets the rectangle's right edge.**

By elongating the incoming text area, you make room for Paint to display the text that you type in the next step.

7 **Type** Party Time!!! **in the Text box.**

You may have to try this step several times until the screen looks like Figure 11-6. Just keep pressing the Backspace key to erase your mistakes and start over, and then click the mouse in a slightly different place to give it another try. Eventually, you'll have the text positioned just right.

If you *really* goof, and pressing Ctrl+Z doesn't help, reload the Party Flyer file and start over.

8 **Save your work.**

Copying Art to a File   Lesson 11-6

on the test

You can copy portions of artwork from Paint and save them in separate files. Follow the next few steps to cut out the banner and save it in its own file. (Review Unit 10 if you're not familiar with the "cut and paste" concept.)

1 **Click on the Select tool.**

That's the one with the dotted rectangle, as shown in Table 11-1.

2 **Select the Party Time!!! banner from the Paint screen.**

To select your work, point your mouse above the banner's top-left corner. Then, while holding down the mouse button, move the mouse until it points just below the banner's bottom-right corner. Let go of the mouse button, and a dotted rectangle surrounds your banner.

3 **Choose Copy to from the Edit menu.**

A familiar-looking box appears.

4 **Save the file as Banner in your Dummies 101\Windows 95 folder.**

Don't be afraid to refer to Lesson 8-2 if you don't recall how to save a file in a certain folder. By saving the banner, you can use it in other pieces of art.

Drawing Circles and Ovals   Lesson 11-7

To add to the festive atmosphere, use some other tools to draw balloons:

1 **Click on the Ellipse tool icon.**

Table 11-1 lists all of Paint's tools. You're going to be drawing balloons below your banner, so you may want to click on the scroll bar so that you have room to draw them down there.

Notes:

Figure 11-7: Your first oval should look something like this.

Figure 11-8: Draw the second oval so that it slightly overlaps the first.

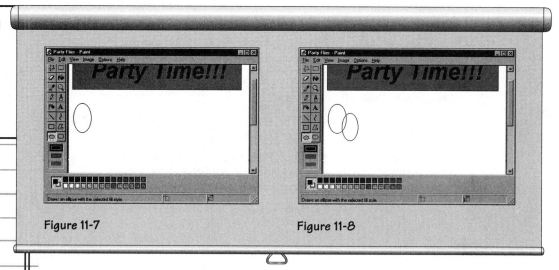

Figure 11-7   Figure 11-8

2 **Draw an oval beneath the banner.**

Click beneath the banner's left side and hold down the mouse button. Then, while holding down the button, move the mouse down and slightly to the right; an oval forms. When it looks pretty close to the one in Figure 11-7, let go of the mouse button. (If you mess up, press Ctrl+Z and try again.)

3 **Draw another oval that slightly overlaps the first.**

Make it about the same size as the one in Figure 11-7. Remember, you're not creating fine, hand-made art here, so it doesn't have to look identical to the picture. The second oval should look roughly like the one in Figure 11-8.

That creates the two balloons. To get rid of that overlapping area, you use the Eraser/Color Eraser tool, described in the next lesson.

4 **Save your work.**

hold down shift while making an oval to make a perfect circle

Lesson 11-8   Erasing Artwork

See that little area where the first and second balloons intersect? Paint's Eraser tool can get rid of it, as the following steps show:

1 **Click on the Eraser/Color Eraser tool.**

That's the button with the little eraser, shown back in Table 11-1.

2 **Click on the smallest square in the tool size box.**

on the test

Many of Paint's tools let you change their size. For example, see the little black squares just below the tool box? Clicking on the big square makes the eraser larger; clicking on the smaller square makes the eraser smaller. Because you're erasing a tiny area here, you want the smallest eraser you can get, so click on the smallest square. Changing the size of your eraser is one of the best ways to effectively rub out unwanted graphics.

3 **Erase the overlapping lines.**

Point at the line that juts into the other balloon and, while holding down the mouse button, move the mouse. The line disappears as the mouse pointer touches it.

Don't worry if you accidentally erase too much. Just press Ctrl+Z to undo your mistake and start over. When the overlap is gone, the balloons should look like those in Figure 11-9.

4 **Save your work.**

Notes:

Drawing Lines

Lesson 11-9

The newly drawn balloons will float away unless you anchor them down, so draw some strings with the Paint tool:

1 **Click on the Brush tool, which looks like a paintbrush.**

The Brush tool isn't named very well, because it doesn't paint. Rather, it lets you draw freehand like you would with a pencil. I'm not going to have you use the Line tool because lines are straight and, well, look boring.

2 **Click on the smallest circle in the brush size box.**

That way, your balloons will look like they have real strings.

3 **Draw a wavy line draping from the base of each balloon.**

Point at the base of a balloon, hold down the mouse button, and slide the mouse gently back and forth as you move it down an inch or two. Let go of the button to end the line. Repeat the process for the other balloon.

4 **Save your work.**

Copying Graphics

Lesson 11-10

Your balloons should look pretty good — too good to stop at just two, in fact. But instead of drawing some more, you can just copy your originals to the other side of the page. The following steps show you the easiest way to do so:

1 **Select the balloons.**

Head back to steps 1 and 2 of Lesson 11-6 if you don't remember how to select something with Paint's Select tool. When you see the dotted line around your balloons, you've selected them.

Figure 11-9: Erase the line where the ovals overlap, and they start to look like balloons.

Figure 11-10: Your party flyer should look like this with more balloons.

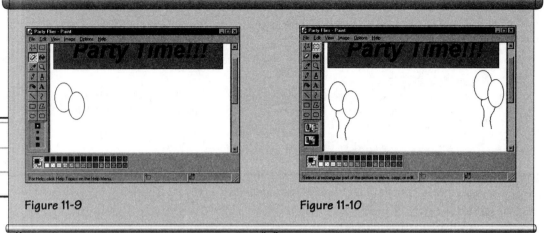

Figure 11-9   Figure 11-10

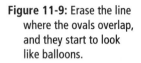

☑ Progress Check

If you can do the following, you've mastered this lesson:

❑ Change the size and colors of your graphics.

❑ Create rectangular borders.

❑ Fill in rectangles with different colors.

❑ Add text of varying sizes.

❑ Copy art to and from a drawing.

❑ Draw ovals and lines.

❑ Erase mistakes.

2 **Hold down Ctrl and drag and drop the balloons several inches to the right.**

Paint instantly makes a copy of the balloons and lets you drop the copy on the other side of your picture. Like where you dropped them? Click anywhere away from the newly dropped balloons, and the dotted lines disappear, leaving the picture looking like Figure 11-10.

3 **Save your work.**

Unit 11 Quiz

Circle the letter of the correct answer or answers to each of the following questions. (Remember that some questions have more than one right answer.)

1. **Do this to turn your mouse pointer into a drawing tool:**

    A. Choose a tool from the pull-down menu.

    B. Choose a tool from a file.

    C. Choose a tool from the icons along Paint's left side.

    D. Choose a tool from the icons along Paint's bottom edge.

2. **This action undoes any mistake you make in Paint:**

   A. Pressing F1.

   B. Pressing Alt+Backspace.

   C. Pressing Ctrl+Z.

   D. Pressing Ctrl+Delete.

3. **When in Paint, you should save your work at the following times:**

   A. Before you start.

   B. Whenever you think of it.

   C. Whenever you complete something you're happy with.

   D. Whenever you make a mistake.

4. **Although primarily a drawing program, Paint also lets you use a variety of fonts, sizes, and special effects.**

   A. True.

   B. False.

5. **You can copy a piece of artwork from Paint and save it in a separate file.**

   A. True.

   B. False.

   C. True, but only with an expensive computer.

   D. True, but only on floppy disks.

6. **Doing this erases unwanted graphics most effectively:**

   A. Varying the size of your Eraser tool.

   B. Increasing the size of your Eraser tool.

   C. Using a small Eraser tool.

   D. Using a medium-sized Eraser tool.

7. **The Brush tool functions like this object more than like a brush:**

   A. A squirt gun.

   B. A spray-paint can.

   C. A pencil.

   D. A paint roller.

Unit 11 Exercise

1. Try some of the different fonts when using text.

2. Use the Airbrush tool to add spray-painted effects.

3. Create one border that's slightly inside another border, and then fill the area between them with a lively color.

4. Add some text between the balloons of the flyer.

5. Print out the flyer, hand-draw a map along the bottom, and head for the copy machine.

WordPad (Writing a Letter)

Prerequisites
- ♦ Using the Start menu (Lesson 4-2)
- ♦ Navigating windows with a mouse (Lesson 2-1)
- ♦ Opening a file (Unit 7)
- ♦ Saving a file (Unit 8)
- ♦ Printing a file (Unit 9)

Objectives for This Unit

- ✓ Using the WordPad word processor
- ✓ Creating letterhead
- ✓ Writing letters
- ✓ Selecting text
- ✓ Centering text
- ✓ Adding boldface and italics
- ✓ Changing the size of letters (font size)
- ✓ Searching for and replacing words

on the disk   ♦ Eau de Froggie

*O*f all the little "free" programs that Microsoft tossed into the Windows 95 box, WordPad may carry the biggest bang for the buck. This word processor lets you write letters, create resumés, and do other stuff that used to cause headaches in the pre-correction fluid days.

This unit shows you how to create letterhead — fancy-looking stationery with your name and address preprinted across the top of your letters. Then you'll learn how to put that letterhead to use by creating an actual letter.

Creating Letterhead   Lesson 12-1

To add a distinguished touch, you can either add the word *esquire* to the end of your name or use letterhead. The Windows word processor, WordPad, can create letterhead and automatically attach it to the top of your letters whenever you want.

Figure 12-1: Your letter-head should start to take shape.

Figure 12-2: WordPad can move text to the center of the page.

Notes:

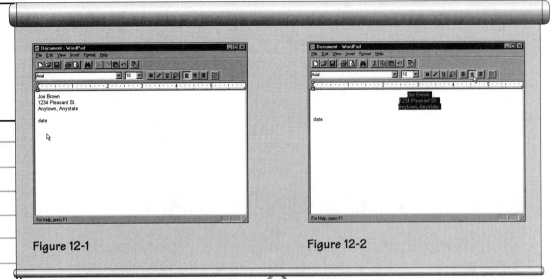

Figure 12-1   Figure 12-2

Follow these steps to enter the world of professional word processing:

1 **Open WordPad from the Start menu.**

2 **Type your name and address, pressing Enter after each line.**

3 **Press Enter again, type the word** date**, and press Enter twice.**

The WordPad screen should look like Figure 12-1 (with your own name and address typed into it, of course).

4 **Select the lines containing your name and address.**

As you learned in Lesson 10-1, you can select the text by pointing at the beginning of the first word, holding down the mouse button, and sliding the mouse cursor to the end of the last line. The text becomes highlighted, changing color.

5 **Click on the Centered tool from WordPad's menu bar.**

See the three icons with the little lines on them near the top of WordPad? Click on the middle icon, as shown in Figure 12-2, and WordPad moves the text to the center of the page. Be sure not to click anywhere in your document while navigating the menus, or WordPad unhighlights your lines; you need them to remain selected for the remaining steps.

Prefer menus to mice? Then choose Format from WordPad's top menu, choose Paragraph, and select Center from the Alignment box.

6 **Choose 14 from WordPad's Font Size box.**

The Font Size box contains a number in it; the bigger the number, the larger your characters grow on-screen. Choosing 14 causes your name and address to increase in size, making them look more important.

7 **Highlight your name and choose 20 from the Font Size box.**

Your name grows, looking most important of all.

rest mouse pointer
over tool icon to see
tool's name

8   **Click on the B button to apply boldface to your name.**

Finally, this step adds bold emphasis to your name, making your finished letterhead look like that in Figure 12-3.

9   **Save your work.**

Save this file as Letterhead in the Dummies 101\Windows 95 folder. Then, whenever you want to use your letterhead, just open that file and save it under the name of your new letter. After you finish typing your new letter, save it again and print it.

heads up

Save your original Letterhead file under a different name *before* you start typing your new letter. That way, you won't accidentally overwrite your letterhead with your newly composed letter.

10   **Close WordPad.**

The next few lessons show you how to use your newly created letterhead for writing professional-looking letters.

on the test

WordPad can add **boldface**, *italics*, and underlining to words.

Writing a Letter

Lesson 12-2

Now that you've created your letterhead in Lesson 12-1, here's how to put it to use:

1   **Open WordPad.**

2   **Open the Letterhead file from your Dummies 101 folder's Windows 95 folder.**

Opening files was covered in Lesson 7-1; because you just saved the Letterhead file, you'll see it listed by name on the File menu. Click on its name, and WordPad brings it to the screen.

3   **Choose Save As from the File menu.**

4   **Save the file as** Begging for Cash **in your Dummies 101\Windows 95 folder.**

By quickly saving your new file under a different name, you can preserve your original letterhead in its Letterhead file, yet still use its contents for your new file.

5   **Double-click on the word date near the bottom of the file.**

Double-clicking on the word selects it so that you can change today's date quickly in Step 6.

6   **Type today's date and press Enter twice.**

The highlighted *date* disappears, replaced by the incoming text.

> WordPad saves a list of recently opened files in its File menu; clicking on the file's name loads it quickly

Figure 12-3: WordPad lets you add boldfacing to words as well as change the size of the letters.

Figure 12-4: WordPad works well for creating letters.

Notes:

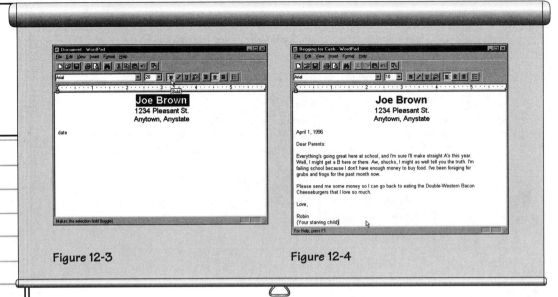

Figure 12-3

Figure 12-4

7 **Type** Dear Parents: **and press Enter twice.**

Until now, you've been pressing Enter after each line. However, that's not normally the case with WordPad or most other word processors. So for Step 8, don't press Enter until the *end of each paragraph.* Then press Enter twice. (That puts a blank line between paragraphs, making the letter look nicer.)

8 **Type the following paragraphs, pressing Enter twice after each paragraph:**

Everything's going great here at school, and I'm sure I'll make straight A's this year. Well, I might get a B here or there. Aw, shucks, I may as well tell you the truth. I'm failing school because I don't have enough money to buy food. I've been foraging for grubs and frogs for the past month now.

Please send me some money so I can go back to eating the Double-Western Bacon Cheeseburgers that I love so much.

9 **Type the following lines, pressing Enter twice after Love, and once after Robin:**

Love,

Robin

(Your starving child)

10 **Save your work.**

Your letter should look like Figure 12-4.

Unlike fancier (and more expensive) word processors, WordPad doesn't have a spell-checker. That means you have to proofread your work yourself.

Figure 12-5

Figure 12-5: Type the word or words you'd like to replace in the Find what box, followed by the word or words you'd like to use as a replacement in the Replace with box.

Searching for and Replacing Words

Lesson 12-3

If your parents don't come through with the cash, perhaps you can drum up some extra coins by opening a word processing service. In fact, here's how you could sell the letter you created in Lesson 12-2 to other students in the same predicament, merely by changing the names. WordPad's Search and Replace feature automatically searches for your name and replaces it with somebody else's name.

1 **Open WordPad.**

2 **Open the Begging for Cash file from the C:\Dummies 101\Windows 95 folder.**

The letter that you created in Lesson 12-2 appears on-screen.

3 **Choose Replace from the Edit menu.**

A box appears, as shown in Figure 12-5.

4 **Type the name** Robin **in the Find what box, and type the name** Bill **in the Replace with box.**

5 **Click on the Replace All button.**

WordPad immediately goes through the file, replacing every instance of *Robin* with *Bill*.

WordPad offers a few other sneaky options as well. For example, if you want to watch and approve all the changes, choose the Find Next button instead of the Replace All button. Then WordPad stops for your approval before making the changes. (If you're making changes in a long document, Find Next is often the safest way to go.)

The Match whole word only option tells WordPad to change the word *Robin* only if it's a separate word — otherwise, WordPad would change the *Robin* in *Robinson Crusoe* to *Billson Crusoe,* which doesn't have quite the same charm.

Finally, the Match case option tells WordPad to keep an eye on the word's capitalization. That makes it change *Robin* the name and not *robin* the bird.

☑ Progress Check

If you can do the following, you've mastered this unit:

❑ Create letterhead.

❑ Write a letter.

❑ Select text.

❑ Center text.

❑ Add boldface and italics.

❑ Change the size of letters (type size).

❑ Search for and replace words.

Unit 12 Quiz

Circle the letter of the correct answer or answers to each of the following questions. (Remember that some questions have more than one right answer.)

1. **WordPad can spruce up a letter with these features:**

    A. Adding **boldface.**

    B. Adding *italics.*

    C. Adding underlining.

    D. Making letters and words bigger or smaller.

2. **The lack of this main feature sets WordPad apart from most other word processors:**

    A. It doesn't have a spell-checker.

    B. It can't do Search and Replace functions.

    C. It can't change type sizes and styles.

    D. It can't create letterhead.

3. **When you search and replace text, WordPad always keeps the text's type size and style the same.**

    A. True.

    B. False.

    C. Hmm, I'd better test it and see.

    D. Sometimes.

4. **In Lesson 12-3, how would Bill's parents know that the letter wasn't legit?**

    A. Bill can't type.

    B. Bill can't spell.

    C. Bill eats only deep-fried grubs.

    D. The name at the top of the letterhead doesn't match the name at the bottom.

Unit 12 Exercise

1. Spend a little extra time on your letterhead; add a border that you created in Paint, for example, or add a monogram. Keep it simple, though, or your letters will look amateurish.

2. Create a resumé by mixing words of different sizes. You can also move a margin in or out by changing the indentation from the Format menu's Paragraph section.

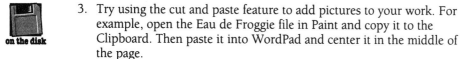

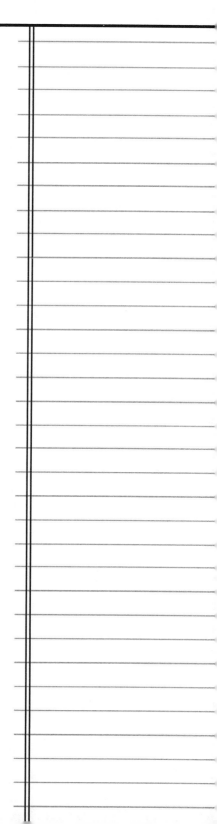

3. Try using the cut and paste feature to add pictures to your work. For example, open the Eau de Froggie file in Paint and copy it to the Clipboard. Then paste it into WordPad and center it in the middle of the page.

. . . .

Notepad (Jotting Down a Quick Phone Message)

Prerequisites
- Controlling windows with a mouse (Lesson 2-1)
- Using the desktop (Unit 4)
- Starting a program (Unit 6)
- Saving a file (Unit 8)

Objectives for This Unit

✓ Using Notepad

✓ Typing and saving quick notes

Notepad is the computerized equivalent of a napkin, matchbook, or scrap of newspaper: It's the quickest way to jot down some thoughts before they evaporate.

But because it's quick, it's also dirty. You can't do much with it, and it's sometimes awkward to use.

If you're looking for the computerized equivalent of a notepad for your computerized desktop, however, then Notepad is the program to use. This unit teaches you how to put it to work.

Jotting Down a Quick Phone Message

Lesson 13-1

Quick — the phone rings and you need to jot down the name and address of that new restaurant your friend discovered the other night. Practice this lesson, and you'll know what to do.

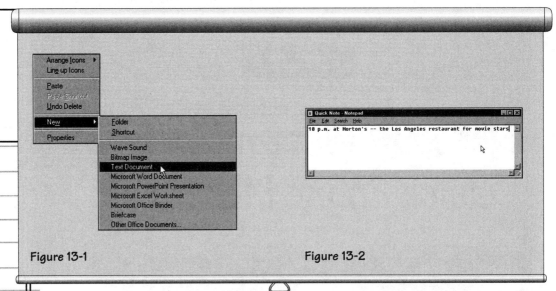

Figure 13-1   Figure 13-2

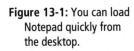

1 **Click on a blank portion of your desktop with your right mouse button.**

The usual menu appears.

2 **Choose New from the menu.**

3 **Choose Text Document from the New menu.**

The screen should look like Figure 13-1.

4 **Type** Quick Note **as a title for your new file, and then press Enter.**

Your file appears as an icon on your desktop, ready to be opened and put to work.

5 **Double-click on your new Quick Note file, and start typing your notes.**

That's it. Nothing fancy here. Just keep typing the incoming information. In this case, type the following information (shown in Figure 13-2):

10 p.m. at Morton's — the Los Angeles restaurant for movie stars

6 **Save your work.**

Quick and dirty, but effective. You may want to create a folder called Random Notes on your desktop, and then drag and drop your new note into it. Or you may want to keep the Quick Notes icon on your desktop as a reminder.

You can go back and clean up the note later — WordPad works well when you want to get fancy. Notepad's just a sponge for soaking up the information as it comes in. Then, when you need to remember what you typed, just open up the file again (provided that you remember what you named the file, of course).

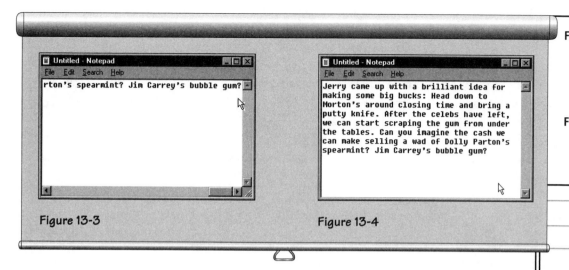

Figure 13-3

Figure 13-4

Figure 13-3: Notepad doesn't normally wrap your text down to the next line.

Figure 13-4: Pressing Alt+E and then pressing W wraps the text so that it fills Notepad's window.

on the test

WordPad and Notepad are both word processors, but they have different features. WordPad is designed more for writing letters, while Notepad works best for jotting down quick notes.

As Lesson 8-3 discusses, Notepad saves files in a special ASCII format, making the files readable by almost any other word processor.

Making the Words Wrap

Lesson 13-2

If the phone conversation starts running a bit long — and you start typing more than a few words into Notepad — you'll notice one thing right away: All the words stay on one line, as you'll see in this lesson.

Unlike WordPad or other normal word processors, Notepad doesn't automatically wrap your text down to the next line. In fact, you may be tempted to press the Enter key when it looks like your words are about to run off the edge of Notepad's window. Don't do it, though. Just keep typing, and the words will wrap, as the following steps show you:

1 Open Notepad.

In the next step, you type a short paragraph into Notepad. Notice how all the words run off the edge of the window. Follow your computer's traditions, though, and don't press Enter until you finish typing the paragraph.

At the end of Step 2, Notepad should look like Figure 13-3.

2 Type the following paragraph in Notepad without pressing the Enter key:

Jerry came up with a brilliant idea for making some big bucks: Head down to Morton's around closing time and bring a putty knife. After the celebs have left, we can start scraping the gum from under the tables. Can you imagine the cash we can make selling a wad of Dolly Parton's spearmint? Jim Carrey's bubble gum?

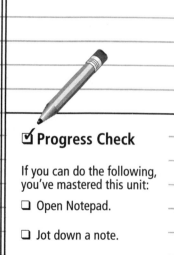

☑ Progress Check

If you can do the following, you've mastered this unit:

❑ Open Notepad.

❑ Jot down a note.

❑ Make the words wrap.

on the test

3 **Choose <u>W</u>ord Wrap from the <u>E</u>dit menu.**

Or use a quick flick of your fingers to press Alt+E, followed by the letter W. Notepad automatically wraps your words so that they fit into the window, as shown in Figure 13-4.

Notepad has a few other problems. For one thing, it can't hold a large amount of text. Eventually, you see an error message saying that you're trying to open a file that's too large for Notepad to swallow. The solution? Open that chunky file in WordPad or another word processor.

Also, Notepad makes you stick with the same old font. Nothing fancy or italicized here, not even for Dolly Parton's spearmint.

on the test

Notepad can't handle large files; leave those for WordPad.

Unit 13 Quiz

Circle the letter of the correct answer or answers to each of the following questions. (Some questions have more than one right answer.)

1. **To make Notepad wrap sentences at the end of the line, you do this:**

   A. Press Alt+E and then the letter W.

   B. Choose Word Wrap from the Edit menu.

   C. Notepad can't wrap sentences.

   D. Use heavier gauge string.

2. **Which word processor works better for large files?**

   A. Notepad.

   B. WordPad.

3. **Which word processor works better for jotting down quick notes?**

   A. Notepad.

   B. WordPad.

4. **Notepad saves files in this format:**

   A. ASCII.

   B. WordPad format.

   C. The Right format.

   D. Cyrillic.

5. **Most other word processors can read files saved by Notepad.**

   A. True.

   B. False.

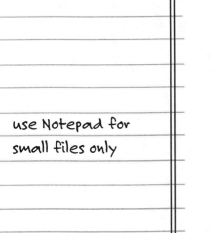

use Notepad for small files only

Unit 13 Exercise

1. Open Notepad.
2. Type a To Do list of tasks you'd like to accomplish today.
3. Minimize Notepad as an icon on your taskbar.
4. Double-click on the minimized icon to take phone notes today.
5. At the day's end, check to see how much of your To Do list you've accomplished.
6. Save your To Do list for tomorrow.

• • • • • • • • • • •

Exploring Internet Explorer

Objectives for This Unit

✓ Connecting to the Internet

✓ Moving from place to place on the World Wide Web

✓ Going to a specific Web page

✓ Searching for subjects on the Web

✓ Returning to favorite places on the Web

Prerequisites

▸ A modem (This unit)

▸ A phone line (This unit)

▸ An Internet Service Provider (This unit)

▸ Internet Explorer software (This unit)

▸ Navigating windows with a mouse (Lesson 2-1)

▸ Using the Start menu (Lesson 4-2)

▸ Using the My Computer and Explorer programs (Unit 5)

▸ Starting a program (Unit 6)

You've probably seen funny words like http://www.cocacola.com/ peering at you from a can of Coca-Cola. Coworkers in neighboring cubicles talk about grabbing satellite weather pictures from the "Internet" before heading to work in the morning. Magazine and television advertisements assault the world with oodles of other strange "http" buzzwords.

Sometimes it seems like you're the only one who's not sitting in front of a computer, logging on to the Internet and "Surfing the Web."

Today's world belongs to the *Internet* — that huge string of computers circling the globe. Now, with the slick sounds and groovy graphics of the World Wide Web riding on top of the Internet, millions of people are pointing and clicking their way onto various "Web pages" and grabbing the goods.

This chapter explains just what the Internet and its World Wide Web are supposed to do, how to use the Windows 95 Internet Explorer *Web browser* to connect to them, and most important, how to turn everything into valuable tools for finding good stuff.

Lesson 14-1   # Connecting to the Internet

Notes:

Web browser lets you surf the Web

Internet Service Provider=ISP

You need three basic things to connect to the Internet:

▶ **An Internet Service Provider (or ISP):** A service, much like your electric company, that lets you connect your computer to the Internet's network of computers. (And just like the electric company, Internet Service Providers charge for their services: The going rate seems to be about $20 a month for unlimited usage, but it often varies.) Ask your friendly computer store owner for the names of some Internet Service Providers; somebody at the store can probably give you a company name and local phone number.

▶ **A computer, phone line, and a modem:** A *modem* is the gadget that lets your computer connect to the telephone lines. (The friendly computer store owner can also sell you a modem, if you need one.)

▶ **A Web browser:** Software that lets you move to different areas on the Internet's World Wide Web. The latest versions of Windows 95 come with a free version of the Microsoft *Internet Explorer* Web browser. The Microsoft Plus package of add-ons for Windows 95 also came with a version of Internet Explorer.

Several other companies market Web browsers; in fact, the Netscape Navigator Web browser currently has about 80 percent of the market. In an effort to catch up, Microsoft is giving away Internet Explorer with the current version of Windows 95.

Setting up your computer to use the Internet's World Wide Web can be a little tricky, so you might want to bring over a computer-savvy friend or Web-head kid. Luckily, you only have to set everything up once. Some ISPs offer tech support over the phone lines, as well. (Don't throw away all the papers with the fine print, because that's usually where the phone number hides.)

The following steps show you how to connect to the Internet's World Wide Web and start surfing its waves, from wacky to wise.

1 **Double-click The Internet icon on your computer's desktop.**

Double-clicking The Internet icon, shown in Figure 14-1, launches your Web browser's phone dialer, which is shown in Figure 14-2.

2 **Click the Connect button.**

Depending on the way Internet Explorer is set up, you might first need to type your password into the Password box.

A click on the Connect button starts dialing your Internet Service Provider. (Internet Service Providers are often called *ISPs* by hip computer folk.) You can usually hear your computer's modem dial the phone and, if you're calling at an opportune time, you hear your ISP's modem answer with an odd hissing sound.

The computer used in Figure 14-2 connects to the Internet through the CompuServe online service.

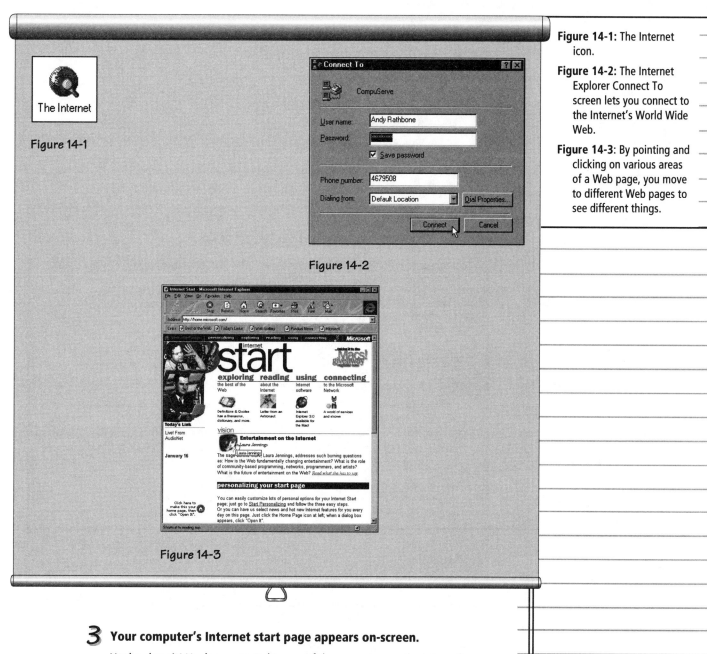

Figure 14-1

Figure 14-2

Figure 14-3

Figure **14-1:** The Internet icon.

Figure **14-2:** The Internet Explorer Connect To screen lets you connect to the Internet's World Wide Web.

Figure **14-3:** By pointing and clicking on various areas of a Web page, you move to different Web pages to see different things.

3 Your computer's Internet start page appears on-screen.

You've done it! You've connected to one of the computers on the Internet's World Wide Web. Those computers display information on *Web sites* that are stuffed full of *Web pages.* And the page of information you're currently viewing is somberly called the *start page.* (It's where you're "starting." Get it? Those raucous computer engineers, eh?)

You can set up your computer to use *any* Web page as its start page, but Microsoft Internet Explorer usually starts you down the road with one of the Microsoft Web pages, like the one shown in Figure 14-3. The Microsoft Web page's content changes constantly, varying with the Internet news.

From here, you're ready to start traveling around on the Internet's World Wide Web — and the very next lesson shows you how to start moving from place to place. ***Hint:*** It's easier than you think.

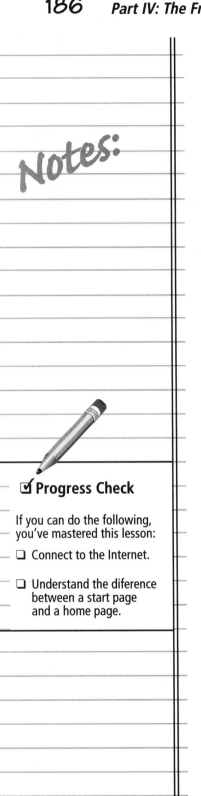

Progress Check

If you can do the following, you've mastered this lesson:

❑ Connect to the Internet.

❑ Understand the diference between a start page and a home page.

on the test

A *start page* is the page your computer automatically displays when your Web browser connects to the World Wide Web. Sure, Web browsers let you change your start page to any Web page you want, but you have to start somewhere — so that page is called your start page. Then when you click a button and move to a different Web site full of information, you start at that Web site's home page. The *home page* is simply a menu that lets you begin moving around within that Web site. A start page and home page don't really differ much, and they can even be the same thing. But Web hippies expect you to know the difference.

Q/A Session

Question: Just what *are* the Internet and the World Wide Web?

Answer: The U.S. Government, worried in the 1960s that a single bomb could wipe out its favorite computers, moved them far apart. It hooked up some powerful computers over some fast phone lines for a speedy way of moving information around. If a computer blows up — or simply crashes — other computers quickly take over, and the messages still get through. Academic institutions hopped aboard to push the technology forward.

Known as the *Internet,* this vast network of computers still runs today. In fact, it's going commercial: The *World Wide Web* is a subset of the Internet's computers that's letting just about anybody join in the fun.

The World Wide Web looks sort of like a convention center kiosk, where you push buttons to find out which booth is serving a quick hamburger. On your computer, by contrast, special *Web browser* software connects to the Internet's vast network of computers, where you can point and click your way from location to location.

By pointing and clicking on various places on your screen, you move to different *Web sites,* visiting things like real estate ads, newspapers, the FBI's Most Wanted list, fan clubs, restaurant menus, and thousands of other subjects, from serious to somber, from weird to wildly wacky.

Many people simply click from page to page, "Surfing the Web" like television's "Channel Surfers." Others use the Web's fast indexes to research specific subjects.

Either way, it's a fast-growing field with a promising future.

on the test

A *Web address*, also known as a URL, begins with the letters `http://` and describes the location of a *Web site* of information within the World Wide Web. When you arrive at the Web site, you'll be greeted by that Web site's *home page* — a "Welcome" menu that describes your location and its features. Finally, when you move around within that Web site, you will see that Web site's *Web pages*.

Moving from Place to Place on the World Wide Web

Lesson 14-2

Thankfully, the World Wide Web is much easier to navigate than most worldwide journeys. No lost luggage, hour-long delays in fogged-in airports, or lost cash in cruise ship casinos. In fact, it's almost too easy to navigate: You can easily find yourself lost at first. (Don't worry; it's easy to get back home, as you'll find out later in this lesson.)

Like most things in Windows, the mouse provides the easiest way to control events. When you point and click on a Web page's various buttons, the Web takes you to the place represented by that button. The strange part is that the buttons can take such a variety of different shapes. Sure, some buttons look like buttons; but others look like underlined words, pictures, spinning balls, or other oddities.

buttons take a variety of different shapes

The following steps will teach you how to recognize a button when you see one and to know what will happen *before* you click on it.

1 **Complete Lesson 14-1 and connect to a Web page.**

Any page will do; you can use the Start page your computer dumps you at.

2 **Without clicking a mouse button, slide the mouse slowly over the screen at random.**

Keep an eye on the mouse pointer — it might surprise you.

3 **When the mouse pointer changes shape, it's hovering over a button.**

When the mouse pointer transforms into a little hand like the one shown in Figure 14-4, it's found a button and it's straining to "push" it.

4 **Click the mouse button while pointing at the button you've found on-screen.**

The Web browser goes to work, fetching the Web page assigned to the button you clicked. You've done it — you've moved to a new page on the World Wide Web! That's all there is to navigating the World Wide Web; just a lot of aiming at weird things on-screen and clicking the mouse.

5 **Click the mouse button on the button marked Back in Internet Explorer's upper-left corner. (It has a left-pointing arrow above it.)**

The Web browser goes to work again, but this time it simply takes you back to the page you just departed from. If you point and click on the Web page's buttons — and use the Back arrow button to cycle back to familiar territory when you get lost — you needn't worry about getting stuck in foreign caverns.

There's more: If you decide you *liked* that Web site you just visited, click the Forward arrow button right next to the Back arrow button. That takes you forward along the path of Web sites you've been walking, while the other button takes you backward.

Finally, if you stumble across a Web page you want to revisit easily the next time you fire up your computer, be sure to check out Lesson 14-5.

Figure 14-4: A Web-button-revealing hand.

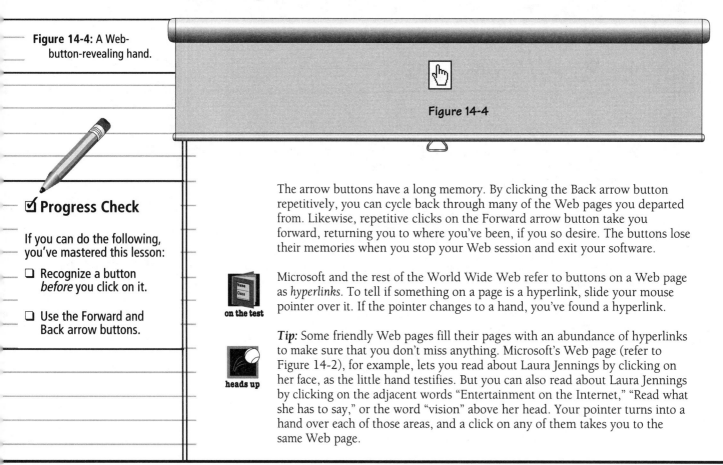

Figure 14-4

☑ **Progress Check**

If you can do the following, you've mastered this lesson:

❑ Recognize a button *before* you click on it.

❑ Use the Forward and Back arrow buttons.

The arrow buttons have a long memory. By clicking the Back arrow button repetitively, you can cycle back through many of the Web pages you departed from. Likewise, repetitive clicks on the Forward arrow button take you forward, returning you to where you've been, if you so desire. The buttons lose their memories when you stop your Web session and exit your software.

Microsoft and the rest of the World Wide Web refer to buttons on a Web page as *hyperlinks*. To tell if something on a page is a hyperlink, slide your mouse pointer over it. If the pointer changes to a hand, you've found a hyperlink.

Tip: Some friendly Web pages fill their pages with an abundance of hyperlinks to make sure that you don't miss anything. Microsoft's Web page (refer to Figure 14-2), for example, lets you read about Laura Jennings by clicking on her face, as the little hand testifies. But you can also read about Laura Jennings by clicking on the adjacent words "Entertainment on the Internet," "Read what she has to say," or the word "vision" above her head. Your pointer turns into a hand over each of those areas, and a click on any of them takes you to the same Web page.

Lesson 14-3

How Do I Move to a Specific Web Page?

Notes:

Somebody passed you a business card with their Web page listed on it? Or do you just want to check out Coca-Cola's Web page? Well, if you can type that weird `http://` stuff with your computer's keyboard, you can move to that specific Web page. This lesson shows you how.

1 Complete Lesson 14-1 to connect to the World Wide Web.

You'll be deposited at your Start page. Now, look at the top of the Internet Explorer for a long box marked Address. Inside, you'll see the Web address for your Start page. If you're starting at the Microsoft Web site, for example, you might see something like `http://home.microsoft.com/`.

2 Click anywhere on the words in the Address box.

The strip of letters becomes highlighted.

3 **Type the new address into the Address box.**

The first letter of the new address knocks the old address out of the Address box. Be very careful not to make any typographical errors while typing your new address, however. Nothing will explode, but your Web browser will just tell you it can't find that particular address. The Internet can be a cranky, exact science.

4 **Press Enter.**

The Internet will do its best to connect with the computer that runs your desired Web page. Usually, it gets there. Sometimes it doesn't. (Better make sure that you typed that name right.) Also, don't be surprised if a much-desired Web page just vanishes: Sometimes Web Pages' caretakers stop taking care of them, and they pull them off the computers. Or maybe they switched to a different Internet Service Provider, changed their Web address, and didn't tell anybody.

But there's still a way to find specific Web pages, as Lesson 14-4 demonstrates.

Tip: Looking for a place to get a little practice in? Then choose Web <u>T</u>utorial from the Internet Explorer's <u>H</u>elp menu. It answers some questions and takes you on a gentle path through the networks.

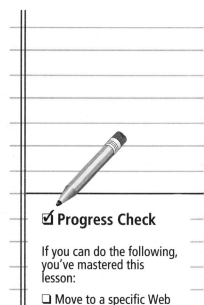

☑ **Progress Check**

If you can do the following, you've mastered this lesson:

❑ Move to a specific Web page.

Searching for Specific Subjects on the Web

Lesson 14-4

Browsing can be the most fun on the World Wide Web. Pop yourself in front of a computer and start wandering through the world's computer networks, looking at people's pets, shopping at trendy stores, and reading magazines and newspapers. *Browsing* means spending your time pointing and clicking your way across the network with no destination in mind.

Most Web sites contain hyperlinks to other Web sites; some of those hyperlinks carry related information, and others are listed just for fun.

But if you're searching for specific information, quick and speedy, these steps show how to find it.

1 **As shown in Lesson 14-1, connect to the World Wide Web.**

That should be a breeze by now; if not, it's time to bring a friend over to get set up.

2 **Click on the Internet Explorer Search button along the center of its top bar.**

The Web browser takes you to the Microsoft Internet Search area. Shown in Figure 14-5, the Internet Search area is a librarian's electronic catalog for performing detailed searches.

3 **Type a few words describing your subject and press Enter.**

For example, if you're looking for information on wine tasting courses, you'd type **wine tasting courses** and press Enter. In a few moments, the Index program reveals the results of its search, as shown in Figure 14-6.

(margin notes, handwritten)
browsing = pointing and clicking across the network without a destination in mind

Internet Search area = librarians' electronic catalog for performing detailed searches

Figure 14-5: By typing a few words into Internet Explorer's Search area, you perform detailed searches of the vast Internet.

Figure 14-6: The results of a search for wine tasting courses.

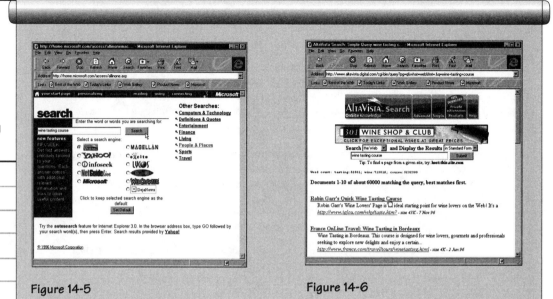

Figure 14-5   Figure 14-6

on the test

As shown in Figure 14-5, Internet Explorer features several different Internet indexes, all run by different companies that use slightly different methods of indexing. If you're having trouble finding what you want with one index, switch to another: Click the Yahoo! button, for example, or search on the AltaVista index. Although both indexes usually carry many of the same sites, you'll also usually find a few different Web sites pertaining to your quest.

Tip: Searching for specific things can be as difficult as a college statistics course. If you're having trouble remembering your AND but NOTs, click on the index's Help or Tips area for a quick refresher.

Lesson 14-5

Returning to Favorite Places on the Web

Finally found a favorite place on the Web? Want to make sure that you can find it again? No problem. Thankfully, you don't have to write down Web addresses on scraps of paper by your computer. Here's how to add your favorite Web sites to a quick-and-easy Internet Explorer pull-down menu.

1 Connect to the Internet, as shown in Lesson 14-1.

2 Move to a site you know you'll want to revisit.

Either stumble across a winner by browsing or locate a specific chunk of information in an index. When you locate a Web site you know you'll want to revisit — or at least show off to friends — you're ready for Step 3.

3 **Click on F̲avorites from along the top of the Internet Explorer and choose A̲dd to Favorites when the menu falls down.**

4 **Click the OK button.**

Now, whenever you click the Internet Explorer F̲avorites button, that Web page will be listed on the pull-down menu. Click on the Web page's description, and the Internet Explorer will whisk you to the page.

on the test

To keep things tidy, Internet Explorer lets you organize your favorite Web sites into different folders within its pull-down menu.

Tip: Spot a favorite graphic or wallpaper on a Web site? Click on it with your right mouse button, and a menu appears, letting you copy it to your own computer for turning into wallpaper. You can also copy text from a Web page just as you would copy it from a word processor: Highlight the text with the mouse and choose C̲opy from the E̲dit menu.

☑ **Progress Check**

If you can do the following, you've mastered this lesson:

❑ Add web sites to the internet Explorer favorites menu.

❑ Access Web sites by clicking the Internet Explorer Favorites button.

Unit 14 Quiz

Circle the letter of the correct answer or answers to each question.

1. **A start page is what I see when I turn on my computer.**

   A. True

   B. False

   C. No, it's what I see when I load the Internet Explorer.

   D. No, it's what I see when I first connect to the World Wide Web for a Web session.

2. **A Home page is the first page you see when you connect to a Web site.**

   A. True

   B. False

3. **Which of the following looks the most like a Web address.**

   A. `osopretty:`

   B. `(teepee)`

   C. `4936 Arachnid Ave.`

   D. `http://www.gibson.com`

Notes:

Notes:

4. **This button is a "safety" for returning you to the Web page you just left:**

   A. Back

   B. Home

   C. Stop

   D. Search

5. **Internet Explorer comes with an index for looking up subjects.**

   A. No, it comes with two indexes.

   B. No, it comes with more than five indexes.

   C. Actually, it comes with several different indexes that should all be tried.

   D. The Internet can only be browsed aimlessly.

6. **When your Internet Explorer's pull-down menu becomes crowded with favorite Web site addresses, you can do the following:**

   A. Delete the ones you're not visiting anymore.

   B. Organize the sites into pop-out folders, much like the Start menu.

Unit 14 Exercise

1. Subscribe to the Internet.

2. Connect to the World Wide Web.

3. Spend an hour simply pointing and clicking on pages, clicking when your mouse pointer turns into a hand.

4. Right-click on graphics, and turn them into wallpaper on your own computer.

5. Add favorite Web pages to your Favorites menu.

Media Player, Sound Recorder, and CD Player (Turning the Computer into an Entertainment Console)

Objectives for This Unit

✓ Playing movies

✓ Playing sounds

✓ Playing music

Prerequisites

▶ Navigating windows with a mouse (Lesson 2-1)

▶ Loading and exiting programs (Unit 6)

▶ Loading and saving files (Units 7 and 8)

▶ Using the Start menu (Lesson 4-2)

▶ Using My Computer and Explorer (Unit 5)

on the disk

▶ Screaming Monster

▶ Very Berry

▶ Buzzed

▶ Cranky Volume

Ten years ago, computers looked like high-tech TV sets, but they could display only low-tech words and numbers. TV sets, on the other hand, dished out fun stuff like *Taxi* and *Soap*. Today, the boring stuff on TV is looking worse and worse, while the computer is looking more and more exciting.

Today's computer can not only play back sounds and movies, but it can also record them, giving you a studio in your den. Sounds! Movies! Microwave popcorn!

Although the computer still has a few hurdles to clear before it replaces your TV, this unit shows you how to prepare your computer to be the TV set of the '90s.

Lesson 15-1   Playing Movie and Music Files

Notes:

Windows can play back movies, but don't throw away your VCR yet. The computer still has a few problems. First, the movies rarely fill the screen, and when they do, they tend to look grainy.

Second, movie files are *huge*. Just a few seconds' worth of *Casablanca* can fill an entire floppy disk.

Finally, movies aren't the easiest thing to get into a computer. Some snippets of movies come on compact discs; smaller ones can fit on a floppy. If you're patient — and you find the right online service, as described in Unit 14 — you can download a video. Or if you have enough money, you can make your own videos by using a video capture card and a camcorder.

Fortunately, a movie comes included on this book's disk, so you have something to play with during this lesson. The following steps show you how to play back the video:

1 **Click on the Start button and choose Accessories from the Program menu.**

2 **Click on Multimedia and then click on Media Player.**

The Windows 95 Media Player program comes to the screen, as shown in Figure 15-1.

3 **Choose Video for Windows from the Media Player's Device menu.**

A familiar-looking box appears; you use this same box when opening files in any other program. This time, however, the box lists only files containing movies. (Those types of files end with the letters *AVI*, although Windows 95 usually hides those letters.)

on the disk

4 **Open the Screaming Monster file from the Windows 95 folder in your Dummies 101 folder.**

A window opens up, with the first picture from the Screaming Monster movie peering out at you.

5 **Click on the Play button.**

As shown in Figure 15-2, that's the first button on the far-left side; the video begins to play.

on the test

For perpetually running videos or songs, choose the Auto Rewind and Auto Repeat options from the Edit menu's Options area. Or if your video is already repeating, click in those options' boxes to deactivate them.

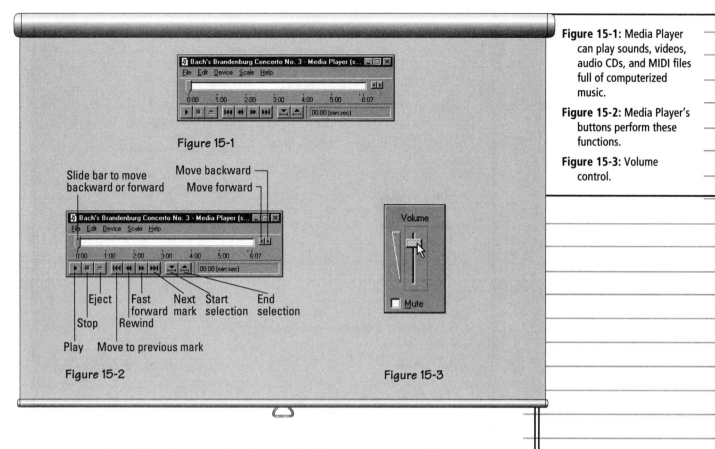

Figure 15-1

Slide bar to move backward or forward

Move backward

Move forward

Volume

Eject   Fast   Next   Start   End
        forward mark selection selection
Stop   Rewind

Play   Move to previous mark

Figure 15-2

Figure 15-3

To change the volume quickly, click on the little speaker in the taskbar's bottom-right corner and slide down the volume knob, shown in Figure 15-3.

Playing Sounds

Lesson 15-2

If your computer has a sound card installed, Windows can play back sounds and music. Although Media Player can play back sound files, we'll use Sound Recorder — another Windows program — to hear some guitar solos packaged on the disk that came with this book.

1 Click on the Start button and choose Accessories from the Program menu.

2 Click on Multimedia and then click on Sound Recorder.

The Windows 95 Sound Recorder program comes to the screen, as shown in Figure 15-4.

on the disk

3 Open the Very Berry file from the Windows 95 folder in your Dummies 101 folder.

Q/A Session

Question: What are some of Media Player's advanced features?

Answer: Choose Options from the Edit menu to see several of Media Player's extra options, as the following list shows:

▶ **Auto Rewind:** Click on this box to make Media Player return to the movie's opening shot after showing the movie.

▶ **Auto Repeat:** Click here, and Media Player repeats the movie over and over.

The other options take place when you paste movies into documents, as the following list describes:

▶ **Control Bar On Playback:** Choose this option, and the Media Player controls appear when you start playing the movie from within the document.

▶ **Border around object:** A check mark in this box inserts a thin border around the movie as you paste it inside a document.

▶ **Play in client document:** Click here, and the video plays from within the document — it won't leap into its own box on-screen.

▶ **Dither picture to VGA colors:** This one's sort of complicated. Don't bother with it unless your colors look strange. If the colors look strange, try clicking on this box.

Finally, the Properties setting under the Device menu lets you control the size of the window in which the movie plays. (The bigger the window, the less realistic the video, however.)

4 Click on the Play button.

As Figure 15-4 shows, that's the big button in the middle with the triangle on it. A quick click on that button, and Sound Recorder starts playing the song.

on the disk

Sound Recorder can add special effects to sounds as well. For example, open and play the Buzzed file. Then choose Reverse from the Effects menu and play it again. Be sure and try the Add Echo feature, too.

on the test

Although the program is called Sound Recorder, it can also *play* sounds.

on the test

MIDI files contain synthesized music or songs. WAV files, by contrast, contain actual recordings of sounds. Sound Recorder can play only WAV files, not MIDI files.

while in My Computer or Explorer, simply double-click on sounds and movies to hear them

---

Lesson 15-3   Recording Sounds

If you have a sound card, Sound Recorder can record sounds as easily as it plays them. You need a microphone for recording most sounds, but you can skip the mike if you're recording off of a home stereo or CD-ROM drive.

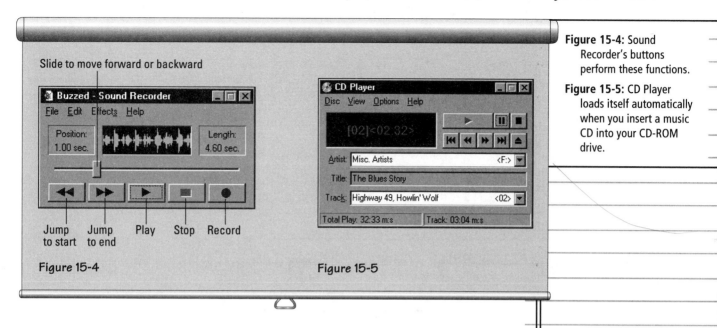

Figure 15-4: Sound Recorder's buttons perform these functions.

Figure 15-5: CD Player loads itself automatically when you insert a music CD into your CD-ROM drive.

1 **Open Sound Recorder.**

You did this step in Lesson 15-2.

2 **Prepare to record the sound.**

This step is different for everybody. If you're recording with a microphone, make sure that the mike is plugged into the sound card's microphone jack. If you're recording from a CD, make sure that the CD-ROM drive is set up correctly. If your setup isn't working right — and I hate to say this — you may have to dig out the manuals that came with your CD-ROM drive and sound card. (Or if you want to try to fix the problem yourself, look at *Multimedia & CD-ROMs For Dummies* (IDG Books Worldwide, Inc.) in the bookstore to see whether it's the book for you.)

Finally, most sound cards come with special mixer programs; make sure that yours is set up to route the sounds to the Sound Recorder.

3 **Click on the Sound Recorder's Record button.**

You see a picture of Sound Recorder's buttons in Figure 15-4.

4 **Start making the sound you want to record.**

Belch fervently, play your favorite CD, or turn on your home stereo. If everything's hooked up right, a little green line quivers inside Sound Recorder. The more energetic the quivering, the louder the incoming sound.

5 **Click on the button with the little black square to stop recording.**

Sound Recorder gives you 60 seconds to record; after that, it simply stops.

6 **Click on the Rewind button.**

7 **Click on the button with the single black triangle — the Play button — to hear the recording.**

If everything sounds great, move on to Step 8. If things sound off, choose New from the File menu to erase everything and start over at Step 2.

Rewind button

Play button

8 **Save your file.**

After you save your file, feel free to add the special effects described in the preceding lesson, like Echo and Reverse.

Also, Sound Recorder's Copy feature, found in the Edit menu, lets you mix files. Record the rain, record yourself singing, mix the two together, and you can be Gene Kelly without getting your overcoat wet.

on the test

Sounds that you record can be assigned to Windows "events." For example, the Control Panel, described in Unit 17, can play back one of your recorded sounds every time you turn on or off your computer.

> Sound Recorder
> can play and
> record only sounds;
> Media Player can
> play sounds, music,
> compact discs,
> and video

Lesson 15-4   Playing Music CDs

If your computer has a CD-ROM drive, Windows can play your old Led Zeppelin favorites in two different ways through two different programs. The easiest way by far, though, is to use the CD Player. The following step shows you just how easy using the CD Player is:

1 **Slide "Houses of the Holy" (or any other music CD) into your CD-ROM drive.**

And the music starts to play — that's it! See, Windows 95 is smart enough to distinguish a music CD from a computer CD. So when it spots a music CD in the drive, it automatically loads the CD Player program, as shown in Figure 15-5. You don't even have to push a Play button.

However, CD Player can do a lot more than that. The following steps show you how to make CD Player play your favorite CD over and over, playing songs in random order:

1 **Load CD Player.**

Usually, putting a music CD into your CD-ROM drive brings CD Player to the screen automatically. But you can also load it from the same menu as Media Player, described in Lesson 15-1.

2 **Choose Random Order from the Options menu.**

That tells CD Player to rearrange the songs on the CD so that you don't get tired of hearing them all in the same order.

3 **Choose Continuous Play from the Options menu.**

That tells CD Player to play the songs continually until you're tired of them.

4 **Click on the Play button to make CD Player play your songs in random order.**

Tip: Choose Edit Play List from the Disc menu and type the songs' names, as well as the CD's title. CD Player automatically remembers the songs' names and lists them the next time you insert that CD into your CD-ROM drive.

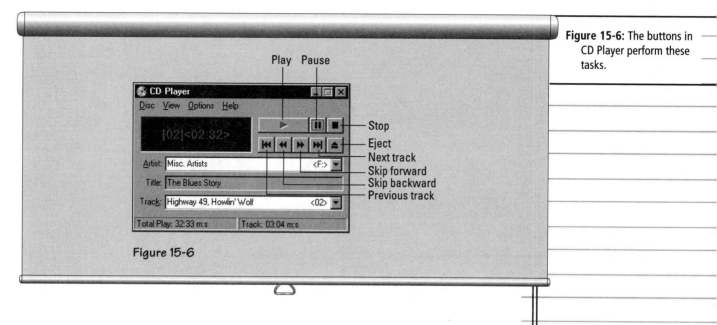

Figure 15-6: The buttons in CD Player perform these tasks.

Figure 15-6

Rest your mouse pointer over the buttons on the CD Player program to see their function. Or if you're impatient, refer to Figure 15-6.

Note: If you still can't hear any sound, check your sound card's volume by clicking on the little speaker in the bottom-right corner of your taskbar. Sliding the little bar up the pyramid increases the volume. If that still doesn't fix the problem, you may need to open your computer and make sure that the proper wires lead from your CD-ROM drive to your sound card. (Leave that stuff for the office computer guru or people who own a copy of *Upgrading and Fixing PCs For Dummies,* 2nd Edition, IDG Books Worldwide, Inc.)

Don't have a copy of CD Player? That's probably because the program only came with the compact disc version of Windows 95. If you have a modem, a copy of internet Explorer and you've read Unit 14, you can probably figure out how to download CD Player from the Microsoft web site at www.microsoft.com.

Viewing Sounds and Movies Quickly

Lesson 15-5

Loading movies and sounds the "normal" way can be tedious. You need to open Media Player or Sound Recorder, load a file through its menu system, and then push the play button. All that pointing and clicking can take some time when you're searching through a bunch of files for that explosion sound you want to stick on your answering machine message. Windows provides several down-and-dirty ways to load files quickly.

on the disk

First, you can simply double-click on the file's name in My Computer or Explorer. Double-click on the Buzzed file in the Dummies 101\Windows 95 folder, for example, and the Sound Recorder appears, ready to play your file.

Figure 15-7: Type the following characters into the <u>F</u>ind program's <u>N</u>amed box, and Windows 95 finds all your sound, music, and video files.

Figure 15-8: Move the My Computer window above Media Player, and then drag and drop sound and video files onto Media Player for quick browsing.

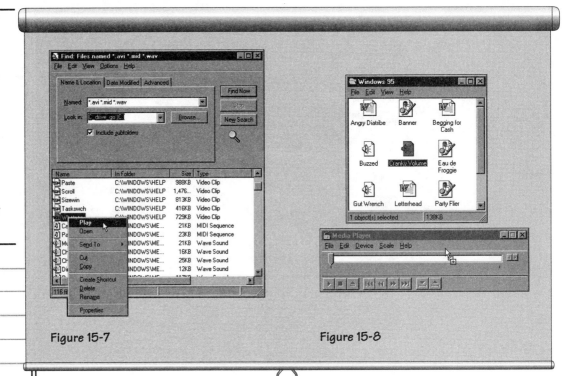

Figure 15-7   Figure 15-8

☑ Progress Check

If you can do the following, you've mastered this lesson:

❑ Play a movie in Media Player.

❑ Play and record a sound in Sound Recorder.

❑ Play a MIDI music file in Media Player.

❑ Play files by double-clicking on their names.

An even faster way is available, however. Follow these steps:

1 Load the My Computer program.

2 Bring the Dummies 101\Windows 95 folder to the screen.

3 Load Media Player.

extra credit

Playing multimedia files

You can quickly play sound, video, and music files from just about any Windows 95 program. Whenever you see a file's name, click on it with your right mouse button and then choose Play from the menu. Try doing so from My Computer, Explorer, or even the Open box that appears when you're opening files from within a program.

For a quick way to see all the fun media files on your C drive, use the Start menu's

Find Files and Folders program described in Unit 5. Type the characters ***.WAV *.AVI *.MID** in the Named box and press Enter. The program then lists all the sound, video, and music files on your C drive, as shown in Figure 15-8.

Double-click on any filename, and Windows 95 immediately plays it. Or click on a filename with your right mouse button and choose Play from the menu.

4 Arrange the Windows 95 folder and Media Player so that they're both visible on-screen.

The Taskbar's Tile command can quickly position programs and folders on-screen for easy "drag and drops."

5 Drag and drop the Cranky Volume file from My Computer to Media Player (see Figure 15-7) to hear the sound or view the movie.

on the disk

Unit 15 Quiz

Circle the letter of the correct answer or answers to each question.

1. **To keep a sound or video from constantly repeating, you do this:**

   A. Exit Media Player.

   B. Deactivate the Auto Repeat option from the Edit menu's Options area.

   C. Unplug the computer.

   D. Turn off the monitor.

2. **Sound Recorder can only record sounds, not play them.**

   A. True.

   B. False.

3. **WAV files contain recorded sounds or music.**

   A. True.

   B. False.

4. **Sound Recorder can record MIDI files.**

   A. True.

   B. False.

5. **Which multimedia files can Media Player play?**

   A. Videos.

   B. MIDI files.

   C. Recorded sounds.

   D. Text.

6. **Which of these can a multimedia computer record with Windows?**

   A. Sound.

   B. Movies.

   C. Text.

   D. Songs.

Unit 15 Exercise

on the disk

1. Open My Computer and Media Player.

2. Drag and drop each multimedia file onto your Media Player icon.

3. Open the Very Berry file in Sound Recorder.

4. Choose the <u>A</u>dd Echo option from the Effect<u>s</u> menu.

5. Repeat Step 4 three more times.

6. Choose Reverse from the Effect<u>s</u> menu.

7. Choose Play to hear how Chuck Berry would have sounded if he had been produced by Jimi Hendrix.

Part IV Review

Unit 11 Summary

- **Paint:** Paint, the drawing tool of Windows, lets you draw both color and black-and-white pictures. It can handle straight lines, curved lines, circles, and ellipses, as well as add special effects such as spray paint. Paint also lets you add text to your creations, making it a popular program for creating fliers.

- **Cutting and pasting Paint graphics:** Graphics created in Paint can also be cut and pasted into other programs, letting you add a monogram to a letter in WordPad, for example.

- **Displaying pictures on-screen:** You can use Paint to display previously drawn pictures on-screen.

Unit 12 Summary

- **WordPad:** One of the most powerful programs that comes with Windows 95, WordPad can handle most of your word processing needs. It can emphasize your words with **bold**, *italics,* and <u>underlining</u>, as well as change the styles and sizes of your characters.

- **No spell-checker:** WordPad doesn't have a spell-checker, however, which keeps it from seriously threatening the more full-featured word processors.

Unit 13 Summary

- **Notepad:** A handy program for jotting down quick notes, Notepad also stores its information in ASCII format — meaning that nearly every other word processor can read its files. Notepad doesn't work well for formatting text, however.

- **When to use Notepad:** If you want to keep your notes off of paper and on the computer screen, Notepad works well. But if your words are meant for the printer, use WordPad instead.

Unit 14 Summary

- **The Internet:** The *Internet* is a huge network of computers around the world. Your computer becomes part of this network when it joins the *World Wide Web* — a portion of the Internet set aside for sending information through words and graphics.

- **Internet Explorer:** Microsoft Internet Explorer is one of many *Web browsers* — software for navigating the World Wide Web and exploring its many pages of information. Internet Explorer currently comes free with Windows 95.

- **How to navigate Web pages:** Web pages contain *hyperlinks* — special buttons that lead the Web browser on to even more pages of information. By pointing and clicking on these hyperlinks, Web users can browse their way across computer networks, much like television's channel surfers flip through various television stations.

Unit 15 Summary

- **Media Player and Sound Recorder:** The flashiest parts of Windows, Media Player and Sound Recorder don't need much maintenance or training. They pop up when needed, ready to play back videos, music, or recorded sounds.

Part IV Test

The questions on this test cover all the material presented in Part IV, Units 11 through 15.

True   False

T   F   1. If your computer has a CD-ROM drive, Media Player can play music from music CDs.

T   F   2. You can cut all or part of a picture from Paint for later pasting.

T   F   3. When you type in Notepad, the words always roll off the edge of the window.

T   F   4. If your computer has a sound card and a microphone, Windows can record sounds.

T   F   5. The Microsoft Exchange program comes already set up to work with the most common online services like CompuServe, America Online, and Prodigy.

T   F   6. You can copy information from the World Wide Web onto your own computer.

T   F   7. MIDI files sound the same on every brand of sound card.

Multiple Choice

For each of the following questions, circle the correct answer or answers. Remember, each question may have more than one right answer.

8. **Media Player can play these types of files:**

   A. Videos in AVI format

   B. Songs in MIDI format

   C. Sounds in WAV format

   D. Music in compact disc format

9. **To make a perfect circle or square in Paint, you hold down this key while drawing with the Pencil tool:**

   A. Alt

   B. Ctrl

   C. Shift

   D. Spacebar

10. **Paint can add these things to a picture:**

    A. Text

    B. Color

    C. Spray paint effects

    D. Oil or acrylic paint

11. **The WordPad word processor includes these features:**

    A. A spell-checker

    B. Adjustable margins

    C. Capability to incorporate graphics

    D. Capability to use different fonts

12. **You connect to the Internet with the following things:**

    A. A computer and modem

    B. A telephone line

    C. An Internet Service Provider

    D. Internet browser software

Part IV Test

Matching

13. **Match up the following pieces of computer gear with the programs that control them:**

    A. Sound card and microphone　　1. Sound Recorder

    B. Sound card and Speakers　　2. Media Player

    C. CD-ROM drive

14. **Match up the following tasks with the programs that accomplish them:**

    A. Sending and receiving e-mail　　1. Exchange bulletin boards

    B. Playing recorded sounds　　2. Media Player

    C. Playing synthesized sounds　　3. Sound Recorder

15. **Match up these file formats with their contents:**

    A. MIDI　　1. A computerized video, either captured from a camera or created by using computer animation

    B. WAV　　2. A picture or drawing

    C. AVI　　3. A microphone-based recording of an actual sound

    D. BMP　　4. Instructions for creating music by using a sound card's synthesizer

Part IV Lab Assignment

Because this huge lab assignment spans five units, it's a little different. Instead of telling you to create more projects, it encourages you to go back over the units you've mastered, changing them subtly to meet your needs more fully.

Step 1: Create your own party flyer

Using the skills that you learned in Unit 11, create a customized party flyer for your own party. Experiment with different fonts and balloon styles. Try drawing a crude map that shows your house's location, and then paste it into the flyer.

Step 2: Create new letterhead in Paint

Use Paint to create a new letterhead, complete with a monogram of your initials in the corner. Save the file and paste it into a WordPad file whenever you need some letterhead.

Part IV Lab Assignment

Step 3: Join an online service

Join an online service like CompuServe that still works with text-based telecommunications programs like HyperTerminal. (America Online, Prodigy, and The Microsoft Network don't work with HyperTerminal, unfortunately.)

Step 4: Spend some time Web browsing

Drop a little television time at the door and spend some time moving about on the libraries of the World Wide Web, visiting zoos, museums, craft fairs, and educational institutions.

Fixing Problems

Part V

In this part . . .

They were picked last at dodge ball during elementary school, but now they're the trendiest people on the block. Today's computer nerds are not only trendy, they're overworked, and they're never there when you need them.

This part of the book teaches you how to perform some basic Windows 95 fixes yourself. You'll learn how to change how Windows appears unleash its screen savers, and adjust your computer's mouse and keyboard. Plus, you'll learn how to install new programs.

Finally, this part teaches you how to use the next best thing to a personal computer guru: the help system built into Windows 95.

Organizing Your Desktop

Prerequisites
▶ Loading a file (Unit 7)
▶ Navigating windows with a mouse (Lesson 2-1)
▶ Dragging and dropping (Unit 10)
▶ Using Explorer and My Computer (Unit 5)

Objectives for This Unit

✓ Moving things around on your desktop

✓ Arranging strategic shortcuts

✓ Doing tasks quickly

✓ Starting programs automatically with Windows

Even after learning how to drive a car, you need to look at a map once in a while. Sure, you can just point in a certain direction and put the pedal to the metal — but that's rarely the fastest or most fuel-efficient way to arrive at the destination.

Because Windows 95 offers so many different ways to do things, setting it up efficiently is difficult. Which desktop setup works best? No one real answer exists, of course. Just as everybody's desktop differs at least slightly in real life, all Windows 95 users will want their own assemblage of shortcuts, icons, and folders.

This unit shows you a few setups to sample; perhaps by picking and choosing from the different lessons, you'll come up with the desktop you've always wanted. Don't feel that you have to use any of these ideas; if you think that some of them are trash, feel free to drag them to the Recycle Bin. (That's what it's there for.)

Lesson 16-1

Creating Desktop Shortcuts

Notes:

Although Windows 95 makes a decent effort, it doesn't leave much in the way of a desktop, as shown in Figure 16-1.

First, everything's hidden — you need to start clicking to find most of the buttons. And because Windows 95 doesn't know what sort of tasks you'll be doing most often, it doesn't know which buttons to move to the forefront. This lesson shows you how to customize Windows 95 to meet your own special needs.

1 **Read the Welcome screen tip.**

When Windows 95 first starts up, it persistently flashes a "helpful tip" onto the screen, as shown in Figure 16-1. Give the tips a chance to soak in — some of them can be useful down the road. In fact, clicking on the box's Next Tip button lets you flip through all the tips as fast as you can read and click.

2 **Click in the Show this Welcome screen next time you start Windows box, and then click on the window's Close button.**

Following Step 2 turns those little tip windows off so that they won't pop to the front of the screen each time you reload Windows.

3 **Double-click on the My Computer icon.**

The My Computer window opens up.

4 **With your right mouse button, drag and drop your A drive icon to the top-right corner of your desktop.**

A menu appears, as shown in Figure 16-2, asking whether you want to Create Shortcut(s) Here or Cancel.

5 **Choose the Create Shortcut(s) Here option.**

Putting a shortcut to your floppy disk drive on your desktop gives you easy access, as shown in Figure 16-3. To move or copy to a floppy, just drag and drop it to your new shortcut. Do the same for your B drive, if you have one.

create desktop
shortcuts to floppy
drives

Shortcuts can be valuable time-savers if you take the time to set them up. Feel free to put shortcuts to your most commonly used programs and directories on your desktop by dragging and dropping them with the right mouse button.

on the test

deleting shortcuts
doesn't hurt the
original files

Deleting a shortcut deletes only the button that starts the program, not the program itself. The program stays in the same location.

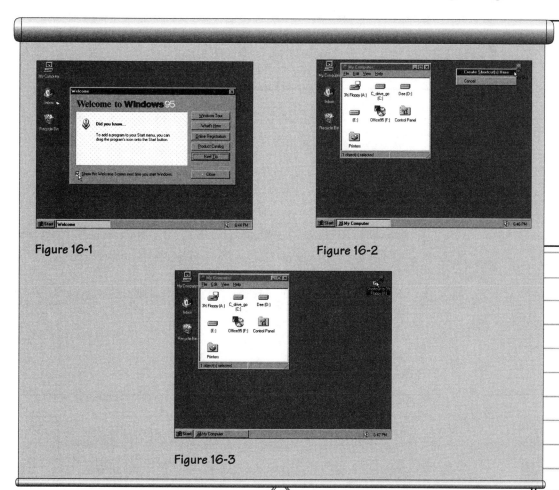

Figure 16-1: Most desktops in Windows 95 start out looking somewhat like this.

Figure 16-2: Dragging and dropping with the right mouse button always brings up a menu that gives you more control over your actions.

Figure 16-3: Drag and drop files to your floppy drive's shortcut to save time.

Figure 16-1

Figure 16-2

Figure 16-3

extra credit

Q/A Session

Question: I turned off my Welcome Tip screens! How can I turn them back on?

Answer: To turn those daily tips back on, click on your desktop's background, press F1 to bring up the Help menu, and click on the Help window's Index tab.

Next, click in the first box and type **Tip of the Day**, and then click on the Display button. Another box appears. Huff, puff.

Double-click on the Tips: Viewing the Welcome screen again listing, and yet *another* box appears. Click on the little arrow in that box, and the Tip of the Day returns.

Now, click in the Show this Welcome Screen next time you start Windows box; a check mark appears. That check mark ensures that the tip stays there, and you won't have to repeat this nonsense until you get tired of the tips again.

Lesson 16-2

Organizing Folders

Notes:

Like it or not, just about everybody uses their computer for work. That's why having a work directory is so important. By creating a folder on your hard drive called Work — and then storing all your work files inside it — you'll always know where to find them.

The next few steps show you how to make your own, easily accessible, Work Folder:

1 Open My Computer and double-click on your C drive icon.

The My Computer program shows you the folders currently stored on your C drive.

2 Choose New from the newly opened window's File menu, and choose Folder.

A blank folder appears in the window.

3 Type Work.

Windows 95 assigns the word *Work* to the folder.

4 Open your new Work folder, and create two folders inside it for your two current work projects.

Make one of those folders for **John's Harebrained Marketing Plan** and the other for **Alice's Crossword Puzzle Scores.**

5 Create a shortcut on your desktop that leads to the folder.

You can create this shortcut just as you did in the preceding lesson — with the ol' drag and drop with the right mouse button.

Now, whenever you're ready to work, just double-click on your desktop icon. That puts you right at your Work folder, with no hemming or hawing. You'll immediately have your two important work projects in front of you.

As your projects change, change your folders. Create an Old Projects folder in your Work folder, for example, and move the completed projects into it as you finish them.

Shortcuts can summon folders just as they can launch programs.

to remove
shortcuts, drag
them to the
Recycle Bin

on the test

Starting Programs Automatically with Windows 95

Lesson 16-3

Ever find yourself using just one program over and over? In fact, the first thing you do when you start Windows 95 is to load that single program and get to work?

on the test

The eager-to-please Windows 95 is happy to load that program for you automatically when it loads itself — if you adhere to the following steps:

1 Click on the Start button with your right mouse button, and then choose _O_pen from the menu.

The My Computer program hops to the screen, showing you the folders and programs currently stored on your Start menu.

2 Double-click on the Programs folder.

A new box pops open.

3 Double-click on the StartUp folder.

A window pops open, listing the programs currently listed in the StartUp folder. Those programs, if any are listed, currently load themselves and run automatically whenever you load Windows 95.

4 Drag and drop your program's icon into the StartUp folder.

You can drag and drop that program's icon from Explorer or My Computer — the program automatically turns into a proper shortcut when you let go of the mouse button.

Close down all the open windows, and you're through. The next time you restart Windows 95, your favorite program will be on-screen waiting for you.

☑ **Progress Check**

If you can do the following, you've mastered this unit:

❑ Create a shortcut.

❑ Organize a folder.

❑ Add a program to the Windows StartUp folder.

Unit 16 Quiz

For each question, circle the letter of the correct answer or answers. Remember, a question may have more than one right answer.

1. **Deleting a shortcut does this:**

   A. Deletes a push-button that starts a program or opens a folder.

   B. Deletes the push-button and the program or folder.

   C. Deletes the push-button, but only moves the program or folder to the Recycle Bin.

   D. Moves the shortcut to the Recycle Bin.

2. **Windows 95 can do these things when you first load it:**

    A. Load a program.

    B. Crash.

    C. Open folders.

    D. Open doors.

3. **Shortcuts can bring the following things to the screen:**

    A. Programs.

    B. Folders.

    C. Files.

    D. Accusations of cheating.

Unit 16 Exercise

Because this unit was more a series of tips than a sequential lesson plan, the exercise follows suit. Try out the following tips and circle the ones you want to remember:

1. To reopen a recently opened file, click on the Start button and choose Documents. Chances are, your file's name will be sitting there, waiting to be clicked into action.

2. To keep incoming material from spreading all over your desktop or hard drive, create a Junk folder on your hard drive. When new files come in, just store them there until you decide on a more organized place to put them.

3. Icons looking a little spread out across the desktop? Click on the desktop with your right mouse button and choose Line up Icons from the menu. Windows 95 immediately scoots the icons into straight, evenly spaced lines.

4. Want to peek inside a file really quickly? Click on the file's name in Explorer or My Computer (or the Open File box of just about any Windows 95 program) and choose Quick View from the menu. Windows 95 immediately gives you a look-see without actually opening the file.

5. Some part of Windows 95 has you baffled? Click on the desktop's background, press F1, and click on the Help window's Contents tab. Double-click on the book icon marked Troubleshooting, and Windows 95 lists the problems that it's ready to help with. If you're lucky and your problem is on the list, then Windows 95 can unleash a software troubleshooter program that will help to solve the problem.

Changing Settings

Objectives for This Unit

- ✓ Changing color schemes and wallpaper
- ✓ Changing sound assignments
- ✓ Adjusting the mouse and keyboard
- ✓ Changing the screen saver
- ✓ Changing video modes

Prerequisites
- ▶ Loading a file (Unit 7)
- ▶ Navigating windows with a mouse (Lesson 2-1)
- ▶ Using My Computer and Explorer (Unit 5)

on the disk
- ▶ Very Berry
- ▶ Buzzed
- ▶ Eau de Froggie

Your personal computer is your personal robot: Both are electromechanical beasts designed to do your bidding. To liven things up, Windows 95 lets you add personality to your computerized robot.

Push a few buttons, and it wears a black leather jacket and makes snarling noises. Push a few more to coat your desktop with autumn leaves.

This unit not only teaches you how to change your robot's appearance, but it also shows you how to adjust the way you talk to your robot — through the mouse and keyboard.

Finally, you'll learn how to add some sparkle to the screen by making Windows use the most colorful display possible — if your computerized robot is powerful enough to handle it, that is.

Lesson 17-1

Changing Wallpaper and Color Schemes

In Windows, *wallpaper* is that picture stuck to the back of the screen. Once you learn how to change your wallpaper, you'll want to change it over and over again. It's easy, and no glue is required.

Color schemes — the colors of Windows borders, menu bars, and other screen elements — aren't nearly as flashy, but they're fun and easy to change as well. This lesson's two sections show you how to change both areas.

Changing the Windows wallpaper

These steps change your current wallpaper to a file called Eau de Froggie that comes on the disk in the back of this book:

1 Click on a blank part of your desktop with your right mouse button and choose Properties from the menu.

The desktop's menu comes to the screen, as shown in Figure 17-1.

2 Click on any file's name listed in the Wallpaper box.

The menu shows you a preview of your selection in the little monitor.

3 Click on Apply to apply the wallpaper to the screen.

Like what you see? Then click on the OK button to return to work. Otherwise, return to Step 2 and try a different file. Windows 95 automatically shows you the wallpaper files — plain old bitmaps — stored in your Windows folder.

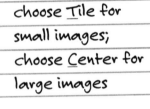

choose Tile for small images; choose Center for large images

4 Click on the Browse button.

A Browse box similar to the one covered in Unit 7 comes to the screen.

5 Double-click on the C:\ folder at the top of the box's Folder section.

The C:\ folder is "shorthand" for your C drive folder — the one that contains all the other folders on your drive.

6 Double-click on the Dummies 101 folder.

You may need to use the scroll bars to see it; a double-click opens it up.

7 Double-click on the Windows 95 folder.

That reveals the Eau de Froggie file.

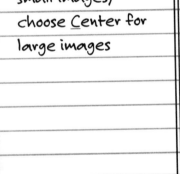

on the disk

8 Double-click on *Eau de Froggie* and then click on OK.

The frog hops onto the little preview monitor.

9 Click on the OK button to make Eau de Froggie your wallpaper.

Tip: Like what you just created in Paint? Save it and choose one of the two Set As Wallpaper options from Paint's File menu. Windows 95 copies the image from the Paint screen to your desktop.

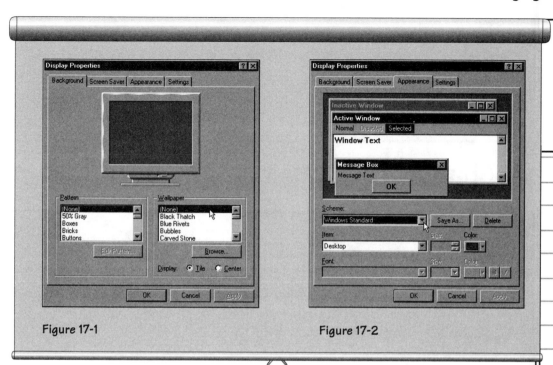

Figure 17-1: You can customize the desktop to your liking through its Properties setting.

Figure 17-2: Choose a new color scheme from the Color box.

Notes:

Figure 17-1   Figure 17-2

Tip: Choosing the Apply button immediately applies your choice to your desktop so that you can see your choice in real life. The selection window remains open so that you can change your choice if you don't like the results. Choosing the OK button, on the other hand, immediately applies your choice to the desktop and closes the window.

Changing the Windows color scheme

Wallpaper coats your Windows 95 desktop. The color scheme, on the other hand, consists of the colors Windows 95 uses for basic windows paraphernalia: menus, scroll bars, and other assorted flotsam. Follow these steps to change the basic colors that Windows uses:

1 Click on a blank part of your desktop with your right mouse button and choose P̲roperties from the menu.

The same box that appeared in Figure 17-1 comes to the screen.

2 Click on the Appearance tab.

The Appearance window pops up, as shown in Figure 17-2.

3 Choose a new color scheme from the S̲cheme area.

Clicking on the downward-pointing arrow makes the choices fall out. Clicking on a choice gives you a preview in the window.

4 Click on Apply for a "real desktop" preview; then click on OK when you're satisfied with the new colors.

Windows uses the new colors until you change them.

on the test

Wallpaper comes from a specific file that Windows uses to cover your screen's background.

on the test

The Windows color scheme isn't a file but a list of colors that Windows uses for embellishing borders, menus, and other areas.

Lesson 17-2   Changing the Screen Saver

Notes:

Screen savers are munchkins that come out to play. When you haven't touched the computer for a while, and the monitor's getting hot for no reason, the screen suddenly turns black — and a man on a lawnmower starts chasing a cat across the screen.

Actually, Windows 95 doesn't come with a man on a lawnmower, but it has several other screen savers to keep your unused monitor dark and safe from prying eyes. The following steps teach you how to put them to use.

1 **Click on a blank part of your desktop with your right mouse button and choose Properties from the menu.**

Yep; same as the first step in Lesson 17-1.

2 **Click on the Screen Saver tab at the top of the box.**

A picture of a monitor appears, as shown in Figure 17-3.

3 **Click on the downward-pointing arrow in the box marked Screen Saver.**

A menu drops down, listing the screen savers installed on your computer.

4 **Click on Flying Windows.**

A preview of the Flying Windows screen saver appears on the miniature monitor in the box, as shown in Figure 17-4.

5 **Click on the Preview button.**

The screen saver takes over your screen. Decide whether you can live with the display, and then wriggle the mouse or push your spacebar to come back to the menu.

6 **If you like the screen saver, click on the OK button; otherwise, go back to Step 3.**

You can customize the Flying Windows screen saver — and the other screen savers that come with Windows 95 — by clicking on the Settings button during Step 5. Although different screen savers come with different settings, most let you adjust things like their speed or the number of objects that appear when the screen saver kicks in.

If you get bored with the built-in Windows screen savers, many third-party companies sell screen savers. (Check out the Berkeley Systems After Dark series.)

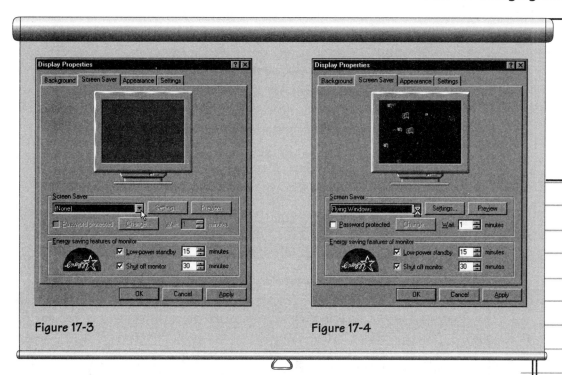

Figure 17-3

Figure 17-4

Figure 17-3: The Windows
    screen savers come to
    life when you aren't
    using your computer.

Figure 17-4: Windows 95
    shows a preview of
    the screen savers
    on the little monitor
    in the box.

Tip: Windows 95 doesn't automatically install all the screen savers that come
with it. To make sure that they're all installed, check out Unit 19. It shows you
how to add and remove portions of Windows 95.

Changing the Screen's Size   Lesson 17-3

Sometimes Windows acts more like a dining room table than a desktop. Just as
the table can expand or contract for dinner guests, Windows can make its
desktop bigger or smaller.

But this expansion is an optical illusion. Instead of making the desktop larger,
Windows simply makes all the programs smaller.

Nevertheless, spreading out is nice sometimes. The following steps teach you
how to make Windows adjust its desktop to fit your current needs:

**1 Click on a blank part of your desktop with your right mouse button
and choose Properties from the menu.**

Once again, this is the first step in Lessons 17-1 and 17-2.

2 Click on the Settings tab.

The Settings box appears, as shown in Figure 17-5.

write down original settings here

3 **In the margin of this book, write down the numbers that appear in the <u>C</u>olor palette box and the <u>D</u>esktop area box.**

You may want to change them back to their original settings after you do this lesson.

4 **Slide the bar in the <u>D</u>esktop area box all the way over to the right.**

That tells Windows to pack as many programs onto the screen as possible. Different computers have different parts, so yours may not look exactly like the one in Figure 17-5.

extra credit

Q/A Session

Question: What do the other screen saver settings do?

Answer: You can customize all the Windows screen savers, as the following list shows:

Password protected: Going to lunch and want to keep prying eyes out of your computer files? Click here and type in a password. Then only people who type in that password can make the screen saver give up its hold on the monitor.

<u>W</u>ait: This setting controls how many minutes Windows 95 waits

before turning on the screen saver. It ranges from 1 to 60 minutes.

Low-power standby: You can power down monitors with special energy-saving features to save electricity. Set the number of minutes here before the screen saver is turned off and the monitor's screen goes blank.

Sh<u>u</u>t off monitor: This option works similarly to the Low-power standby mode, but it completely turns off the monitor. (It, too, works only with special energy-saving monitors.)

5 **Click on the <u>C</u>olor palette box and choose the selection at the bottom of the list.**

This action tells Windows to pack as many colors onto your monitor as possible. (Normally, you should stick with 256 colors — anything higher tends to slow down all but the fastest computers.)

6 **Click on the <u>A</u>pply button.**

Windows may have to restart itself in order to wake up with its new size or colors. Or it can switch to the new video mode and ask you whether you like it, as shown in Figure 17-6.

If Windows 95 asks whether you like the new video mode — and you do like it — click on the Yes button. If you don't click on the Yes button within 15 seconds, Windows assumes either that you don't like it or that the change has hopelessly distorted your monitor and you can't read it. So that savvy Windows 95 switches back to your original settings for safety's sake.

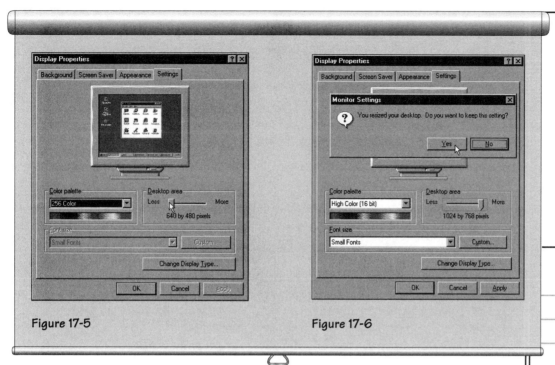

Figure 17-5

Figure 17-6

Figure 17-5: The Settings box lists thte number of colors your computer can display and the size of the screen in which it can display them.

Figure 17-6: Sometimes Windows switches to your newly chosen screen settings immediately; other times Windows has to reboot before switching to those new settings.

Tip: Video cards can display different-sized screens, rated by the number of little dots they display in a grid. Monitors of 17 inches or larger will probably like 1024 × 768 mode; smaller monitors should stick with 800 × 600 or 640 × 480.

Changing Sound Assignments   Lesson 17-4

Forget about the stuff you hear on the sci-fi shows. Computers still can't talk very well, much less calculate shortest routes and gas mileages between planets. Your computer can toss out more than a simple beep, though, as long as the computer has a sound card and speakers.

This lesson shows you how to turn on the built-in sounds in Windows 95, as well as hear some of your own creations.

1 Load the Control Panel.

Click on the Start menu, and then click on the Control Panel from the Settings menu. Shown in Figure 17-7, the Control Panel lets you adjust almost all the settings in Windows 95. (You can even adjust your screen savers, colors, and screen size by double-clicking on the Display icon.)

2 Double-click on the Control Panel's Sounds icon.

The Sounds Properties box appears, as shown in Figure 17-8. The box lists which sounds are "linked" to play during certain events, such as when you turn the computer on or off.

Figure 17-7: By double-clicking on the Control Panel's icons, you can adjust almost every aspect of Windows 95.

Figure 17-8: Windows can play back sounds during certain Windows events.

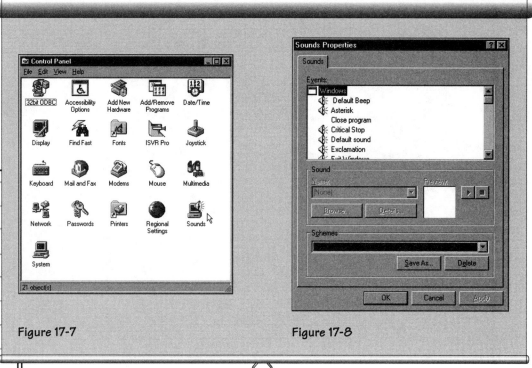

Figure 17-7   Figure 17-8

3 **Click on Start Windows in the Sound box's Events list.**

4 **Click on the Browse button.**

Doing so brings up the standard Browse box you learned about in Unit 7.

on the disk

5 **Move to the Windows 95 folder of your Dummies 101 folder and double-click on the Very Berry file.**

6 **Click on the triangular Preview button to hear the sound.**

Windows plays your selection.

7 **Click on OK to close the Sounds Properties box.**

Now, whenever Windows starts, a guitar riff will accompany that first sip of coffee.

Note: Don't assign an event to a file that lives on a floppy disk. If you remove the disk when Windows tries to make a noise, your computer may not be happy.

Lesson 17-5   Setting the Clock

Unlike most jewelers, Clock offers only two models: digital or no clock at all. And unless you turn off the clock or drag and drop your entire taskbar, that little digital clock stays in the bottom-right corner of your screen.

Clock does let you play with one aspect, though, thank goodness: It lets you adjust its time setting. The following steps show you how to set the clock if you find that it needs adjusting:

1 Double-click on the clock at the edge of the taskbar.

The Date/Time Properties box rises to the screen.

2 Click on the digital clock numbers, and then press the up or down arrows to adjust the time.

For example, if the clock says 9:00 and it's really 10:00, click on the 9 and press your up-arrow key to advance the clock an hour. Repeat the steps for the minutes and seconds.

3 Adjust the date in the same way.

Click on the current month, year, and date in the box to the right of the clock.

4 Click on the Time Zone tab.

The Time Zone window comes to the screen. If you're a laptop user, you may need to adjust this area during your travels. Most desktop users won't ever need to adjust it.

Are you under Daylight Savings Time? Better click that box so that Windows 95 will automatically adjust your computer's clock at the appropriate times.

5 Click on the OK button.

The window closes, and your computer's clock now displays the proper time and date.

Finally, if you want to turn off the clock, click on it with your right mouse button and then choose Properties from the menu. Click on the Show Clock button to remove the X, and then click the OK button. Whoosh! The clock disappears from the screen. (Click on the Show Clock button again to bring it back to life.)

rest mouse pointer over clock to see current date

Adjusting the Mouse and Keyboard   Lesson 17-6

Your computerized robot may try to speak to you with beeps and growls, but 99 percent of the conversation is one-way: You're the one talking to the computer through its mouse and keyboard.

This lesson shows you how to adjust the mouse and keyboard to your liking, hopefully making your robot more understanding when you talk to it.

Figure 17-9: The Control Panel's Mouse Properties box lets you fine-tune your mouse's behavior.

Figure 17-10: The Keyboard controls let you adjust the keys' responsiveness.

Notes:

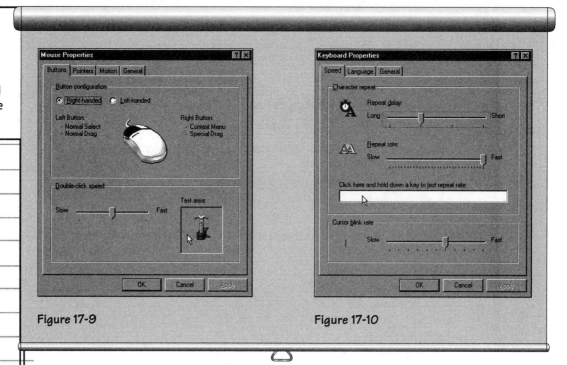

Figure 17-9

Figure 17-10

Fine-tuning the mouse

1 Double-click on the Mouse icon in the Control Panel.

Bring the Control Panel to the screen the same way you did in Step 1 of the preceding lesson, and then double-click on the Mouse icon to see the box shown in Figure 17-9.

2 Slide the Double-click speed bar to Slow, and double-click on the little jack-in-the-box.

Lil' Jack hops into the box when you complete a successful double-click at that speed, and then he hops back out for the next double-click.

3 Slide the Double-click speed bar to Fast, and double-click on the little jack-in-the-box.

Notice the difference? You probably won't be able to click fast enough to make ol' Jack jump in or out.

4 Slide the bar to the middle, adjusting it to your personal preference.

You'll probably want to leave the bar somewhere close to the middle. But if you're having trouble making a recognizable double-click, keep it on the Slow side.

If you're a left-hander, click on the Left-handed button; that way you can make right-clicks just like everybody else — even though you're holding the mouse with your left hand.

5 Click on OK.

Doing so saves your settings for future work.

Left-handers can make Windows swap their left and right mouse buttons.

on the test

Q/A Session

Question: What do all the other mouse settings stand for?

Answer: Although you probably won't need to change these settings, the following list explains what the other pages on the Mouse Properties windows can do.

Pointers: Windows provides several different mouse "schemes," which use different types of mouse pointers. Choose the Extra Large pointers, for example, if you're having trouble spotting your current-sized mouse pointer. (*Note:* Some of these options are available only to people who installed Windows 95 from a compact disc rather than floppies.)

Motion: Pointer speed controls how your mouse moves in comparison to your hand movements. Slide the bar to Fast, click on Apply, and the mouse roars; move to Slow, click on Apply, and the mouse crawls.

Can't spot your mouse on a laptop or crowded monitor? Choose Show pointer trails to make your mouse leave a trail of visible images as it travels across the screen.

General: Don't change this one unless you've bought a different brand of mouse and want to install it. (General brings up the same box you'll read about in Unit 21.)

Fine-tuning the keyboard

1 Double-click on the Keyboard icon from the Control Panel.

You learned how to load the Control Panel in the preceding lesson.

2 Adjust the controls.

The Keyboard Properties box, shown in Figure 17-10, lets you adjust two things that happen when you hold down a single key. And the only way to learn how it works is to experiment.

The Repeat delay controls how long Windows waits before it starts repeatingggggggg your key.

The other option, Repeat rate, controls how quickly the key rrrrrrrrraces across your screen.

3 If your experimenting made the keyboard behave better, click on OK; if it made things worse, click on Cancel.

Unless you've suddenly moved to a foreign country and want to use a foreign language, you probably won't need to click on the Language tab. (But now you know where it is, just in case you find yourself moving to or from Belgium.)

And don't bother clicking on the General tab, either, unless you've bought a new keyboard. (And even then, you'll find more information about adding and removing computer parts in Unit 19.)

☑ **Progress Check**

If you can do the following, you've mastered this unit:

❑ Change the Windows color scheme.

❑ Switch to different wallpaper.

❑ Assign different sounds to Windows actions.

❑ Adjust the "feel" of the mouse.

❑ Change the screen saver.

❑ Switch the screen's size or video mode.

Unit 17 Quiz

Notes:

For each question, circle the letter of the correct answer or answers. Remember, the questions may have more than one right answer.

1. **Wallpaper does these things in Windows:**
   A. Decorates your screen's background.
   B. Fits in one file.
   C. Determines the color of your screen's menus.
   D. Often peels in the corners under heavy use.

2. **Which of these color schemes doesn't come with Windows?**
   A. Eggplant.
   B. Rainy Day.
   C. Pumpkin (Large).
   D. Glow in the Dark.

3. **Left-handers can make Windows swap their left and right mouse buttons.**
   A. True.
   B. False.

4. **Windows can't display all the video modes that it lists.**
   A. True.
   B. False.

Unit 17 Exercise

1. Change your Windows wallpaper to Red Blocks, tiled.
2. Change your Windows wallpaper to Red Blocks, centered.
3. Experiment with some of the other files listed in your Windows folder.

on the disk

4. Assign the Buzzed sound file to the Exclamation event.
5. Test all your screen savers.
6. Change among your video card's video modes to see which one you like best — and which one makes your computer run the most quickly.

Using the Windows 95 Help Program

Objectives for This Unit

✓ Finding help in Windows 95

✓ Finding help for Windows programs

✓ Customizing the Help program

✓ Finding help for specific problems

Prerequisites

▶ Navigating windows with a mouse (Lesson 2-1)

▶ Using the Start menu (Lesson 4-2)

▶ Loading and running programs (Unit 6)

Computers can do just about everything, according to the sales guy on TV. But then how come computers can't help you change the margins in your funky new word processor?

Well, at least Windows makes an effort. Microsoft built a Help system into Windows 95 that's supposed to be as welcome to baffled users as the Auto Club is to stranded motorists.

Unfortunately, the system's advice rarely rates full-fledged computer geek status; on the contrary, the hints often sound like an electrical engineer's bare-bones notes.

Although the Windows 95 Help system is overly complicated, it's much better than the underpowered versions that came with earlier versions of Windows. This unit shows you how to drag the most help from it as possible.

Figure 18-1: Pressing F1 in programs like Notepad brings up the Help program.

Figure 18-2: Double-click on a book icon to see its list of pages.

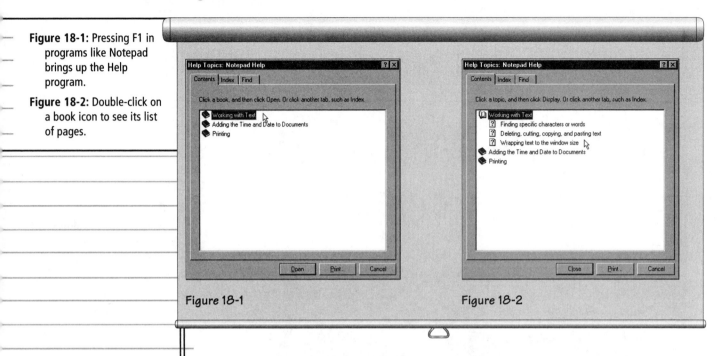

Figure 18-1 Figure 18-2

Lesson 18-1

Using the Windows Help Program

Notes:

Just as some neighborhoods don't get all the good cable TV channels, not all Windows programs come with a built-in Help system. But follow these steps to see if your current program offers Help — and how helpful it will be.

1 Load a program — Notepad, in this case — and press F1.

Sometimes just pressing F1 instantly summons a helpful bit of advice, as shown in Figure 18-1. The little book icons work like folders; double-click on the book icon that sounds the most helpful to see its contents.

2 Double-click on the Help program's Working with Text book for information about that subject.

The book opens up, spilling its list of more specific subjects, as shown in Figure 18-2.

3 Click on Wrapping text to the window size.

The Help program brings a window explaining how to perform that task to the screen, as shown in Figure 18-3.

By double-clicking on the various book icons and reading bits and pieces of different helpful explanations, you should eventually solve the problem that's bugging you.

Unfortunately, not all programs come with a built-in Help system. If your program is one of those unlucky few, pressing F1 won't summon a helpful bit of advice. Pressing F1 twice won't do anything, either.

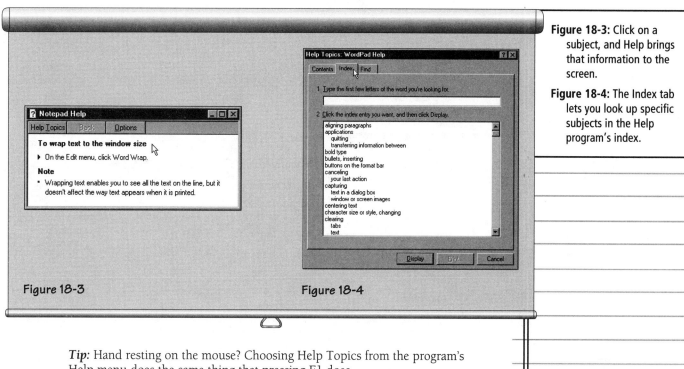

Figure 18-3

Figure 18-4

Figure 18-3: Click on a subject, and Help brings that information to the screen.

Figure 18-4: The Index tab lets you look up specific subjects in the Help program's index.

Tip: Hand resting on the mouse? Choosing Help Topics from the program's Help menu does the same thing that pressing F1 does.

If you don't see your subject listed in the contents page, chances are that the Help program doesn't have anything to say about it. The Help system is pretty basic.

on the test

Pressing F1 brings up Help in most programs, but not all of them.

Finding Help for General Problems

Lesson 18-2

Probably the fastest way to find help for a nagging problem is to simply jump around, clicking on the words that you see in the Help program shown in Figure 18-1. But if you want to be *sure* that the Help program doesn't have an answer for your problem, the following steps teach you how to make more precise searches for certain subjects.

For example, here's how to forage for help on setting margins in WordPad:

1 Load WordPad and press F1.

The Help program box, similar to the one in Figure 18-1, appears.

2 Click on the Index tab.

An indexed list of the Help program's contents appears, as shown in Figure 18-4.

Figure 18-5: Type the first few letters of the subject, and the Index section looks it up.

Figure 18-6: Double-click on the Settings page margins topic for even more information.

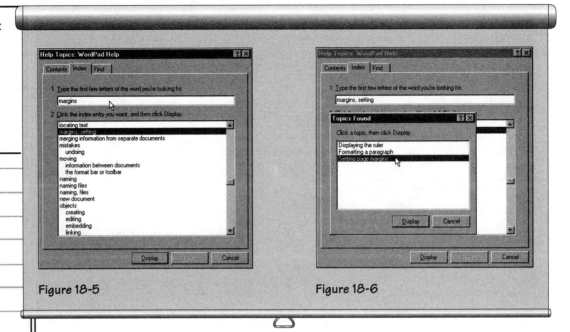

Figure 18-5

Figure 18-6

3 **Type the first few letters of the word** margins **in the box.**

The Help program starts showing you the indexed entries beginning with the word *margins,* as shown in Figure 18-5. See how it found an index entry for *margins, setting?*

4 **Double-click on the margins, setting entry.**

A box that brings up more specific margin-related tasks appears, as shown in Figure 18-6.

5 **Double-click on the Setting page margins topic for even more information.**

A box appears, giving you explicit instructions for setting page margins in WordPad.

Tip: If you stumble across some helpful Help information, place an electronic note on the spot so that you can find it later. Just choose Annotate from the Options menu and type your note. Click on the note's Save button, and a little paper clip is attached to that Help page. Clicking on the paper clip brings up the note for future reference.

Remember: Windows searches alphabetically by subject, so search by generalities. For example, search for *margins* instead of *changing margins.*

click on blank part of desktop and press F1 for help with Windows 95 itself

$1 2^3$

ABC

#

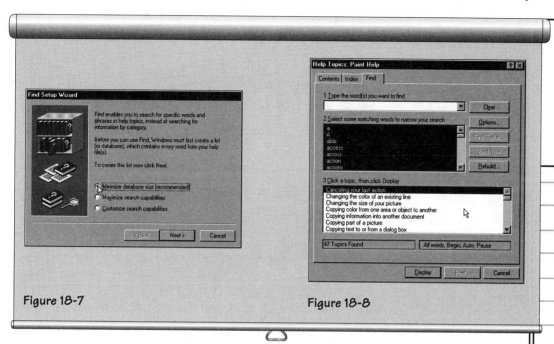

Figure 18-7

Figure 18-8

Figure 18-7: The Find Setup Wizard can search for help by specific words and phrases instead of general categories.

Figure 18-8: The Find program narrows your search to a specific topic.

Finding Help for Specific Problems

Lesson 18-3

Sometimes you want help for a specific problem now, and you don't want to mess around with general, subject-oriented menus. The solution? Tell Windows to make an index of *every* word in its help system, no matter how insignificant it may appear. Then search through that complete index.

The advantage, of course, is that you'll know whether Windows 95 mentions your problem. After all, you've told it to update its index to include every word, not just generalities like *margins*. The disadvantage is that these complete indexes take some time to create and can consume a lot of space on your hard drive.

But if you want to make sure that help is available if you want it, follow these steps (I'll use Paint as an example):

1 Load Paint, press F1, and click on the Find tab.

The Find Setup Wizard program appears, as shown in Figure 18-7, ready to create your index.

2 Click on the Next button to choose <u>M</u>inimize database size.

3 Click on the Finish button.

Your hard drive makes whirling noises as Windows rummages through the Paint Help file, sorting through all its contents. After it's through, the Find window comes to the screen, as Figure 18-8 shows.

Notes:

Figure 18-9: Resting your mouse pointer over confusing buttons often reveals clues as to their function.

Figure 18-10: Clicking on the question mark and then clicking on an option can reveal clues as to the option's function.

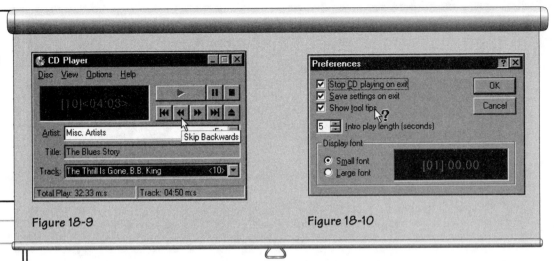

Figure 18-9   Figure 18-10

4 **Type** line **in the Type the word(s) you want to find box.**

As you type the letters, the Find program narrows down your search until it comes up with entries that contain the word *line.*

Double-click on any topic that the Find program came up with to see whether it solves your questions. If it does, great. If it doesn't, head back to the Find program — you only have to make the index once, and it's always there for your use.

Lesson 18-4   Finding Help in a Dialog Box

☑ Progress Check

If you can do the following, you've mastered this unit:

❑ Find help about Windows 95.

❑ Find help for Windows 95 programs.

❑ Customize the Help program.

❑ Find help for specific problems.

Dialog boxes can be confusing with their buttons, forms, and unlabelled icons. What does what? Here's a quick way to figure them out:

1 **Load the CD Player program.**

2 **Rest your mouse pointer over the buttons on the CD Player program.**

After a few seconds, a box appears and explains the button's function, as shown in Figure 18-9.

3 **Choose Preferences from the Options menu.**

The Preferences box appears, listing various settings that you can make for the program.

4 **Click on the little question mark icon in the Preference box's top-right corner, and click on any item, as shown in Figure 18-10.**

Unit 18 Quiz

Circle the letter of the correct answer or answers to each of the following questions. Remember that some questions have more than one answer to keep you from coasting. (After all, you're almost done with the book.)

1. **Pressing F1 always brings up the Help program.**

   A. True.

   B. False.

2. **Does Windows let you mark helpful pages with electronic annotations?**

   A. Yes.

   B. No, that's ridiculous.

3. **How does the Windows Help system display topics across the screen?**

   A. It sorts them alphabetically by first word.

   B. It sorts them alphabetically by category.

   C. It sorts them numerically by creation date.

   D. It doesn't sort them.

4. **To search for help in Paintbrush about drawing straight lines, which phrase would work best?**

   A. Drawing straight lines.

   B. Straight lines.

   C. Line.

   D. Avoiding squiggles.

Notes:

Unit 18 Exercise

With 18 units under your belt, you've probably punched the F1 key a few times. Therefore, these exercises are tips more than they are mandatory study aids. Nevertheless, give them a run-through before moving on to the next unit.

1. Click on a blank part of your desktop, press F1, and double-click on the Troubleshooting book icon. If you see any topics that are giving you problems, double-click on them. Windows 95 leads you through steps that may improve the situation.

Notes:

2. Load Help and experiment with it *before* you have a problem.

3. For either a good way to practice or create supreme confusion, load Help and try out Help's Help program, which shows you how to use Help.

4. Keep an eye out for the little question mark icon in the corner of some dialog boxes. That icon can be handy for finding help when you're filling out confusing Windows forms.

Installing Programs and Drivers

Prerequisites

▶ Navigating windows with a mouse (Lesson 2-1)
▶ Using the Start menu (Lesson 4-2)
▶ Using the Control Panel (Lessons 17-4 and 17-5)
▶ Opening a program (Unit 6)

Objectives for This Unit

✓ Installing programs
✓ Adding or removing parts to Windows 95
✓ Adding Microsoft Windows 95 programs

Congratulations! You've passed the course. By now, you know enough about Windows 95 to keep it on the road with only a few swerves.

The lessons in this unit are a little rougher than usual, but they're here for two reasons. First, you can consider this unit to be a Master's course — an entirely optional opportunity for extended education. Or because this unit puts nearly all your newly learned skills to work, you can consider it a challenge.

It's entirely up to you. Finally, you may find these skills important later on down the road if you need to install a program or additional portion of Windows 95.

Installing a Program

Lesson 19-1

on the disk

You may already be an old hand at this procedure, having installed the disk that comes with this book. If you have never installed a program, or lost or spilled coffee on its instructions, these steps will help you get the program's files onto your hard drive.

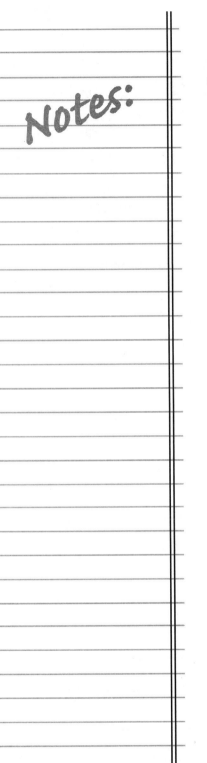

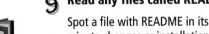

Some programs come with an installation program that tucks the program neatly onto your hard drive and sets it up automatically. Other programs make you do all the work, creating folders and moving files yourself.

This lesson shows you how to treat both types of programs:

1 Find the program's disk or disks.

Root through the box of software until you find the disk marked Disk 1, Setup, Installation, or something similar.

2 Put the disk (or the first disk) in the disk drive.

Whether you're putting a floppy disk into a disk drive or a CD into a CD-ROM drive, make sure that you put it in right-side up. (The label always faces upward.)

3 Double-click on the Control Panel's Add\Remove Programs icon.

You learned how to use the Control Panel in Unit 17. (If you fell asleep during that class, look for the Control Panel in the Start menu's Settings area.) The Add/Remove Programs Properties window jumps to the screen, as shown in Figure 19-1.

4 Click on the Install button and then click on Next.

Windows 95 searches your floppy disk drives and, if you have one, your CD-ROM drive for the program you want to set up. If it finds that program's setup program, click on Finish — you're done. Answer the program's questions, and Windows 95 installs the program for you.

You only have to follow these first four steps to install most Windows 95 programs. But if Windows 95 can't find an installation program, move on to Step 5.

5 Click on Cancel to remove the Install window.

6 Click on Cancel to remove the Add/Remove Programs Properties window.

7 Close the Control Panel and double-click on the My Computer icon.

8 Double-click on drive A in the My Computer window to view the disk's contents.

As shown in Figure 19-2, double-click on My Computer's drive A icon to view the disk's contents. (Unit 5 covers this stuff.) If your disk fits in drive B, double-click on My Computer's drive B icon instead.

9 Read any files called README.

Spot a file with README in its name? Double-click on the file to read any last-minute changes or installation tips. Either Notepad or WordPad usually pops to the screen, ready to help you read the file.

10 Create a new folder on your hard drive.

Create a new folder on your hard drive, as you learned in Unit 5.

Tip: When adding folders, organize them and give them logical names. For example, keep your new *Zonkar the BelchFire* game in a Games folder.

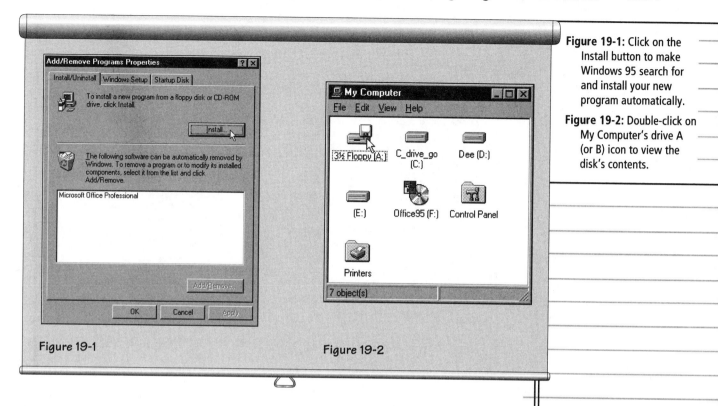

Figure 19-1: Click on the Install button to make Windows 95 search for and install your new program automatically.

Figure 19-2: Double-click on My Computer's drive A (or B) icon to view the disk's contents.

Figure 19-1

Figure 19-2

11 Copy the program's files to the new folder.

Drag-and-drop the files from the floppy disk or CD-ROM drive to the newly created folder, as you learned in Unit 5. Then save the floppy disk as a backup copy in case something goes wrong.

save the floppy as a backup

12 Put the program's icon in the Start menu.

Unit 4 teaches how to place a new program's icon in the Start menu: Drag and drop the file's name from the My Computer or Explorer programs onto the Start menu. The program's icon will appear at the top of the Start menu the next time you click on the Start button.

on the test

An installation program is a second program designed to install the first program. Not all programs come with installation programs; some require you to install them manually.

extra credit

Advanced Start menu setups

Dragging and dropping a program's icon onto the Start button is the quickest way to add the icon to the Start menu, but it's not always the best. The icons simply stack themselves up near the top of the menu where they're easy to reach, but bulky.

These steps show you how to arrange a program's icon in the Start button's Game menu.

1. **Click on the Start button with your right mouse button and choose Open.**

    A window that looks and works just like My Computer appears.

2. **Double-click on the Programs icon.**

3. **Double-click on the Accessories icon.**

4. **Double-click on the Games icon.**

5. **Drag your game's icon from the My Computer folder to the Games folder.**

6. **Close all your windows.**

Your new game is then listed on the Start menu's Game menu.

Lesson 19-2   Installing a Hardware Driver

Added a new piece of gadgetry to your computer? Congratulations! Now, comes the big question: Can Windows 95 hold a computerized conversation with your new piece of computer hardware?

See, when Windows wants to talk to a piece of your computer's hardware — a new sound card or CD-ROM drive, for example — it needs a translator called a *driver*. Specially written to control a certain brand or type of hardware, software drivers let Windows communicate with various parts of your computer.

If you're lucky, Windows 95 automatically notices when you've installed a new piece of equipment to your computer. It might recognize a new modem, for example, and automatically set itself up to begin talking to the modem.

If you're not lucky, you need to install the driver yourself. Either way, this lesson should help you out.

1 First, install the computer part.

Make sure that the computer is turned off, of course; then install the modem, sound card, CD-ROM drive, video card, mouse, printer, or monitor. (Unit 17 gives additional information about changing the modes of a video card and monitor.)

2 **If Windows 95 automatically recognizes the part, follow the on-screen instructions.**

You must be lucky — Windows 95 can sometimes recognize your new part and automatically install all the appropriate software. If Windows 95 doesn't say anything about seeing the new part, move to Step 3.

3 **Choose Control Panel from the Start menu's Settings area.**

The Control Panel appears on the screen.

4 **Double-click on the Add New Hardware icon and click Next.**

The Windows 95 Add New Hardware Wizard looks through your computer, searching for the new part. When Wizard finds the part, it usually asks you to insert one of your original Windows 95 disks or compact disc so that it can copy the driver onto your hard drive.

Other pieces of hardware come with installation programs that completely bypass the ways in which Windows normally installs drivers. Either way, one of the two methods should make the new hardware feel at home.

extra credit

My version of Windows 95 doesn't have the right programs!

Depending on the buttons you punched when installing Windows 95, you'll find different varieties of programs installed on your hard drive. Very few people get all the programs installed. If you feel left out and want some of the optional programs mentioned in this unit, follow these steps:

1. Double-click on the Control Panel's Add/Remove Programs icon.

You can load the Control Panel by choosing Settings in the Start menu.

2. Click on the Windows Setup tab.

It's the tab in the middle of the three along the top; a box appears showing the various components of Windows 95, as well as the amount of space they need to nestle onto your computer's hard drive.

3. Click in the little boxes by the programs or accessories you'd like to add.

A check mark appears in the box of the items you select. To select part of a category — a portion of the accessories, for example — click on the category's name and click on the Details button. Windows 95 lists the items available in that category so that you can click on the ones you want. If you clicked on the Details button, click on the OK button to continue back at the main categories list.

4. Click on the OK button and insert your installation disks when asked.

Windows 95 copies the necessary files from your installation disks onto your hard drive. You can remove Windows 95 accessories the same way, but by *removing* the check mark from the box next to their names.

Unit 19 Quiz

Circle the letter of the correct answer or answers to each of the following questions. (Remember that some questions have more than one right answer.)

1. **What's an installation program's filename?**

   A. INSTALL.COM

   B. GO.EXE

   C. SETUP.EXE

   D. KETCHUP.COM

2. **Which file usually contains last-minute information or installation tips?**

   A. INSTRUCT.TXT

   B. LASTMIN.TXT

   C. TIPS.DOC

   D. README

3. **An installation program is a second program designed specifically to install another program.**

   A. True

   B. False

4. **All programs come with installation programs.**

   A. True

   B. False

Unit 19 Exercise

Unless you run out and buy that big, new monitor, fast video card, and cool sound system for your computer, you probably won't have much to exercise with for this unit. That means that this unit has no practice exercises.

But hey, don't take it hard. After all, you've finished the entire book, and you deserve a break.

Once again, congratulations.

Part V Review

Unit 16 Summary

▶ **Customizing your desktop:** Just as everybody's real desk differs a little in organization, so should Windows 95. Feel free to create folders for your current work projects and create shortcuts to those folders on your desktop. Use a program constantly? Put a shortcut for it in your StartUp folder so that it loads itself automatically whenever you load Windows 95.

Unit 17 Summary

▶ **Customizing Windows:** You can customize Windows 95 to fit your tastes, both practically and aesthetically. For example, you can change the color schemes and add sounds to be played during certain events. You can switch between video modes, allowing more colors to be displayed on-screen and at different resolutions. And you can adjust the mouse's clicking speeds, allowing for more relaxed double-clicks.

▶ **Using wallpaper:** On the more artistic side, Windows allows you to "paste" a picture on your desktop as a background for all your programs. This *wallpaper* can be any file that Paint can read.

Unit 18 Summary

▶ **The Windows 95 Help program:** Windows comes with a built-in help program designed to offer assistance when you're in a jam. Sometimes it's helpful, but it's often filled with jargon that's difficult to understand. Luckily, the Help program includes a built-in glossary, letting you click on a word to see its definition.

▶ **Helpful Wizards:** Also, the Help program comes with built-in Wizards and Troubleshooters — pieces of software that ask you questions and use your answers to try to solve the problem.

▶ **Press the F1 key:** When you're confused, try pressing F1 for advice. If you see a question mark icon within a program, click on it, and then click on the part of the program that confuses you. Sometimes that action brings helpful hints as well.

Unit 19 Summary

▶ **Installing programs:** Installing a Windows program isn't always easy. The most helpful programs come with an *installation program* — a second program custom-written specifically to install the first one. Others make you do the dirty work yourself; you must create a folder, copy files, and set up the program to work on your computer.

▶ **Drivers:** Windows 95 needs *drivers* — specially written pieces of software — to talk to the pieces of hardware installed on your machine. Like Windows programs, drivers often come with their own installation programs. If they don't, you're forced to do the work yourself, increasing the chances of problems. Luckily, Windows 95 comes with most of the drivers you need.

▶ **Computer parts:** Windows 95 can automatically recognize and set itself up to use many popular computer parts like modems and sound cards.

Part V Test

The questions on this test cover all the material presented in Part V, Units 16 through 19.

True   False

T   F   1. All Windows programs install themselves automatically.

T   F   2. You can make your own wallpaper in Paint.

T   F   3. Windows lets left-handed people switch their left and right mouse buttons.

T   F   4. Clicking on an underlined word or phrase in the Windows Help program brings up more helpful information pertaining to that word.

T   F   5. If you have a sound card, Windows can play sounds when it starts up.

T   F   6. A screen saver keeps dust off the monitor.

T   F   7. Windows comes with several different color schemes, letting you change the colors of the borders, menus, and other areas.

T   F   8. New computer equipment occasionally requires the installation of a new Windows driver as well.

T   F   9. Windows comes with several built-in files that you can use for wallpaper.

T   F   10. Windows can usually use all the video modes that it lists on its menu; in fact, testing different display sizes rarely causes your computer to crash.

Multiple Choice

For each of the following questions, circle the correct answer or answers. Remember, each question may have more than one right answer.

11. What is a Windows program's installation program called?

A. INSTALL.COM

B. LOAD.COM

C. SETUP.COM

D. SETUP.EXE

12. Which of these functions does a screen saver perform?

A. It darkens the screen when nobody is using the computer.

B. It entertains.

C. It keeps the screen clean.

D. It prevents an image from "burning" itself into the monitor.

13. Which of these keys usually brings up the Windows 95 Help program?

A. F2

B. F?

C. F1

D. F7

14. What does a file called READ.ME usually contain?

A. Computerized junk mail.

B. Last-minute tips and instructions that didn't make it into the program's manual.

C. Programmer's poetry.

Part V Test

15. **The label on a disk containing a program's installation program usually says one of these things:**

    A. Disk 1.

    B. Installation disk.

    C. Startup disk.

    D. Setup.

16. **Which of the following is easiest to install?**

    A. Drivers.

    B. Programs.

    C. The one that comes with an installation program.

Matching

17. **Match up the following words with the corresponding definitions:**

    A. Color scheme

    B. Wallpaper

    C. Screen saver

    D. Video mode

    1. The number of colors that Windows displays on-screen.

    2. A program that "blanks" or adds animation to the screen when you're not using the computer.

    3. A picture that serves as the desktop's background.

    4. The assortment of colors that decorates the borders and menus in Windows.

18. **Match up these types of Windows files with their probable uses:**

    A. Troubleshooter

    B. Answer Wizard

    C. Icon

    D. Shortcut

    E. Folder

    1. An icon that loads a Windows program, folder, or file.

    2. A symbolic button.

    3. A program that helps install something.

    4. A Help program that fixes problems.

    5. A storage area for files.

Part V Lab Assignment

Congratulations! But don't tell your friends or coworkers that you've finished the course, or they'll be calling *you* when they're struggling to install a new piece of software. Then again, isn't it nice to be on the other end of the struggle for a change?

Anyway, now that you're an Official Windows 95 User, don't be afraid to customize Windows a little bit. Use what you've learned in this unit to spruce up Windows 95, making it look more like your personal work area. This lab assignment should give you some ideas, but don't be afraid to experiment — that's the best way to learn.

Step 1: Hang some wallpaper

Try out the wallpaper files that come with Windows. The program comes with about a dozen files. Or if you feel artistic, make your own file in Paint and use it for wallpaper by using Paint's File menu.

Step 2: Assign some sounds

If you have a sound card, try assigning different sounds to Windows functions.

Step 3: Try a screen saver

Try the screen savers built into Windows 95; it comes with a half-dozen or so.

Step 4: Practice using the Help program

Budget 15 minutes of practice time for using the Help program. You'll get the most use out of Help if you practice with it *before* you need to use it.

Appendix

Answers

Unit 1 Quiz Answers

Question	Answer	If You Missed It, Try This
1.	A, B, C	Review Lesson 1-1.
2.	A	Review Lesson 1-1.
3.	C, D	Review Lesson 1-3.
4.	B	Review Lesson 1-3.

Unit 2 Quiz Answers

Question	Answer	If You Missed It, Try This
1.	B	Review Lesson 2-1.
2.	B, C, D	Review Lesson 2-1.
3.	B	Review Lesson 2-1.
4.	B, C	Review Lesson 2-1.
5.	D	Review Lesson 2-2.
6.	D	Review Lesson 2-2.

Unit 3 Quiz Answers

Question	Answer	If You Missed It, Try This
1.	C	Review Lesson 3-1.
2.	A	Review Lesson 3-1.
3.	A, B, C	Review Lesson 3-1.

Question	Answer	If You Missed It, Try This
4.	A	Review Lesson 3-5.
5.	B	Review Lesson 3-1.
6.	B	Review Lesson 3-3.
7.	B	Review Lesson 3-4.

Part I Test Answers

Question	Answer	If You Missed It, Try This
1.	True (although some rare computers make you type exit to leave DOS mode)	Review Lesson 1-1.
2.	False	Review Lesson 1-2.
3.	False	Review Lesson 1-3.
4.	False, although a mouse is much handier	Review Lesson 2-1.
5.	False	Review Lesson 3-1.
6.	False	Review Lesson 3-3.
7.	False	Review Lesson 3-3.
8.	True	Review Lesson 2-1.
9.	False	Review Lesson 3-3.
10.	True	Review Unit 3.
11.	A, B, D	Review Lesson 2-1.
12.	A, D	Review Lesson 3-1.
13.	A, B, C, D	Review Lesson 1-2.
14.	A, B, C, D	Review Lesson 2-1 and Table 2-1.
15.	B	Review Lesson 3-5.
16.	C	Review Lesson 3-4.
17.	A, B, C	Review Lesson 3-3.
18.	A, B, C, D	Review Lesson 2-1.
19.	A, 4	Review Lesson 2-2.
	B, 1	
	C, 2	
	D, 3	
	E, 5	

Question	Answer	If You Missed It, Try This
20.	A, 5	Review Lesson 3-1.
	B, 4	
	C, 3	
	D, 2	
	E, 1	
21.	A, 3	Review Lesson 3-4.
	B, 1	
	C, 4	
	D, 2	
	E, 5	

Unit 4 Quiz Answers

Question	Answer	If You Missed It, Try This
1.	A, D	Review Lesson 4-1.
2.	A, B, C	Review Lesson 4-1.
3.	A	Review Lesson 4-2.
4.	A	Review Lesson 4-2.
5.	D	Review Lesson 4-3.
6.	A	Review Lesson 4-3.
7.	B	Review Lesson 4-3.
8.	A, C	Review Lesson 4-3.
9.	D	Review Lesson 4-3.

Unit 5 Quiz Answers

Question	Answer	If You Missed It, Try This
1.	C	Review Lesson 5-1.
2.	A, B	Review Lesson 5-1.
3.	C	Review Lesson 5-1.
4.	A, B, C	Review Lesson 5-1.

Question	Answer	If You Missed It, Try This
5.	A	Review Lesson 5-1.
6.	A	Review Lesson 5-1.
7.	A	Review Lesson 5-2.
8.	D	Review Lesson 5-2.
9.	D	Review Lesson 5-2.
10.	D	Review Lesson 5-2.
11.	A, B, C, D	Review Lesson 5-3.
12.	A	Review Lesson 5-3.
13.	B	Review Lesson 5-3.
14.	A, but only if the files are all next to each other	Review Lesson 5-4.

Part II Test Answers

Question	Answer	If You Missed It, Try This
1.	False; very few CD-ROM drives can write to compact discs	Review Lesson 5-1.
2.	False	Review Lesson 4-3.
3.	True	Review Lesson 4-1.
4.	True	Review Lesson 4-1.
5.	True	Review Lesson 4-3.
6.	True, but a mouse is much handier	Review Lesson 4-3.
7.	False	Review Lesson 4-3.
8.	True	Review Lesson 5-3.
9.	True	Review Lesson 5-5.
10.	True	Review Lesson 5-6.
11.	A	Review Lesson 4-1.
12.	A, B, C	Review Lessons 4-1 and 5-4.
13.	A, B, C, D	Review Lesson 5-1.
14.	A, B, D	Review Lessons 4-3, 5-3, and 5-4.
15.	C	Review Lesson 5-1.

Question	Answer	If You Missed It, Try This
16.	A, B, D	Review Lesson 5-1.
17.	A, B, C	Review Lesson 5-6.
18.	B	Review Table 5-1.
19.	A, 3	Review Lessons 4-1 and 5-1.
	B, 4	
	C, 1	
	D, 2	
	E, 5	
20.	A, 1	Review Lesson 5-2.
	B, 2	
	C, 3	

Unit 6 Quiz Answers

Question	Answer	If You Missed It, Try This
1.	A, B	Review Lesson 6-2.
2.	A	Review Lesson 6-1.
3.	A, B, C	Review Lesson 6-2.
4.	B	Review Lesson 6-2.
5.	B, C, D	Review Lesson 6-3.

Unit 7 Quiz Answers

Question	Answer	If You Missed It, Try This
1.	C	Review Lesson 7-1.
2.	A, B	Review Lesson 7-1.
3.	D	Review Lesson 7-1.

Unit 8 Quiz Answers

Question	Answer	If You Missed It, Try This
1.	A, B, C, D	Review the Unit 8 introductory text.
2.	A	Review Lesson 8-1.
3.	D	Review Lesson 8-2.
4.	A, B, C	Review Lesson 8-2.
5.	B, D	Review Lesson 8-3.

Unit 9 Quiz Answers

Question	Answer	If You Missed It, Try This
1.	A, B, C	Review Lesson 9-1.
2.	A, D	Review Lesson 9-1.
3.	A, D	Review Lesson 9-4.

Unit 10 Quiz Answers

Question	Answer	If You Missed It, Try This
1.	C	Review Lesson 10-2.
2.	A, B	Review Lesson 10-1.
3.	B	Review Lesson 10-1.
4.	A, B, C	Review Lesson 10-1.
5.	A, B, C	Review Lesson 10-3.
6.	A	Review Lesson 10-3.
7.	A, B, C	Review Lesson 10-4.

Part III Test Answers

Question	Answer	If You Missed It, Try This
1.	False; *double*-click on the icon	Review Lesson 6-1.
2.	False	Review Lesson 6-2.
3.	True	Review Lesson 10-2.
4.	True	Review Lesson 9-3.
5.	False	Review Lesson 8-2.
6.	True	Review Lesson 8-3.
7.	True	Review Lesson 10-1.
8.	False	Review Lesson 8-3.
9.	True	Review Lesson 8-3.
10.	True	Review Lesson 8-3.
11.	A, B, C, D	Review Lesson 7-1.
12.	A, C	Review Lessons 6-1 and 6-2.
13.	A, B, C	Review Lesson 7-1.
14.	C	Review Lesson 8-3.
15.	B, C (Notepad saves in ASCII format)	Review Lesson 8-3.
16.	A	Review Lesson 6-1.
17.	B, C	Review Lesson 6-1.
18.	A, 4	Review Lesson 7-1.
	B, 3	Review Lesson 7-1.
	C, 1	Review Lesson 9-4.
	D, 2	Review Lesson 8-2.
	E, 5	Review Lesson 1-2.
19.	A, 3	Review Lesson 7-1.
	B, 1	
	C, 2	
	D, 4	

Unit 11 Quiz Answers

Question	Answer	If You Missed It, Try This
1.	C	Review Lesson 11-1.
2.	B, C	Review Lesson 11-2.
3.	C	Review Lesson 11-4.
4.	A	Review Lesson 11-5.
5.	A	Review Lesson 11-6.
6.	A	Review Lesson 11-8.
7.	C	Review Lesson 11-9.

Unit 12 Quiz Answers

Question	Answer	If You Missed It, Try This
1.	A, B, C, D	Review Lesson 12-1.
2.	A	Review Lesson 12-2.
3.	A, C	Review Lesson 12-3.
4.	D	Review Lesson 12-3.

Unit 13 Quiz Answers

Question	Answer	If You Missed It, Try This
1.	A, B	Review Lesson 13-2.
2.	B	Review Lesson 13-1.
3.	A	Review Lesson 13-1.
4.	A	Review Lesson 13-1.
5.	A	Review Lesson 13-2.

Unit 14 Quiz Answers

Question	Answer	If You Missed It, Try This
1.	D	Review Lesson 14-1.
2.	A	Review Lesson 14-1.
3.	D	Review Lessons 14-1 and 14-3.
4.	A	Review Lesson 14-2.
5.	B, C	Review Lesson 14-4.
6.	A, B	Review Lesson 14-5.

Unit 15 Quiz Answers

Question	Answer	If You Missed It, Try This
1.	B	Review Lesson 15-1.
2.	B	Review Lesson 15-2.
3.	A	Review Lesson 15-3.
4.	B	Review Lesson 15-2.
5.	A, B, C	Review Lesson 15-2.
6.	A, B, C, D	Review Lesson 15-2.

Part IV Test Answers

Question	Answer	If You Missed It, Try This
1.	True	Review Lesson 15-4.
2.	True	Review Lesson 11-6.
3.	False	Review Lesson 13-2.
4.	True	Review Lesson 15-3.
5.	False	Review Lesson 14-4.
6.	True	Review Lesson 14-5
7.	False (The sound depends on the quality of the sound card's synthesizer.)	Review Lesson 15-1.

Question	Answer	If You Missed It, Try This
8.	A, B, C, D	Review Lessons 15-1 and 15-2.
9.	C	Review Lesson 11-7.
10.	A, B, C	Review Lesson 11-1.
11.	B, C, D	Review Lesson 12-1.
12	A, B, C, D	Review Lesson 15-1
13.	A, 1	Review Lesson 15-3.
	B, 2	Review Lesson 15-1.
	C, 2	Review Lesson 15-4.
14.	A, 1	Review Lesson 14-1.
	B, 2, 3	
	B, 2,3	Review Lesson 15-2.
	C, 2	Review Lesson 15-1.
15.	A, 4	Review Lesson 15-1.
	B, 3	Review Lesson 15-2.
	C, 1	Review Lesson 15-1.
	D, 2	Review Lesson 15-2.

Unit 16 Quiz Answers

Question	Answer	If You Missed It, Try This
1.	D	Review Lesson 16-1.
2.	A	Review Lesson 16-3.
3.	A, B, C	Review Lesson 16-1.

Unit 17 Quiz Answers

Question	Answer	If You Missed It, Try This
1.	A, B	Review Lesson 17-1.
2.	D	Review Lesson 17-1.
3.	A	Review Lesson 17-4.
4.	B	Review Lesson 17-5.

Unit 18 Quiz

Question	Answer	If You Missed It, Try This
1.	B (but almost always)	Review Lesson 18-1.
2.	A	Review Lesson 18-2.
3.	B	Review Lesson 18-2.
4.	C	Review Lesson 18-2.

Unit 19 Quiz

Question	Answer	If You Missed It, Try This
1.	A, C	Review Lesson 19-1.
2.	D	Review Lesson 19-1.
3.	A	Review Lesson 19-1.
4.	B	Review Lesson 19-1.

Part V Test

Question	Answer	If You Missed It, Try This
1.	False	Review Lesson 19-1.
2.	True	Review Lesson 17-1.
3.	True	Review Lesson 17-4.
4.	True	Review Lesson 18-1.
5.	True	Review Lesson 17-2.
6.	False	Review Lesson 17-3.
7.	True	Review Lesson 17-1.
8.	True	Review Lesson 19-2.
9.	True	Review Lesson 17-1.
10.	True	Review Lesson 17-3.
11.	D	Review Lesson 19-1.

Question	Answer	If You Missed It, Try This
12.	A, B, D	Review Lesson 17-3.
13.	C	Review Lesson 18-1.
14.	B	Review Lesson 19-1.
15.	A, B, C, D	Review Lesson 19-1.
16.	C	Review Lesson 19-1.
17.	A, 4	Review Lesson 17-1.
	B, 3	Review Lesson 17-1.
	C, 3	Review Lesson 17-3.
	D, 1	Review Lesson 17-5.
18.	A, 4	Review Lesson 17-5.
	B, 3	Review Lesson 17-1.
	C, 2	Review Lesson 19-2.
	D, 1	Review Lesson 19-1.
	E, 5	Review Lesson 17-2.

Index

Symbols

Q

R

▸S◂

IDG BOOKS WORLDWIDE, INC.

END-USER LICENSE AGREEMENT

Read This. You should carefully read these terms and conditions before opening the software packet(s) included with this book ("Book"). This is a license agreement ("Agreement") between you and IDG Books Worldwide, Inc. ("IDGB"). By opening the accompanying software packet(s), you acknowledge that you have read and accept the following terms and conditions. If you do not agree and do not want to be bound by such terms and conditions, promptly return the Book and the unopened software packet(s) to the place you obtained them for a full refund.

1. **License Grant.** IDGB grants to you (either an individual or entity) a nonexclusive license to use one copy of the enclosed software program(s) (collectively, the "Software") solely for your own personal or business purposes on a single computer (whether a standard computer or a workstation component of a multiuser network). The Software is in use on a computer when it is loaded into temporary memory (i.e., RAM) or installed into permanent memory (e.g., hard disk, CD-ROM, or other storage device). IDGB reserves all rights not expressly granted herein.

2. **Ownership.** IDGB is the owner of all right, title, and interest, including copyright, in and to the compilation of the Software recorded on the disk(s)/CD-ROM. Copyright to the individual programs on the disk(s)/CD-ROM is owned by the author or other authorized copyright owner of each program. Ownership of the Software and all proprietary rights relating thereto remain with IDGB and its licensors.

3. **Restrictions on Use and Transfer.**

   (a) You may only (i) make one copy of the Software for backup or archival purposes, or (ii) transfer the Software to a single hard disk, provided that you keep the original for backup or archival purposes. You may not (i) rent or lease the Software, (ii) copy or reproduce the Software through a LAN or other network system or through any computer subscriber system or bulletin-board system, or (iii) modify, adapt, or create derivative works based on the Software.

   (b) You may not reverse engineer, decompile, or disassemble the Software. You may transfer the Software and user documentation on a permanent basis, provided that the transferee agrees to accept the terms and conditions of this Agreement and you retain no copies. If the Software is an update or has been updated, any transfer must include the most recent update and all prior versions.

4. **Restrictions on Use of Individual Programs.** You must follow the individual requirements and restrictions detailed for each individual program in the Introduction of this Book. These limitations are contained in the individual license agreements recorded on the disk(s)/CD-ROM. These restrictions may include a requirement that after using the program for the period of time specified in its text, the user must pay a registration fee or discontinue use. By opening the Software packet(s), you will be agreeing to abide by the licenses and restrictions for these individual programs. None of the material on this disk(s) or listed in this Book may ever be distributed, in original or modified form, for commercial purposes.

5. **Limited Warranty**.

   (a) IDGB warrants that the Software and disk(s)/CD-ROM are free from defects in materials and workmanship under normal use for a period of sixty (60) days from the date of purchase of this Book. If IDGB receives notification within the warranty period of defects in materials or workmanship, IDGB will replace the defective disk(s)/CD-ROM.

   (b) **IDGB AND THE AUTHOR OF THE BOOK DISCLAIM ALL OTHER WAR-RANTIES, EXPRESS OR IMPLIED, INCLUDING WITHOUT LIMITATION IMPLIED WARRANTIES OF MERCHANTABILITY AND FITNESS FOR A PARTICULAR PURPOSE, WITH RESPECT TO THE SOFTWARE, THE PROGRAMS, THE SOURCE CODE CONTAINED THEREIN, AND/OR THE TECHNIQUES DESCRIBED IN THIS BOOK. IDGB DOES NOT WARRANT THAT THE FUNCTIONS CONTAINED IN THE SOFTWARE WILL MEET YOUR REQUIREMENTS OR THAT THE OPERATION OF THE SOFTWARE WILL BE ERROR FREE.**

   (c) This limited warranty gives you specific legal rights, and you may have other rights which vary from jurisdiction to jurisdiction.

6. **Remedies**.

   (a) IDGB's entire liability and your exclusive remedy for defects in materials and workmanship shall be limited to replacement of the Software, which may be returned to IDGB with a copy of your receipt at the following address: Disk Fulfillment Department, Attn: *Dummies 101: Windows 95,* 2nd Edition, IDG Books Worldwide, Inc., 7260 Shadeland Station, Ste. 100, Indianapolis, IN 46256, or call 1-800-762-2974. Please allow 3–4 weeks for delivery. This Limited Warranty is void if failure of the Software has resulted from accident, abuse, or misapplication. Any replacement Software will be warranted for the remainder of the original warranty period or thirty (30) days, whichever is longer.

   (b) In no event shall IDGB or the author be liable for any damages whatsoever (including without limitation damages for loss of business profits, business interruption, loss of business information, or any other pecuniary loss) arising from the use of or inability to use the Book or the Software, even if IDGB has been advised of the possibility of such damages.

   (c) Because some jurisdictions do not allow the exclusion or limitation of liability for consequential or incidental damages, the above limitation or exclusion may not apply to you.

7. **U.S. Government Restricted Rights**. Use, duplication, or disclosure of the Software by the U.S. Government is subject to restrictions stated in paragraph (c) (1) (ii) of the Rights in Technical Data and Computer Software clause of DFARS 252.227-7013, and in subparagraphs (a) through (d) of the Commercial Computer — Restricted Rights clause at FAR 52.227-19, and in similar clauses in the NASA FAR supplement, when applicable.

8. **General**. This Agreement constitutes the entire understanding of the parties and revokes and supersedes all prior agreements, oral or written, between them and may not be modified or amended except in a writing signed by both parties hereto which specifically refers to this Agreement. This Agreement shall take precedence over any other documents that may be in conflict herewith. If any one or more provisions contained in this Agreement are held by any court or tribunal to be invalid, illegal, or otherwise unenforceable, each and every other provision shall remain in full force and effect.

Installing the Dummies 101 Disk Files

To use the files on the disk that comes with this book, you first have to *install* them on your computer. Follow these steps to do so:

1 Insert the Dummies 101 disk in your computer's 3¹/₂-inch floppy disk drive (the only drive in which the disk will fit).

2 Double-click on the My Computer icon.

3 Double-click on the Control Panel icon.

4 Double-click on the Add/Remove Programs icon.

5 Click on the <u>I</u>nstall button.

6 Click on the <u>N</u>ext button.

7 Follow the directions on-screen.

Unless you *really* know what you're doing, accept the settings that the installation program suggests. If you decide to forge into the unknown and change the folder in which you install the files that you'll use with this book, write the pathname of that folder here.

Folder in which this book's files reside:

_____

(Problems with the installation process? Call the IDG Books Worldwide Customer Support number: 800-762-2974.)

IDG BOOKS WORLDWIDE REGISTRATION CARD

RETURN THIS
REGISTRATION CARD
FOR FREE CATALOG

Title of this book: **Dummies 101™: Windows® 95, 2E**

My overall rating of this book: ❑ Very good [1] ❑ Good [2] ❑ Satisfactory [3] ❑ Fair [4] ❑ Poor [5]

How I first heard about this book:

❑ Found in bookstore; name: [6]   ❑ Book review: [7]

❑ Advertisement: [8]   ❑ Catalog: [9]

❑ Word of mouth; heard about book from friend, co-worker, etc.: [10]   ❑ Other: [11]

What I liked most about this book:

What I would change, add, delete, etc., in future editions of this book:

Other comments:

Number of computer books I purchase in a year: ❑ 1 [12] ❑ 2-5 [13] ❑ 6-10 [14] ❑ More than 10 [15]

I would characterize my computer skills as: ❑ Beginner [16] ❑ Intermediate [17] ❑ Advanced [18] ❑ Professional [19]

I use ❑ DOS [20] ❑ Windows [21] ❑ OS/2 [22] ❑ Unix [23] ❑ Macintosh [24] ❑ Other: [25]_____
(please specify)

I would be interested in new books on the following subjects:
(please check all that apply, and use the spaces provided to identify specific software)

❑ Word processing: [26]   ❑ Spreadsheets: [27]

❑ Data bases: [28]   ❑ Desktop publishing: [29]

❑ File Utilities: [30]   ❑ Money management: [31]

❑ Networking: [32]   ❑ Programming languages: [33]

❑ Other: [34]

I use a PC at (please check all that apply): ❑ home [35] ❑ work [36] ❑ school [37] ❑ other: [38] _____

The disks I prefer to use are ❑ 5.25 [39] ❑ 3.5 [40] ❑ other: [41]_____

I have a CD ROM: ❑ yes [42] ❑ no [43]

I plan to buy or upgrade computer hardware this year: ❑ yes [44] ❑ no [45]

I plan to buy or upgrade computer software this year: ❑ yes [46] ❑ no [47]

Name: _____ Business title: [48] _____ Type of Business: [49] _____

Address (❑ home [50] ❑ work [51]/Company name: _____)

Street/Suite# _____

City [52]/State [53]/Zipcode [54]: _____ Country [55] _____

❑ **I liked this book!** You may quote me by name in future
IDG Books Worldwide promotional materials.

My daytime phone number is _____

IDG BOOKS

THE WORLD OF COMPUTER KNOWLEDGE

❏ YES!
Please keep me informed about IDG's World of Computer Knowledge.
Send me the latest IDG Books catalog.

SECRETS™

...FOR DUMMIES™
COMPUTER
BOOK SERIES
FROM IDG

MACWORLD
MW
AUTHORIZED
EDITION

AUTHORIZED
PC WORLD
EDITION